LOOK WHO'S TALKING

COLIN BAKER

Colin Baker : Look Who's Talking
First Published December 2009. First reprint February 2010.
by Hirst Books

Hirst Books, Suite 285 Andover House, George Yard, Andover, Hants, SP10 1PB

ISBN 978-0-9557149-2-4

The articles in this compilation originally appeared in the Bucks Free Press between
1995 and 2009.

Compilation and internal design by Tim Hirst.
Cover by Lee Thompson
Proof-reading by Louise McDonald.
Printed and bound by Good News Press

Paper stock used is natural, recyclable and made from wood grown in sustainable
forests. The manufacturing processes conform to environmental regulations.

www.hirstbooks.com

This book is dedicated to my wife, Marion, whose skills as an actress were denied to a nation while she has looked after me and our children. This is doubly noteworthy as her ability to convince me that it was worth it, combined with her continuing tolerance of me, demonstrates just what calibre of actress the audiences of the last quarter of a century have lost.

Contents

Introduction

When I wrote a letter to my local newspaper, The Bucks Free Press, in the summer of 1995, I certainly did not entertain the possibility that it would result in my writing a column for that same paper the following week and then for the next fourteen years (at the date of writing). Nor indeed could I have predicted that anyone might think my ramblings worthy of compilation into a book. But publisher Tim Hirst, approached me earlier this year with precisely that suggestion and convinced me that there were enough people out there who might be interested and so I agreed to give it a go. I was encouraged to make that decision, in part, because Tim has done a superb job in publishing the two volumes of my delightful friend, and former *Doctor Who* companion, Anneke Wills' autobiography, which was one of the best reads I have had in recent years. Since then, he has laboriously sifted through all 750 examples of my hebdomadal sesquipedalianism and presents his personal selection in the pages that follow.

I cannot now remember what it was that provoked me to write to the Bucks Free Press in the first place, but I imagine that I was probably tilting at some windmill of political correctness, bureaucracy or public incompetence. If only I could claim that my writing had just once changed anything – but who knows, it may have occasionally sowed a seed in somebody's mind that may bear fruit one day?

In my local area of South Buckinghamshire, I am gratified to say that I get more people commenting on my column in the paper than I do for my former temporary tenure of the Tardis back in the 1980's. Most people are kind enough to tell me that they enjoy reading my column, although they almost invariably add the qualification that, of course, they don't always agree with everything that I say. And that is just as it should be. If you try to please all of the people all of the time, then it is almost inevitable that you end up pleasing nobody.

Tim's selection starts with a pot-pourri of unrelated articles ranging from nomenclature via *Doctor Who* to sadistic clergymen and insurance, with the intention perhaps of giving a flavour of what is to follow, a sort of smorgåsbord of opinions in the hope that just one

of them might titillate your appetite and induce you to read more. I notice that in making his selection he has contrived to ensure that your attention is grabbed on the very first page by the account of my meeting with Pamela Anderson. And why not? Just don't expect a plethora of pneumatic blondes appearing regularly throughout the rest of the book.

If you notice (and are perplexed by) the differing lengths of these offerings, it stems from the fact that the newspaper has undergone several changes during my time as a columnist. I started off contributing to the entertainment section pull-out, graduating to the body of the paper first of all and then to the editorial and letters page when the Free Press turned from being a broadsheet to a tabloid weekly.

I am thankful that the paper retained its character - a truly local 'news' paper - despite the change. The only difficulty that I encountered during these processes was in reducing the word count. I find I have to edit severely after I have pounded my keyboard into submission each Tuesday (or Wednesday if I am trying patience of Steve Cohen who has been the tolerant editor of the Bucks Free Press during the whole time I have been contributing). But I firmly believe that there are very few first drafts of anything that cannot be improved by a good healthy edit.

Can you imagine then what the following were like before a judicious pruning?

1. Random Jottings

20th February 2009

After my visit to New York last week, I spent the weekend in Los Angeles in the company of a splendid bunch of people who gather together annually to celebrate their affection for *Doctor Who*. It is heartening that they are still prepared to tolerate the old fogies who used to portray the nation's favourite time lord in the age of the new improved programme and the ever youthening Doctor. As if David Tennant hadn't already proved the visibly beneficial power of time travel on the genes, the imminent new one, Matt Smith, we are told, is so young that he is likely to be asked for ID if he tries to purchase an intergalactic gargle blaster in licensed premises either side of the Atlantic. On my day off in LA, I accompanied some friends to Santa Monica, and while the residents of South Bucks were still sliding around on the icy roads, I was strolling in shirt sleeves along the beach among palm trees, by that other ocean the Pacific in temperatures of around 60 degrees. The locals were complaining of the cold, by the way. As we passed a Belgian chocolate shop, one of my companions uttered the word 'Chocolate' in precisely the same tones that Homer Simpson habitually intones "Beer!"

In my current state of self denial – my daughter has decreed a diet and I obey – I protested "No!" She repeated her mantra – and I repeated my denial, two or three times. As we waited for the lights to change to 'Walk' to allow us to escape the seductive temptations of confectionary, I intoned Homer's actual words to indicate my attitude to her demonstration of chocaholicism. An American woman standing at the kerbside turned around and said,

"Now you're talking!" and laughed. We chatted for a moment or two and, as she walked away, I said to my companions who looked, I thought, inexplicably perplexed at my behaviour,

"You know she looked a bit like Pamela Anderson."

"That", replied one of them "…is because she *was* Pamela Anderson!" Apparently the pneumatic star of Baywatch and other perhaps more infamous films bears unique tattoos that everyone, except your columnist, had instantly recognised. I would love to think that as she entered the adjacent interior design outlet, she said to her

female companion that I looked a bit like that bloke who used to play Doctor Who. No, not Tom! The other one!

1st December 2006

Previous generations, as a matter of course, used to name their children after relatives, often their grandparents, and until recently this assured the continuance of names like Edna, Clarence, Ernest and Gertrude long after they became unfashionable. And, after all, given that they are just sounds, why should Wilfred or Monica be less desirable moniker for a young girl than Jack or Chloe, the nation's recent most favoured names? Clearly it is association.

When I was at school there was one poor child whose personal hygiene and habits were, put delicately, not of the highest order. Her name still carries for me memories of the experience of sitting next to her in class. It is one area in which class still rears its visible head in our far from classless society. You don't find many Kylies or Keanus at our public schools, do you Arabella? It is from the ranks of the famous that some parents now choose to name their children and the attraction of fame seemingly extends to products as well as people. Researchers who examined birth records dating back to 1984 report twenty-six children (boys and girls!) named Arsenal, two Reeboks and three Adidas. Sport is also responsible for over a thousand Tigers and thirty-nine Gazzas, heaven help us.

You would think that the rarefied air breathed by some media folk that compels them to come up with names like Peaches, Apple, Brooklyn would not have the same effect on more grounded parents. Think again. All of those names have been hung heavily around the necks of children who will have to carry them in less privileged surroundings than their super rich namesakes, as will thousands of Britneys, Shakiras and Orlandos. Believe it or not, according to a BBC website, there are children in this country saddled with the names Jellyfish McSaveloy, Nigel Bottomface and Toasted T Cake! But then you would think that Colin Baker was a safe, if uninspiring name, wouldn't you? That was the case until the most popular comic of my childhood, The Eagle, included in its weekly school saga, The Three J's, a character called Colin Baker. The three J's were the heroes. Three boys called John, all fine, decent, fun loving young

sportsmen and good eggs. Colin Baker was a 'specky swot' who told tales and 'blubbed'. Why couldn't I have been called Dan Dare?

16th February 2001

Some dozen or so years ago I was taken on a backstage tour of Durham Cathedral by a friend who was a Canon there. We were accompanied by another cleric, who rejoiced under the name of Reverend Precentor of the Ecclesiastical Heraditament or something along those lines. All went well until this benign and solemn gentleman beckoned me to follow him through a small door and I found myself on a narrow ledge hundreds of feet above the high altar. It had a single metal rail around the edge at hip height, which would have been a fairly reassuring sight for Happy, Sleepy or Grumpy, but to me seemed nothing more than a further hazard.

I had always believed that my lungs, heart and other internal organs (I had better not be too specific here) were more or less able to function happily without any significant conscious contribution from me. In a millisecond all that changed. Breathing and staying vertical and AS STILL AS POSSIBLE occupied my immediate horizons. I paid particular attention to the activities of my knees which were insisting that folding up and having a little rest were top of their agenda, please. I faintly heard my holy buddies deriving great amusement from having led another poor acrophobic to the heights of terror. I have viewed dog collars and their seemingly benign owners with deep suspicion ever since. They take 'Closer my God to thee' a little too literally sometimes. Imagine therefore my delight this week, when I stepped off the plane for my first ever visit down under to be told by my welcoming hosts,

"You're climbing the Sydney Harbour Bridge this arvo, cobber!" (Actually their words were far less obviously Australian than that, but then why let the truth spoil a good story?)

My initial terror at the prospect was not lessened by the knowledge that my wife's sister and her husband had done it and survived to strut their stuff about it. How could I face my brother- in-law again if I chickened out? He can already hang a door in the time it would take me to find a sticking plaster after gouging my finger with the

screwdriver at the first hinge. Male pride that has caused the downfall (no pun intended) of many a foolhardy man forced me to stammer,

"Yeah, great, wow, thanks!" whilst my brain was urgently requesting Scotty to beam me up. But, dear reader, I did it.

The first ten minutes was a journey through nightmare to terror. But the climb is meticulously organised. You are attached by cable to the bridge throughout and it's as safe as houses (tell that to the wicked witch of the west!). I even got used to seeing cars between my feet 100 feet below. My knees gradually remembered that they were made of bone and not potty putty; my lungs started to work in the appropriate way. I began to appreciate that I was actually climbing up one of the world's most famous landmarks. I am sure I will still decline to lean over the edge of the white cliffs of Dover to see what's going on down below, but I have actually stood on top of the Sydney Harbour Bridge with an intrepid band of Brits and Aussies and the view was simply stunning, like the country itself.

Note to ed: do you want a permanent Australian correspondent?

17th November 1995

A national charity was recently obliged to take legal advice on a matter involving libel. Through a misunderstanding it appears that the lawyer consulted was not in fact, giving his services free, but only at 'discounted rate' for the charity. After the first month, a bill was delivered. Four meetings, some research, a dozen or so phone calls and letters. Over £8,000 including VAT. (and, appallingly, charities cannot register for and therefore reclaim VAT.) If that's the discounted rate...? Boy, am I in the wrong job. I was recently castigated by a *Doctor Who* fan for not sending him a 10 x 8 photograph of myself, that he had requested in an earlier letter, the basis being that I could afford to do so because I'm "a famous actor, and therefore must be rolling in it". His words not mine. I should bring him with me to see my bank manager this week. One or other of them would learn something to their advantage.

How are these two stories connected? Before I succumbed to the lure of 'shouting in the evening' which was my late and still very much missed friend Patrick Troughton's definition of stage acting, I studied law and was articled to a firm of solicitors in Manchester. Much to most sensible people's astonishment, at the very time I was

supposed to be sitting my final qualifying exams I was auditioning for drama schools in London. 'The rest is history', or is that 'silence'?

But for five years in the sixties I worked in most departments of a busy and large firm of Solicitors. I learnt a lot about the law and even more about human nature. In the area of litigation, I learnt that the wealthier the client the more they were able to use your services to impose their will on the less wealthy, by the simple expedient of running up huge lawyers' bills on both sides until the other party could no longer afford to stay in the game.

The rich have always been able to use the law as their personal bludgeon to advance their own interests and agenda. Legal aid which was only available then to a few truly impoverished is gradually becoming even less accessible. A vast swathe of people from those just above the breadline to the more than comfortable middle classes are effectively prevented from having recourse to the civil law to achieve justice because it involves such a considerable risk to their capital.

I must confess to having been most unprofessional on at least one occasion. A major client wanted to be rid of the tenants of a house, so when the wage earner became ill and had missed several payments, the landlords did not react to letters explaining the problem asking for time but waited for the tenants to reach the point where they were in breach of the terms of their lease, in order to (quite legally) evict them. I am afraid, (or is that proud?), that I telephoned the family anonymously to warn them that their next missed rental payment would result in their imminent eviction. They were able to take action to prevent that.

Those years spent in a solicitor's office left me with an enhanced and almost obsessive regard for justice, which, unfortunately, does not always coincide with what is achieved by recourse to the law. It is a fault, but I am unable to shrug off injustice and can only envy others who refuse to waste their precious time addressing every small wrong they encounter. I also learnt how to write a letter and how powerful a tool the English language can be to express the writer's true meaning. At one time lawyer-speak became ridiculously repetitive and clumsy in its attempt to leave no loophole unplugged, but over the years that has improved. 'Messuages and hereditaments'

are now 'houses', 'curtilages' are 'gardens' and a 'feoffee' is a 'purchaser'.

But a bill is still a bill, which brings me neatly back to the beginning of this article and the certainty that if most actors in this country, including myself, were remunerated at the "preferential rate" of lawyers, we would happily dispense 10 x 8 photographs of ourselves to the world at large, whether they wanted them or not!

7th August 1998

I suspect that I am not alone in being seduced by those glossy catalogues that contain enticing photographs of gadgets which one covets, but which in practice would soon end up gathering dust at the bottom of a cupboard. I am in the process of moving all that goes with what I am pleased to call my study to another room.
I am discovering all sorts of, well – stuff – that I have for a long time resisted chucking away in case it 'comes in useful one day'.

Some of it I have been given by well-intentioned friends and relatives. You know – those things that men traditionally get given for birthdays because the donor is desperately trying to avoid the sock\hanky\tie option. So they go to those shops that only sell things that absolutely nobody ever buys for himself, but which, oddly, they will happily buy for someone else. Seaside gift shops are full of them. A statue of an inebriated golfer with some witty inscription at the bottom involving rather unsubtle play on words; a model car on a plinth with a bonnet that opens to display its lovingly re-created minute plastic engine: a pint tankard bearing an uplifting m.c.p. legend; little plastic feet which hold your socks in pairs in the washing machine, so that you don't have that drawer full of single socks whose partners have gone walkies (or is that hoppies?).

You know the sort of thing. Every now and then I am tempted. Even more rarely I purchase. I once got one of those gadgets that is supposed to restore otherwise non-rechargeable batteries to full vigour and electrical potency. I now have two shoe boxes of batteries, which I fondly believe I will be able to re-charge when I get the state of the art version which I saw recently in another catalogue with a name like 'Indispensables".

I hope I can continue to resist hurling good money after bad, but cannot yet bring myself to throw away the batteries. Perhaps I should

join Hoarders Anonymous, the acronym of which would be a very appropriate HA! I succumbed to an offer in the Radio Times this week. My eyes fell upon a beguiling invitation to purchase a videotape re-winder, the use of which would save wear and tear on my VCR apparently. I was attracted to this offer in particular because the children's machine has declined to rewind for some weeks and I know, just as sure as a child in a car will ask,

"Are we nearly there yet?" while your house is still visible in the rear view mirror, that the cost of repair will probably hover tantalisingly just below the price at which it would be sensible to replace rather than repair. It would cost me £19.95 and with video head cleaner thrown in. It seemed a bargain – and a cheaper option than the repair/replace scenario. I telephoned the order line and was agreeably surprised when, after two rings, a friendly voice explained that I was in a queue and that I would be kept informed as to the length of that queue. After a musical interlude the same friendly voice told me that I was number two in the queue. I was by now planning to congratulate the eventual human recipient of my order on the thoughtfulness of the system. A little more music; a human voice. I explained my desire to purchase. "I'll put you through sir". More music. A ringing phone. It rings and rings and rings. No more friendly voices.

After a total waiting time of 15 minutes, which I would not have contemplated had the opening gambit not been so disarmingly user friendly, I hung up swearing eternal allegiance to real shops and real shopkeepers – if they will forgive my temporary infidelity.

8th March 2002

In case it may have escaped your attention my surname is Baker. It is likely therefore that someone in my ancestry earned his living making bread. Nothing remarkable about that. A vast proportion of the names of those whose families have been resident in these islands for a few centuries bear names that give evidence of occupational connections. All those Thatchers, Smiths, Fletchers, Shepherds, Barbers and Butchers. However, if the modern trend to give people fancier job descriptions as a cheaper alternative to pay rises had been around in the Middle Ages, then my name today might easily be Colin Bread Creation Operative. A combination of political correctness and

a disinclination to tell it how it is has resulted in a bizarre evolution in job descriptions.

The train I was on a couple of weeks ago had a senior conductor, whom I can only imagine is what we might hitherto have called the guard. There was, it has to be said, no sign of anyone who might be described as a junior conductor. Secretaries have all but vanished off the face of the earth; anyone worth their screen radiation filter and ergonomic keyboard is now termed a personal assistant or communications facilitator. And that blight of the BBC – the accountant - has cleaned up his image as a dry-as-dust stifler of creativity, by evolving effortlessly into the new, user friendly, financial executive. At the same time insurance salesmen have shifted the world's perception of their main aim in life, by restyling themselves as financial advisers.

Sell you something? Not us guv, just want to help you, that's all!

And no one must be seen to be doing a job that others might (however unreasonably) consider demeaning. Rat catchers are rodent control operatives; dustmen are refuse disposal contractors; plumbers are sanitary engineers; office odd-job men sport titles like service provision officer. I suspect that the people who perform these very important jobs were perfectly content with their former simpler and more accurate descriptions. The grander sounding names are more often than not yet another way of avoiding paying a decent wage to the worker. Give him a bit of job-description massage, and he might just do the same job for less money.

Words used to be employed simply to describe and inform. Nowadays, they are more frequently used to deceive and confuse, to lull the customer, lure the consumer and, of course, extract a cross in the right place from the voter. That new and unloved phenomenon the spin-doctor evolved to achieve precisely those effects. Funnily enough acting is one profession that has escaped this new speak.
In fact, our job description has got simpler.

We are now commonly known by that awful patronising word that makes my skin crawl – 'luvvies' - just because a handful of high profile, old hams have given the false impression that the bulk of our profession are an insincere bunch of show offs.
And in case you think I've been exaggerating, last year Liverpool Council decided that the term 'road sweeper' was inappropriate. The

men and women who clean that city's streets are now known as 'street scene operatives'.

And did you know that AD and BC are on their way out? Using the same numbering system, our schoolchildren are being taught that we are now in the year 2002 CE (Common Era). It's better to be common than Christian these days.

29th May 2009

I wish someone could explain the attraction of wearing clothes that prominently display the manufacturer or designer's name.

When I went to the USA earlier this year, my youngest daughter made it quite clear that I would not be viewed with great favour if I returned without a t-shirt bearing the legend of a popular American clothing chain, whose mythical status with young teenagers I will not increase here by naming. And yes, I did as I was bid. It saves thinking about what gift to bring back, a dilemma fathers usually resolve by a quick whiz round the shops at the airport from which they are returning home.

The whole brand display trend started, I suppose, when the really expensive brands started to become accessible to a wider public than film stars and the super-rich. To wear something that bore the name of an iconic designer, usually from Italy or France originally, was a way of demonstrating that you hade made it, both in terms of your earning power and your membership of the elite tasteful classes.

But now the branding of clothing, shoes and handbags has spread to include almost every mass market manufacturer as well the stylish designers, it has evolved into something more akin to wearing a club football shirt. "Oh you wear those trainers, do you? Well I wear these!" If you need an argument in favour of school uniform, it must be this. If everyone has to wear the same at school, then no-one can be sidelined, categorised or picked on because of their choice of clothing, at least.

The trend for brand as social identifier has seemed to have replaced other, to me more important, issues when buying, like comfort, cost and appearance. 'Never mind the quality read the label!' seems to be the order of the day now.

I take the opposite view. If it has a visible manufacturer or designer identification that cannot be easily removed – then I don't buy it.

If they gave their stuff away, then I might be persuaded to advertise their products; but how have they succeeded in persuading millions to pay a premium to advertise their products for them? It's quite a neat trick really, I suppose.

Annoyingly, occasionally one does have to succumb. The shoes I wear are particularly identifiable – but so comfortable that I confess I have no option but to break my own rules.

13th November 1999

When I sat in the office of the BBC's head of series and serials in the summer of 1983, he went to great pains to ensure that I fully understood the implications to my future life and career of taking on the most famous role on British television – the Doctor in *Doctor Who*? I, however, was made of the stuff that could not resist the opportunity to play intergalactic Cowboys and Indians for a few years and was unashamed to surrender willingly to the lure of temporary fame.

Even though I knew that there would eventually be a price to pay for my brief time in the spotlight, I am still proud that from 1983 to 1986 I was a hero to a generation of children who dived behind the sofa when the Daleks trundled on screen, waving those sink plungers from their pepper pot casings and, against all logic, striking absolute terror into audiences of all ages.

At this point, I must pay tribute to Raymond Cusick, the BBC staff designer who responded so imaginatively and brilliantly to the one line description of those alien creatures with the obsessive drive to EXTERMINATE. Without his three dimensional realisation of the ominous and implacable Dalek - hate on casters - it is truly arguable that the programme itself might have fallen at the first hurdle. It was only when they appeared, in the second story in 1963 that the nation became glued to their screens every Saturday evening in a way that has never happened since and, indeed, in the age of multiple television channels and videos, never will again. Perversely, Ray Cusick, being a salaried, contract employee at the BBC, never received another penny for his inspirational design, unlike Terry Nation, who wrote the first script and coined the word 'Dalek', thereby securing ownership of the rights to all things Dalek in perpetuity. 'Twas ever thus.

This weekend sees a long overdue re-examination by the BBC of its most famous and successful family entertainment programme ever. My namesake Tom, the oldest surviving Doctor, is hosting a programme this weekend in which there are contributions from many of us who have over the years played a part in the Who legend. Even though science fiction has undoubtedly moved on and expensive special effects are considered by some to have made the BBC's trailblazing time traveller look a little outmoded, nonetheless I still think that it is a great shame that we have a generation of children today who have never had "their" Doctor.

But when the plug was pulled on Sylvester McCoy in 1989, I doubt that many would have predicted that ten years later, when the BBC wanted to convince us all, via advertisements, that it is worth keeping, licence fee and all, the good Doctor in his Tardis and the Daleks are the flags that are unfurled to trumpet Beeb excellence. In the BBC's annual Red Nose Day charity fundraiser, twice in ten years *Doctor Who* has been seen as the perfect vehicle to engage a national audience. Some might think I am engaging in special pleading, but so far down the line, it could even be disadvantageous to me if *Doctor Who* were revived.

But for my children and for all those future generations who might just love to surrender to the delicious thrill of terror at Saturday tea-time after the footie results, there is surely still an opportunity for the Tardis to vwo-orp into life again, with well constructed, imaginative plots showing that hi-tech effects are not essential for good story telling. I vote for Dawn French as the Doctor!

3rd October 2008

If it weren't for the fact that we are all going to end up footing the bill one way or another, there would be more than a small part of me thinking that the financial institutions are getting exactly what they deserve in the current global meltdown.

Every time I dip my toes into the murky waters of the banking, mortgage or insurance market, I end up wanting to do them more or less what they have seemingly just managed to do to themselves fairly comprehensively.

I am small fry in their terms, so they probably don't care about what I think about the way things have changed since I first needed

to insure something or to borrow money. Half of you will remember a time when this could be done simply without hours spent on the phone wading through multiple choices on automated call centres or spending the time it takes to walk from Wycombe to Marlow (on one leg) inputting data on a website, only to be rejected at the end of the process and referred to – yes, you are ahead of me – a call centre, where an automated voice will tell you that you are important to them. Oh yeah? I grew a beard today trying to insure my house, having foolishly responded to a handful of those inducements that plop through the letter box around renewal time.

If you don't fit neatly within the narrow parameters decreed by insurers who really want to only insure those who are least likely ever to need to claim, then you can forget all the 50% off and free pens they are offering. More than three bedrooms? Forget it. Built before 1850? Forget it. How many books? What no armed guards patrolling the perimeter of your garden? No CCTV? And heaven help those poor people who were flooded recently when they come to renew. Wasn't insurance supposed to be about spreading the load, so the lucky majority help out the desperately unlucky few? And when it comes to cars – an actor? Forget it. The reason? Not that we are a bunch of alcohol crazed speed merchants – but we may give a lift to a Hollywood superstar who would get millions for a scratch on their chiselled or silky cheeks.

Oh yes! I'm always nipping down to Asda with Angelina and Brad – they love sitting in straw and sweet wrappers. So does their chauffeur.

2. Grumpy Old Git

I suppose it will come as no surprise to anyone who has met me or spent any time in my company that there is a certain, shall we say, 'grumpiness' bubbling away under my seemingly benign and easy-going exterior. This is apparent, I must admit, in the following selection of examples of frustration venting and downright irascibility.

Some of the targets are obvious, to the point of shooting fish in a barrel, and I see myself as merely articulating what most sane citizens must surely and inevitably feel when confronted by the objects of each rant. Most of us are fed up to our molars and wisdom teeth with appalling customer service, call centre insanity, a steadily increasing number of badly behaved children and a society in which everyone knows their rights but many fewer believe that, hand in hand with those rights, there might be some concomitant responsibilities or duties.

There are some topics that I fulminate about, however, that provoke the occasional adverse response from some readers. I always get the most aggressive response imaginable when I venture to criticise those who indulge in blood sports, for instance. But there are also passions aroused when I suggest that smoking is less than desirable, or that the world of my childhood (when parents supported teachers who disciplined their children because those parents shared their values of good behaviour) was perhaps better than the chaotic, child confusing parenting that results in parents confronting teachers who venture to suggest that their offspring are less than perfect; or when I suggest that cyclists might occasionally be guilty of treating pedestrians in precisely the same way that they often claim they are treated by motorists.

But, as I suggest in the next selection, if only more of us were appropriately grumpy and expressed that grumpiness clearly, repeatedly but politely, then we might just make the odd ivory tower creak a little, lean a little and eventually even tumble down. Well we can all dream, can't we?

The title of the following jottings derives from the epithet my children and (I am chastened to reveal) my wife use (mostly affectionately, I hope) to describe me. You will probably find that hard to believe, dear gentle reader, but I am afraid it is true.

18th April 2008
The makers of the television programme Grumpy Old Men/Women have finally acknowledged its contributors were far

from old and (I would argue) nowhere near grumpy enough. The programme might more accurately have been called 'Slightly Irritated Middle Aged or even Younger Men/Women'. Not as catchy a title, I concede. The series now calls itself '*The Grumpy Guide to....*'

More accurate, though it doesn't yet quite plumb the depths of grumpiness that I share with the majority of my contemporaries - we who are nudging at the threshold of 'old' – the pre-zimmer generation. We have more to be grumpy about than the comparative youths that populate the programme because we can remember those days, that now sound like the stuff of fiction – days when people repaired things, when shops were all different and had different products, when food was fresh and not wrapped in three layers of landfill fodder, when bank managers knew our names and we knew theirs and relationships were built up.

We lived during a time when there were three television channels offering programmes that were excellent, rather than three hundred amongst which you are hard pressed to find something you want to watch, a time when you really could cycle to school or work without being mown down, asphyxiated or find your bike nicked at the end of the day, a time before yellow lines, speed cameras, congestion zones, when victims of crime were given more consideration than the poor deprived criminal, a time before call centres and the 'Help Line' which vies with "For the convenience of our customers…" for the title 'Misleading expression of the decade.' And what do we get hot under the collar about? What mobilises protests and marches?

Nothing much.

The last significant public demonstration of any magnitude was by a bunch of people who like chasing small furry animals and killing them. We don't apparently care a great deal that petrol now costs more in the UK than it does anywhere else in the 'first world' (if such a place exists), that our public transport systems are woefully inadequate, that our direct and indirect national and local taxation soars at the same time as services that we took for granted forty years ago are cut and reduced, that our young people have to put themselves in hock for twenty years to get the university educations our generation got for free.

As Bashful said to Happy,   "Let's get Grumpy!"

25th August 1995

As a regular reader of the letters page of this paper, I am often diverted by the arguments people unblushingly produce to justify their own particular eccentricity, habit, alleged sport or downright unsociable activity, in the face of all informed reason. Last week two correspondents attempted to defend the increasingly indefensible position of the smoker who wishes to smoke in enclosed public places by respectively implying that car driving pots shouldn't throw stones at cigarette-smoking kettles, or indeed call them black (how's that for a mixed metaphor!) and that a lady in her 94th year, could not have achieved that splendid age whilst sharing a home with her smoking offspring in permanent residence, if passive smoking is really potentially life-threatening.

The suggestion that someone who drives a car cannot therefore have an attitude about another person smoking is patently flawed. It emanates from the same school of 'defence by attack' as the argument that "people who protest at the export of live veal calves obviously don't care about child abuse because they would be protesting about that if they did!" The existence of one pollutant does not deny the existence of another. And as 'smoke-screens' go, this one is a little insubstantial because you are not allowed to run a car engine in a restaurant either. Furthermore, cars do at least serve a purpose beyond simply introducing chemicals and tar into the body with the sole and exclusive purpose of making the smoker feel better.

I used my car once to go and visit a friend who was dying of lung cancer in hospital. He was an actor called Mike Pratt, who had had a distinguished career over many years ranging from the Royal Shakespeare Company, via *Randall and Hopkirk (Deceased)* (he was Randall - the living one) to *The Brothers* where I worked with him. When I met him, he had won a lengthy battle to rid his body of a dependence on large quantities of alcohol and other drugs, and was 'clean' for the first time in some years, something of which he was justifiably quietly proud. Within two years of joining the programme he was dead, having succumbed to lung cancer. We visited him shortly before his death. He was bald from the chemotherapy, blind, pitiably emaciated and in great pain. He shared with us his sense of irony that having cleansed his system of all the other toxins which he had inflicted on his body, the one that was killing him was the one

that was least socially unacceptable (certainly in the 1970's) - smoking. I remember his words very clearly. He said,

"Give it up mate, it's a mugs game". I felt a responsibility to Mike, who, like the remarkable Roy Castle many years later, had taken time out from his own very personal death to help others. It would have seemed a betrayal of his death-bed advice had I not tried rid myself of the habit. I succeeded and am now a "reformed smoker" with all that that implies.

It saddens me to see cigarettes being smoked by increasing numbers of young people, who have more information about the very real dangers of ill health and death than my generation did, when peer pressure led us to cough and gasp our way through those first few dozen cigarettes, until we could light up without running the risk of turning green.

Certainly, we have progressed some way since the publication of a heavy volume on Motherhood which my mother possessed. It recommended smoking as an aid to relaxation during pregnancy. It seems to me that the facts are now beyond dispute, despite the contortions of the addicts and the industry to prove otherwise. Only very lucky smokers will not suffer ill health and a shorter life if they become habitual smokers. And once started, like all addictions, it is very hard to give up. As for the 93 year old mother who has survived the smoke so admirably thus far, the idea that her luck and miraculous constitution is proof that exposure to cigarette smoke is of no consequence evokes the image of a man who has played Russian Roulette and pronounces it harmless because he is still alive to tell the tale.

21st November 2008

As a nation that has historically been reticent to do so, we are gradually learning that we have a right to question and even complain if necessary, when as customers we feel the need. We should also take every opportunity to guide retailers and service providers to a clearer understanding of our requirements. After all they do tell us, over and over, again that we are "important to them." I engaged a bemused saleswoman in conversation this week about the way in which shirts and trousers are displayed in stores.

Those of you who know me, or have seen me, will not be surprised to learn that I am no stranger to the size known as XXL. But in order to see what the shop has on offer for me, I have to hunker down to the floor and, sometimes on all fours, delve through the items on the bottom shelf. Is it really beyond the wit of these companies to realise that someone with a need for that particular size is liable to be, perhaps, - well, a little larger and a little less supple than a customer, whose size 'S' item is conveniently stacked at chest level? Being of a slighter build than your columnist and possibly also shorter, they could more easily bend down to the bottom shelf, if necessary. The saleswoman said she saw my point and said she'd pass it on. I'm not holding my breath though.

This shelf stocking policy stems either from the rank size-ism already evident in women's fashion magazines - hiding away the embarrassing porkies' clothing so as not to offend their decent S and M customers - or from some sadistic desire to make us suffer for using up more of the Earth's dwindling resources in order to cover our larger than 'Large' bodies. Maybe a system of giving sizes names might help. This technique is used in some theatres to avoid the unseemly squabbles that occasionally occur between agents about who is entitled to take up residence in the Number One dressing room. Calling them Olivier, Gielgud, Irving and Garrick is an elegant solution adopted by some theatres. Perhaps sizing clothes could follow the same logic. 'S' could be Rooney, 'M' – Cruise, 'L' – Damon, 'XL' - Travolta and 'XXL' maybe Schwarzenegger? "Could I have a Hawaiian shirt in Schwarzenegger, please?" sounds better than 'Extra Extra Large' doesn't it?

3rd November 2000

I have great sympathy for those householders whose homes have been flooded in the recent spate of appalling weather, not just because of the messy disruption to their lives but also because their future relationship with their insurers is, I fear, liable to be problematical. This time last year, seduced by an avalanche of leaflets, I succumbed to the temptation to shop around for my household insurance and indeed saved money by changing to a new insurer. A year later – and that new insurer has sent my renewal notice. It was generated by computer and took the form of twelve sides of

printed information. In bold type on page one were the crucial and acceptable details of price. I was about to confirm my acceptance, but thought I should perhaps plough through the other eleven pages in case they contained something fundamental. In type many times smaller than the details of all the good things I was being offered, lurked the far from insignificant requirement that I should, within 28 days, install an approved burglar alarm system. The cost of this did not compare favourably with the small saving I had made the year before. Outraged telephone conversation achieved nothing. I described the three stranger intolerant dogs who live with us. I told them, truthfully, that the house is very rarely unoccupied and that we have nothing worth much to the average burglar (unless they're fans of damp horse blankets, dogs' bowls, Barbies and pop CDs which seem to occupy more space at Baker Towers than anything else). When you are speaking to the human lackey of a computer, forget it. The computer exgurgitates instructions based on post codes, claims and resident profiles. If you live within a mile or so of an estate that contains the burgled in enough numbers then your profile is adversely affected.

You could have Desperate Dan sitting in your garden 24 hours a day, and a police station across the road, but if your postcode paints a picture of vulnerability, then never mind increased premiums, they just don't want to know. I set about phoning the handful of the 0800 numbers that have dropped onto my mat over the last few pre-renewal weeks. Several wouldn't contemplate me because I claimed two years ago when a broken underground drain resulted in the flooding of my sitting room. They were unmoved when I pointed out that after the installation of new drainage, it could never happen again. Three major insurance names would quite simply not quote to insure an actor's home. A variety of reasons for this were given to me in respectively Glaswegian, Bristol and Geordie accents.

Apparently the entertainment business (including footballers, heaven help 'em,) is policy repellent. According to Tracey (the Bristolian) we're a pretty feckless bunch who regularly lie around drunk and trash our homes. The Geordie damned us big claimers. Miss Hain, the Glaswegian, told me that actors might become big stars and therefore attract the unwelcome attentions of the felonious. She declined to comment on my protestations that only one actor in

ten thousand becomes that famous and the rest of us are at home (guarding our possessions) a lot more than our regularly employed neighbours. We're in the business of risk assessment she told me with some asperity. I replied that she seemed to be in the business of risk avoidance. We parted not on the best of terms.

29th August 2008

A well known actor friend, whom I will not name in the earnest hope that he will regret the action that prompts this rant, sent me an email this week. He started by apologising to the many recipients for forwarding the attached drivel – but he forwarded it nonetheless. It suggested that I might like to benefit from the huge amount of good luck that would shower upon me were I to be sufficiently devoid of common sense as to pass the happy news it contained on to my poor, unsuspecting friends. The message of joy was that a saintly Dutch missionary had initially promulgated his ludicrous message some years earlier and as a result of his generous and altruistic initiative, a man whose life was in tatters suddenly came into countless millions because (we are seriously expected to believe) he forwarded the original missive to eight unsuspecting friends.

More repellently, it told of a colleague of that first recipient whose child became ill because he did not forward the email and who suddenly recovered when that same thitherto sane friend lapsed into temporary mushiness and sent the email onward to another swathe of the gullible. These things have been going round for years but I am genuinely staggered that the 'Just in case...' and 'What if...' factor is still powerful enough to influence people who seem on the surface to be capable of tying their shoelaces and distinguishing talk from mutter.

I wish I could fathom the agenda of the creators of these scattergun emails. Is it idle work for idle hands? Or a means of disseminating viruses? Or a 21st Century version of knocking on doors and running away? It surely cannot be that the originator actually believed what they were writing? I am resolved to punish future offenders by repeating the message I sent my deluded and weak actor friend today.

"Unless you send all your friends including and especially me 200 quid in the next twenty four hours, your eyeballs will explode and your toenails will turn into man-eating purple frogs. A cynical actor in

Buckinghamshire sent this message and never received a piece of tripe like it again – don't you envy him?" I can only urge you, dear sane reader, to punish your weak friends who try to persuade you to clog up the internet in a similar way. You might make a bob or two.

14th November 1997

When I returned home this week, after a couple of days away, one of my messages was to ring an American friend on a London number. When I did, I thought I had been misrouted to Rio de Janeiro, when a voice that sounded like Carmen Miranda on speed said,

"Ellotenkyouferrcallinzeefartypostausotelkenssintonowknaielpyoo?"

After requesting and receiving two repetitions of this rapidly delivered gibberish, I deciphered that she was thanking me for calling her hotel and asking how she could help me. I told her the name of the friend who had left the message and spent the next minute listening to his room phone ringing out. Then a tape recording switched in, offering me the opportunity to leave a message on his voice mail or return to the operator. I chose the former and keyed the appropriate button. I was then treated to more than two minutes of a recorded tape exhorting me to sample the delights to be experienced spending Christmas at the Hotel, telling how very a reasonable a three day break would be, that children were welcome and that the chef would be excelling his already impossibly high standards of cuisine on my behalf. I hung up and tried again. The "Ellotenkyou..." rapid fire ritual was repeated. I explained that I had just been put through to a room and then diverted to an endless recorded tape and before I could finish, she chirruped,

"Haipuchoothrroosah" and I heard the room phone ring again. I hung up and phoned again. "Ellotenkyou..." I was ready this time.

"Do not put me through to anyone. I have just spent two minutes listening to advertising material as a result of phoning you just now. I do not wish to do that again. Listen very carefully to what I have to say. I wish to leave a message with a human being for one of your guests." A momentary silence. I had a mental picture of a female version of Manuel from *Fawlty Towers* pausing in suspicious incomprehension and struggling with a situation for which she did

not have a pre-programmed response available. Manuella dived for the nearest available exit.

"Haipuchoothrroosah!" She put me through to the porter's desk, where I finally got to leave a message for my friend. Leaving aside the advisability of employing telephone receptionists for whom English is a third language, I do most fervently wish that hotel chains wouldn't insist that their staff adhere to formula greetings and valedictions. It is one of those American imports that really do not cross the pond happily. The first time I was encouraged to "Have a nice day!" by a shop assistant in the States, I was sufficiently charmed to thank her warmly and offer lengthy and warm reciprocation. She was visibly alarmed and clearly thought me deranged. Now, I am beginning to wonder whether I don't really have a sneaking preference for the uninterested and thinly disguised disdain of the archetypal English shop assistant's response, characterised by the studied refusal to terminate her current activity to serve you. When she is describing to a colleague the television programme she was watching the night before or chatting on the phone about what her boyfriend's latest excesses, it has an added piquancy. I am, actually less provoked by that indifference, than I am by being asked, as a knee jerk reaction, if I need help when I am perfectly capable of asking for it if I did. I think the preferred English approach is a cheery "Let me know if I can help you sir." which carries the implication that the assistant is aware of my existence but I am under no pressure. And why, oh why, must I be thanked on the telephone for calling someone, when the reason for my call is completely unknown at that point and for my benefit not theirs?

9th November 2007

I was roundly abused by a cyclist this week because I walked in front of him without looking. Fair enough you may think, oh even handed reader. In most circumstances I would agree with you. However, on this occasion I was walking along the pavement in Broad Street in Birmingham. The irritated cyclist was cycling along the same pavement and came from behind me at speed. My failure to signal my intention to turn to the right caused him to swerve slightly in order to avoid a situation in which my breaking bones might have damaged his bike. It is worth noting here that he had protective

headgear on; I did not. Although if this cycle where you like trend continues then, given the vagaries of modern health and safety requirements, doubtless pedestrians will be fined if they fail to wear safety helmets and are mown down by cyclists. In the next half mile five more pavement cyclists wove their way around the homeward plodding commuters and a solitary community support officer whose failure to raise an eyebrow let alone a hand to halt their progress was matched only by their failure to regard her presence as offering any kind of limitation to their dangerous use of what was designed to be a footpath. I was by this time sufficiently apoplectic to suggest to the final cyclist that the road was the more appropriate place for both him and his bike. He made some suggestions of his own, which did not relate to road traffic offences and served to confirm my disinclination to remember him in my will.

It may be that after years of being the hunted, cyclists have evolved to become the hunter. They have had decades of dicing with death and I must admit that cyclists get scant attention from drivers who no longer give them the safe margins that we were afforded when I was a young cyclist. What better way to purge that memory than by asserting their position as top dog in a less frantic pool? I have recently noticed too that urban cyclists seem to have awarded themselves immunity from the restrictions on movement offered by traffic lights, which users of other means of transport obey. Is it perhaps time that the police and other agencies made it clear that pavements are not cycle paths and that the Highway Code applies to all road users?

17th May 1996

I recently took my bubble jet printer into an authorised repairer. As it was not a state of the art model, I wanted to know the potential cost before deciding whether it was worth repairing. Within minutes of entering the Service Agent's showroom I was tempted to dispatch the receptionist to a place where hordes of nail filing, brain dead bimbos would recite a series of formula responses to customer enquiries until she died of boredom. I have a strong suspicion that it would take several thousand years.

"Good morning sir. How can I help you today?" Why, 'today'? Is it in case we hang around for a week obstructing their view of

themselves reflected in the showroom window? I wanted to know how much it might cost me to sort out my problem. In the good old days, Jim the engineer would pop out from the back for a couple of seconds, take a quick look and say either,

"It's probably your grommet return spindle, jamming on the feed uptake bush. Leave it with me and pop back tomorrow" or "To be honest this has had it. I could repair it for you, but it would cost at least sixty or seventy quid for parts alone, it's up to you but you'd be better off getting a new one." Because you have had a personal relationship with a human being called Jim, you were more inclined to take his advice and probably ask good old Jim to supply any new machine for you. By genuinely considering your interests, Jim is also being a good employee. The trouble is that Jim has now been whisked off to a repair depot where the sun doesn't shine and to which there is no customer access. My loony tune in Manchester simply trotted out her rehearsed formula.

"There's a twenty five pound minimum charge for our engineer to look at it and he will do work up to fifty pounds and refer back to you if it's going to cost more than that." She was neither equipped to accommodate any uncertainty on my part nor able to help me make a reasoned choice about the most economical route to take. Twenty five pounds is a lot of money to be told,

"I tightened up the grub screw on the rollers. You won't have any more trouble with it." or indeed "It's knackered mate. You need a new one." I had the same experience today. I telephoned a service agent in Henley to ask about the advisability of continuing to use my microwave oven as the enamel has started peeling off inside the heating compartment. Nobody could discuss it with me. I would have to bring it in. There would be a twenty pound minimum charge, the engineer would do up to forty pounds of work and refer back to me if it needed more. It would take at least ten days.

"You mean I could then be told it would cost two hundred pounds to repair and I would have to pay twenty pounds for the privilege?"

"Yes, but the twenty pounds would be refunded if you bought a new one off us!" Aha!

"Can you not give me even a vague idea of the potential repair cost?"

"No".

"Can I talk to the engineer for a second?"

"No, they're not on the premises and anyway who would be paying for his time while he's talking to you?" The telephone all but melted in my hand. I then called another service agent in Reading, who listened attentively as I described the problem. Although his company had a similar charging policy, at least he suggested that I might very easily and safely rub down the flaking interior myself and repaint it with enamel. I am left with the certainty that I would not use the Henley repairer, even if it meant never having a baked potato again. I would however, if necessary, go to the repairer who tried to help me solve my problem, even though it meant going to Reading! I didn't get his name; but it could have been Jim's son. But where will the minimum charging policy end.

"How much is a ticket to London please?"

"It'll cost you a tenner for me to tell you!"

"How much is that doggy in the window?"

"Our canine costing adviser will be with you in a moment. That'll be twenty quid, sucker!"

14th December 2001

The 'Emperor's New Clothes' syndrome is alive and well and resident in the London artistic community, one that already has a reputation for boldly going where the rest of us have far too much common sense to go. Martin Creed won the £20,000 annual Turner Prize for 'Work 227 – The lights going on and off'. For those of you who have either missed, or still cannot believe, what this piece of so-called conceptual art comprises, - you enter an empty white-painted gallery in the Tate Britain and the lights go on and off every 5 seconds - and erm, - well, that's it, folks!

Now, Turner did certainly get a bit abstract in his later creative life, but his pictures exploring light arrived after an artistic life in which he had demonstrated a mastery of his craft in more conventional ways. Martin Creed's artistry is somewhat more modern in that he has played the art establishment at their own pretentious game. One only hopes that he is doing so deliberately. It would be unthinkable that he should actually believe that turning lights on and off is somehow worthy of bracketing him with the old masters. To compound the dazzling lunacy of rewarding this work, it is a rehash of a former

(literally) flashy piece of work - yes – a light being turned on and off, but every twenty minutes. Next year he's going to have a torch in his pocket, which he may or may not turn on. He is disarming in his admission that he cannot explain what his entry means,

"...except to say that the lights are definitely going on and off", adding, "I don't think it's for me to tell people what to think." Wise move, Martin. Most of us know exactly what to think and can only gaze in wonderment as the art commentators and critics fall over each other trying to mine some nugget of pretentious sense out of this scam. In fact, this is the ultimate nonsense that serves only to prove that the Emperor's skin and flesh are absent, not just his clothes. One of that rarefied breed that works for the Tate – one Simon Wilson – produced a typical piece of arty flim-flam – "I think life is like that work. One minute it's on, the next minute it's off. It's emblematic of mortality. What Creed has done has made minimal art minimal by dematerialising it – removing it from the hectic commercialised world of capitalist culture." Oh yes, and the baby that daubs his apple puree over the wall is expressing his contempt for urban decay and architectural decadence!

No wonder Madonna took the opportunity to heighten her profile with some well-chosen profanity at the Turner award ceremony. I have decided to enter next year. £20,000 would enable Mrs. Baker to get a nice new wheelbarrow, some new green wellies and a mohair rug for the goat. I am going to nail a kipper underneath a table and stand it on a mirror. It will be called 'Reflections of What is Not a Cod.' I can imagine the praise heaped on me by the art pundits as they grapple with the multiple levels of reality and self-awareness, as they see themselves looking down (and at the same time up) at something that is indeed not a cod, whilst simultaneously being precisely that. Who's codding whom? Humbug!

11th October 1997

It's official. I am turning into Victor Meldrew. I am not sure whether it is a function of age or I am an unreconstructed interferer by nature and increasingly unable to disguise my rage at the inconsiderate behaviour of others. My road to Damascus was, somewhat bathetically, more accurately described as a supermarket aisle in Cressex. My mood, I thought, was average; nothing had

happened thus far to waken the slumbering beast of my strong sense of decency and public duty. Then I reached the grapes of wrath. As I approached the display a lady shopper reached over from the rear of the stand and began the ritual search through the bunches to find the best. In doing so, she knocked over a five foot by two foot placard alerting us to the existence of the grapes, which fell on top of them. My assumption that she would, of course, replace the board was ill founded. She was a grape sorter not a damage limitation operative. Irresistible Meldrew's Syndrome arose within me. I walked behind the display as the miscreant was walking away, I replaced the sign with some flourish and, I am afraid to say, I tut-tutted, adding the coup-de-grace, a heavy world-weary sigh, that spoke volumes of the human race's descent into the Slough of Despond and the Staines of Utter Worthlessness. The offender's response, after a suitable moment for thought, was to turn around, walk past me and, without breaking stride, and mutter, "We're not all as perfect as you, Mr Baker!" Wrong footed by the recognition, I heard myself give the unthinking and rather arch response, "Evidently!" - thereby neatly shooting down my alleged perfection. For some reason every piece of jettisoned rubbish in the street, every small example of selfish and thoughtless behaviour provokes more wrath within me than appears to be the case with the more temperate majority. It is probably quite simply that my ire is greater than my fear of violent retribution and I am probably heading for the kind of punishment meted out on my evident role model - the quixotic Victor. Barely a few moments later, I witnessed the spectacle of   a nine or ten year old thug screaming and yelling at his young mother. When she bent over to advise him that his behaviour was unacceptable - I couldn't hear her words but the body language was unmistakable - he launched a salvo of kicks and verbal abuse at her. She was evidently used to it because her face became almost vacant as she mentally retreated from the situation and walked away from him. I next encountered this frightening family group when I saw the tall figure of the mother disappear behind a row of shelves whereupon young Atilla grabbed hold of his four or five year old sister's arm hurled her to the ground and kicked her twice. Girl screamed and sobbed; mother returned and comforted, but said nothing to the spawn of Satan, who stood there looking defiant, with a savage triumph in his eyes which

prophesied a future of joy-riding, drug abuse and domestic violence. As I passed him I told him I thought he was quite the ghastliest piece of work I had ever seen. His look in response registered surprise, which I suppose could be a good omen. No other customer appeared to wish to compound the embarrassment of the mother by registering what was happening at all. On the way out of the store, an enormous tattoo in a vest lit   a cigarette while still some twenty yards short of the exit. I am pleased to report that my sense of self preservation, at least, is greater than Victor's. I neither coughed ostentatiously nor plucked it from his ox-like mitt and stubbed it out on his hairy chest. But Oh! How   I yearned!

22nd November 2002

I was in Poole on Saturday and popped into a branch of my bank to get some cash. I realised that I also had some cheques to pay in, so went over to the teller and transacted my business. Then I went to the cash machine, put my hand in my pocket and encountered emptiness. No wallet. Quick mental rewind to the last place I had used it. Cordially despising citizens who have loud telephone conversations in quiet places, I went out into the street, found a suitably unpopulated spot and phoned the last beneficiary of the Baker plastic. No, my wallet had not been handed in by anyone; she remembered serving me and I definitely had not left my wallet there. My internal organs sank further into my size tens.

The options were few. I had definitely used my credit card less than half an hour earlier. Since then I had been to the theatre at which I was working and parked my car. Then I had walked down to the bank. I ran, well walked briskly -(ish) back to my car, searched under and around the seat. No joy. My wallet, with umpteen credit cards in it was either lost by me or feloniously appropriated by another. Aware that every moment of indecision could be filled by the current possessor of my plastic making inroads into his (or her) Christmas shopping list, I decided to make the call and cancel all the cards. I then had to call the police in order to comply with the terms of the card protection scheme.

Ten minutes later, having returned to the theatre in Poole where I was about to perform in a matinee, my mobile phone trilled at me. It was the Poole branch of my bank. Did I know that I had left my

wallet on the counter in their branch? They had now closed, so I would have to collect it next week when they re-opened. But I will be in Coventry next week! Okay, come down now and ring the bell. I walked briskly (ish) the length of Poole High Street (unwritten law – the branch of your bank in any strange town will always be the furthest bank away from the point at which you start to look for it). I retrieved my wallet, gushed my profuse thanks, accepted their regrets that I was now unable to obtain any cash as all my cards were useless and they had cashed up, learned that the cards' cancellation was – for obvious and compelling reasons – irrevocable and absolute, and walked, not as briskly (-ish), back to the theatre.

As a result of my own failing faculties I had rendered myself cashless in Hampshire, a hundred miles from home, with no means of obtaining funds.

Fortunately, a fellow performer, the perennially generous and talented Louise Jameson, bunged me £40 to fill my tank with petrol and get myself a bite to eat. I had, in case you are as addled as I am and failed to understand, entered the bank, taken out my wallet and, then realising that I cheques to pay in, I had put it on the counter while filling in the paying in book.

A "senior moment" then occurred. I had forgotten taking it out within seconds of doing so and reported its loss when it lay within feet of me. Book me into the Home for Confused Thespians please!

3. Family Life

I have always been absolutely clear about one thing – the reason why I go to work. Yes, I am lucky that I work in a profession that I have always enjoyed being a part of and only rarely have I had to steel myself before going out of the door to earn a crust. The wrench on departure to work away from home is all about what I am leaving, usually – rather than what I am going to. And in that I am under no illusion that I am other than very, very lucky indeed. I know that probably the majority of the working population derive considerably less job satisfaction from their employment than I have over four decades.

My family are my rock and my reason. I am certainly someone who works to live – rather than lives to work. The latter was probably my position before I met my wife and we had children. Losing our first child, Jack, when he was just seven weeks old served to underline for both Marion and me what our priorities were in life. My daughters will, I hope not be too surprised to learn that they occupy such a high position in my list of priorities. In that, I claim to be no different to most other fathers, of course. And I have been luckier than most fathers too, inasmuch as the majority of dads lead variations of the 9 to 5 working life and their weekday interaction with their children can tend to be a quick burst of bedtime stories after struggling back home on the commuter train. I, on the other hand, may have had to be away for weeks at a time when touring or filming, but then, given the vagaries of my unpredictable and unreliable profession, I find myself at home for several weeks at a time, occasionally months – and can then play a full hands-on role as a parent round the clock.

I am therefore happily no stranger to bedtime stories, school runs, school trips, parties and evening activities.

I see that I have written more than once about the vexed question of paying for four daughters' weddings. Am I protesting too much, do you think? People assume I must be joking. But I have never been in a position where I could give my four children everything they needed whilst going through their early years and then their post-18 education whilst at the same time putting aside enough for four weddings. I have supported/ am supporting all of them through University, as far as I am able – and after that… Saving an unexpected Hollywood role or another windfall there is unlikely to be anything left to engage in the kind of fairy tale wedding that everyone seems to expect these days. I just hope they invite me, though.

I know that most of my contemporaries will know exactly what I mean when I say that it has all gone by so quickly. Childhood, viewed from the point of view of the child is almost eternal in its leisurely pace, at a time when you are burning with the desire to rush headlong into life. Childhood viewed from a parent's perspective is like a runaway horse careering down the steepest hill – on a skateboard!

6th March 1998

Ever since I have had children, in common with millions of parents before me, I have had to re-assess all sorts of issues in order to give our children a moral or ethical structure by which to lead their lives. It has sometimes proved a challenge to do this without the whiff of hypocrisy becoming too strong. *Do as I say, not what I do* has never seemed a terribly satisfactory maxim to me. But it is much harder to expect young children to accept that lying about their mistakes or outright villainies makes those offences far worse, if they are constant witnesses of their parent's own economies with the truth. This, I freely admit, has had a salutary effect on my own conduct, which only falters when it would be appallingly impolite to offer unpalatable opinions on friends' new hair styles or, indeed, partners! My children rightly berate me when the car's speedometer indicates that I am exceeding the speed limit, which has had a similarly salutary effect on my driving - for some of the time at least.

My latest dilemma is to do with the certification of films. It is terribly hard to say to a twelve year old that she cannot go to her contemporary's party because you have learned that they are all going to watch a film with a 15 certificate, particularly when it seems the parents of other children do not see a problem in allowing twelve year old girls to watch, say, *The Full Monty*. The film in question is undoubtedly an excellent one. It deals with poignant and important contemporary issues with sensitivity, charm and humour. But I would rather my daughter saw it when she was old enough to understand and enjoy it.

Also, I must confess, I have no desire to unnaturally hasten that headlong rush from childhood through adolescence, to the full Monty of adulthood. Childhood is precious; and even in these knowing, sophisticated pre-millennial days, I am unashamed in my desire to prolong the bliss of ignorance as long as possible. The other

issue is legality. I know that some parents do not see this as a problem, and will happily take eight or nine year olds to see 12 rated films, because they are confident that their children are mature enough to handle the content, which may indeed be the case. But by implication at least you are saying to that child that it is okay, sometimes, when it suits us - to disregard a law or rule which we, from our superior intellectual or social position, view as inconvenient. This sends out all sorts of dangerous messages.

Just as children from violent homes learn the currency of violence, so surely children of parents who feel free to disregard laws that don't suit them can only learn a similar disrespect for the law. Whilst some parents may feel that their children are the exception to the generality whose interests are being protected by the certification of films, those parents are totally irresponsible or arrogant if they feel able to make those judgements for other peoples' children. And this is what happens when they shrug and allow their pre-pubescent children to screen movies at their parties without personally checking with the parents of other children that the films are acceptable to those parents too. It really will not do to force those of us - who may be considered over-protective by some - to be seen as spoil-sports by our children because other parents refuse to acknowledge the possibility that others may not share their liberal views. I am prepared, if that is what it takes, to be seen as very un-modern and square. Just as my children have to face peer pressure, so do we adults, it seems. For my children's sake it is worth it.

5th July 1996

When people learn that I have four daughters they usually feel the need to react sympathetically. Some suggest that I must be dreading the approach of the misunderstood teens and the endless stream of unsuitable boys. I am preparing myself for that. The moat is being excavated; the drawbridge constructed; miniature cameras and tracking devices are being installed; the machine guns are in place. This is a boy free zone. But if any do get through, I am determined not to succumb to a common paternal temptation. I will voice no criticism of the repellent, surly, unwashed lout who communicates in monosyllabic grunts and has the social skills of a flatulent whippet. If asked for an opinion, I shall say that he seems a really nice lad with

hidden depths of intelligence and sensitivity and that he puts me in mind of myself at his age. That should do the trick. Conversely, I will resist all temptation to praise the pleasant, intelligent, clean and polite boy friend. I might even go so far as to suggest an antipathy, based on the fact that he is obviously untrustworthy and unattractive and that he reminds me of the moronic lead singer of one of those awful pop groups - ('Slur' or 'Nowaysis'?) Now is that subtle or what? Of course, somebody or other's law states that my girls, being their mother's daughters too and therefore nobody's fools, will be aware of their father's devious nature and seeing through the ruse, will continue to favour the unsavoury. So maybe I should just opt for the ritual agony of being a conventional Dad and telling it how it is.

"You're not going out with that ghastly Neanderthal with the tattoo and pierced eyebrows again? For heaven's sake your mother and I haven't wasted all these years bringing you up, have we? It only seems five minutes ago that you were an angel in the Playgroup Nativity. And if you think you're going out looking like that, you can think again my girl! All the clothes you've got upstairs - and you're going out looking like a refugee!" I am assured that I -and, more importantly, they - will survive these rites of passage. The other reaction that seems to greet the discovery that I am a father of daughters is a gleeful,

"Well you'd better save up then! Four weddings" This last statement is usually followed by a shake of the head and expulsion of air through pursed lips. I am resolved to challenge a tradition which recalls a time when women were regarded as chattels and responsibilities to be endured by men. In order to off-load your daughters you had to bribe the groom with livestock and promises of advancement. I like my daughters (at the moment) and would therefore rather expect substantial recompense for losing them! But the historical bribe has evolved into marquees, mobile discotheques, poached salmon in mayonnaise and Australian sparkling white wine. The latter is consumed by a group of people, half of whom would rather be watching Grandstand and are only there for the free bar.

The remainder are wishing that they had gone for the pink two-piece and the little hat with the netting on top and regretting the new shoes and blistered heels. Even the children only look and feel sweet for the first half hour. Formal dress and marquee hire companies,

caterers and florists derive more benefit than the couple who are the intended focus of the celebration. You will never of course get someone who has spent £6000 on a wedding for his daughter to say anything other than that it was a wonderful day and worth every penny. Similarly guests and relations are reluctant to admit that they regretted missing Finals Day at Wimbledon in order to spend the day listening to Uncle Eddy tell anyone who stood still long enough about his colostomy. Or indeed that they would much rather have had the unrivalled pleasure of complaining that they hadn't been invited, whilst saving the cost of a present. If when cupid does his work I have any cash to spare, my girls will be welcome to it. But I hope they can wait until they're in their thirties! Surely, nobody will expect a poor old pensioner to stump up for a lavish wedding. Will they?

16th August 1996

A day on the river. What could be nicer? My youngest daughter is a devotee of *Rosie and Jim*, the two rag dolls, who travel with a gentle bearded eccentric up and down the waterways of Britain. My other children have visions of the idyllic river life based on an amalgam of *Wind in the Willows*, *Swallows and Amazons* and *Tales of the Riverbank*. They have not seen *The Poseidon Adventure* or read *Robinson Crusoe*. Their one stipulation was that it should not be a rowing boat. They very sensibly foresaw the possibility that my macho urge to emulate Marlow's finest son might wear off quite soon after pulling muscles that haven't seen active duty for a decade or so. They then envisaged themselves shackled in ranks like galley slaves with me beating a brass gong to keep them in time.

We opted for an inboard-engined no frills motorboat from a hirer in Henley. Our boat was given to us by two young lads who couldn't have been much older than thirteen. They had a thinly disguised casual contempt for day trippers. In the practised delivery of one who could barely bring himself to say aloud anything that was so blindingly obvious, he muttered the (admittedly rudimentary) instructions on the control of the vessel and the lore of the river.

Had I never been in control of a small boat before I might have felt the need to risk the lad's weary disdain and double check. Mercifully I have some limited experience of river and canal cruising. My first

foray into messing about on the wet stuff was some thirty years ago when, as a law student, I joined five others in the purchase of a narrow boat in which we planned a leisurely summer, cruising the waterways of England and visiting as many canal side hostelries as possible. Then we would let the boat out to others of a similar disposition and recoup our costs.

That was the plan anyway. I suppose I should have seen a life pattern forming after our first weekend exploring the canals around Manchester. We left it at its moorings on a spur of the Manchester Ship Canal and a few days later the banks of that section collapsed necessitating its closure for at least six months for repairs. Our already stretched resources couldn't extend to paying for a crane to lift eighty feet of narrow boat out of the canal, so we sold it at a slight loss and ruefully contemplated our rather expensive weekend afloat. Fifteen years later I was tempted by a 12 foot Shetland Cruiser which seemed ridiculously cheap at the time. I did get two or three pleasant summers of chugging up and down the same stretch of the Thames, until the novelty faded and I eventually sold it. The plan was to potter down to Marlow for lunch. However a little while after successfully negotiating Hambleden Lock, we realised that we didn't have time for that and would have to return to Henley. I detached myself from the queue of boats of all sizes waiting at Hurley lock and turned around in the crowded waters to go back upstream. I felt fairly conspicuous in my comparatively small vessel, as I struggled with the ninety three point turn that it took me to be sure of avoiding a collision with the odd floating hotel.

That experience paled into insignificance however on my return to Henley. I was watched by the deadpan pre-adolescent as I rather neatly, I thought, moored up. He waited until I was about to tie up before calling out that he wanted me the other way round at another mooring. It took me some several minutes inelegantly hurtling between forward and reverse gears to achieve this. When we had disembarked, Master super cool then jumped into the boat and with the same casual expertise displayed by those chaps that walk around nausea inducing fairground rides collecting money, nonchalantly returned the boat to precisely the spot where I had originally moored it, but in about ten seconds. I must reluctantly concede that had I had such an opportunity to humiliate an adult when I was his age I might

have been similarly tempted, but it still dents the street cred in front of the daughters.

"Why are those boys sniggering Daddy?"

"Are they? I hadn't noticed!"

24th September 2004

I am constantly obliged to witness my contemporaries spending vast sums of money to mark the occasion of their daughters being carried off by young men. And I continue to fail to understand why, at a time when a young couple needs a great number of very expensive things quite urgently, there is this obsession with feeding and watering vast numbers of friends and relations whom one has not seen or thought of for decades, and moreover doing so in a style so lavish that it bears no relation to the usual standard of living of the families concerned. I am clearly out of step because otherwise intelligent fathers of my acquaintance routinely fail to see any problem with the whole spendfest. But as, in their new suit, uncomfortable shirt and tight shoes, they take their daughters' arms on that long walk between the ranks of two families that will probably only ever meet up again at christenings, surely mingled with all those conflicting emotions of pride, sadness and love, must be nagging doubts about the cost of the whole process.

However much a doting father protests that nothing's too good for his little girl, only a millionaire or a saint could hold steadfastly to that noble thought in the face of the veritable industry that has grown up around the public celebration of a very private intention. The expression 'giving away' in this context is one of the understatements of all time. Historically, families tempted suitors for their daughters by offering them dowries, as an inducement to take on the burden of the support of one of their many dependants. This has resulted in today's father of the bride being responsible for the cost of the whole shebang from the wedding dress and flower festooned impossibly large marquee to the fourteenth pint of lager consumed by the bridesmaid's boyfriend that the father has never met before and whom the bridesmaid only met at the hen night.

This has never seemed entirely fair to me. And I swear I was of this opinion long before I had four daughters. Though it would perhaps be fair to say that my attitude became increasingly crystallised with

the arrival of each successive little lovely, lively lady in my home. Society has changed. Our daughters hold down jobs as well as bringing up families. Indeed, such has been the shift in social structure, that logically it should be the groom's family that carry the cost of whatever celebration they elect to have on the occasion that they deprive me of my daughter and rid themselves of their messy, truculent burden. Sons, after all, tend to be less use around the home. I know; I was one once. They certainly contribute less in terms of communication, effort and emotion and are far less likely to care for their aged parents, when they sink into their armchairs, sprout slippers and start reminiscing about the good old days when television announcers spoke the Queen's English and national service made men of us all.

The time has come for those who wish to deprive us of our gentle, loving daughters to at least have the decency not to expect us to bankrupt ourselves for the privilege at precisely the time when we need to invest in the Sunny Valley Home of Content Savings Plan, so that the daughter of some other bereft couple can eventually soothe our ageing brows.

16th September 2005

I have regularly battled with my daughters over their reluctance to do anything (or worse to allow me to do anything) that may turn out to be 'embarrassing'. Unhelpfully, anything that is visible or audible to a third party seems to fall into that category. I am a great believer in the maxim *Honi Soit qui Mal y Pense*, the motto of the Order of the Garter. Edward III uttered those words (Shame on him who thinks ill of it...) to his courtiers, who sniggered when a lady's garter fell off. He picked it up and put it on his own leg to underline their shallowness, founding thereby the noble order.

However, I do draw the line when my pets embarrass me. And they do so regularly, particularly our 18 year old cat, Rover, who as a fit and feisty black young lad about town caused us considerable embarrassment when he conned two other households into believing that they owned him too, a fact we discovered when we saw him exiting the window of a house half a mile away. We eventually sorted that one out by convincing the well-intentioned would-be adopters that he had been taking bed and board with us for some years, ever

since he and his brothers had joined us as kittens. Now he is ancient and gaga, and has forsaken his ablutions entirely, he wanders around the local tracks looking emaciated and unkempt, despite nine dinners a day, and attempts to convince all and sundry that he is cruelly treated. He does this by simulating death. He lies around the place like a bag of old bones and declines to move even when slavering dogs rush up intent on mayhem. This, of course, confuses them and they back off, while he lolls impassively watching them. A risky, but seemingly effective, strategy.

Today a delightful and kind neighbour knocked on our door to ask my wife if she knew who owned a poor, bedraggled cat that she had seen drinking out of a muddy puddle in the woods. My wife, known as soft touch for the halt, lame and furry guessed immediately the identity of the said bag of bones, but before she could begin to enlighten our concerned Samaritan, the dishevelled spindle-shanks ambled round the corner yelling,

"Where's me dinner", which he does at least forty times a day.

"There it is, poor thing!" she cried. I told you – embarrassing! We hope and trust that she left reassured.

July 26th 1996

Three years ago we were entertaining some friends and their children to Sunday lunch. The weather was glorious; the children were happily playing in the garden. The adults were relaxed. The atmosphere could not have been more pleasant. We had bought one of those rigid framed, blue plastic paddling pools for the children to play in. You know the sort, the ones that never survive intact to be used the next year and very soon begin to look like the inside of an octopus tank that hasn't been cleaned out for months. But it provided precisely what children need on a hot day - somewhere to cool down, splash each other and have fun.

After a fairly definitive family Sunday afternoon, my wife went inside to make tea. Everyone else drifted in after her. After a short time, measurable only in seconds, she noticed that Rosie, our thirteen month old daughter, was absent from the milling throng of children and went back outside to look for her. She then screamed out for help. I met her in the doorway carrying our daughter, limp, blue faced, her eyes open, staring and fixed. She was not breathing. There

was an awful millisecond when the blood in every single artery and vein in the room turned to ice.

Ten years earlier our first baby had been a cot death victim; surely we couldn't have another taken from us? I grabbed Rosie, turned her upside down and shook her. I banged her on the back, lay her on the ground and covered her mouth and nose with my mouth and blew into her tiny lungs. In my panic and uncertainty, and without time for thought, I just did what I had seen done in countless television dramas. After a brief eternity, she started to wake from the living death that had seemed to hold her and would certainly have taken her from us forever had my wife not noticed her absence so soon. She appeared to be in a dream. Slowly her skin changed from that terrifying bluish pallor back to a healthier pinker hue. She was shaking and disorientated for some time and was content to be held wrapped in warm blankets until a doctor came to examine her. In the space of no more than two minutes, Rosie had noticed what we had not - that the other children had lifted her play slide into the water. The three steps were on the grass, the slide itself was in just nine inches of cold water. For five, six and eight year olds - great fun. For a one year old - potentially lethal. Rosie had seen her favourite slide, climbed it, sat on the top and whooshed the few inches down into the water. All she had to do then was sit up and she would have been completely safe, if a little shocked. However she was wearing a nappy which did its efficient water absorption job and weighted her down. And the cold water was such a shock to her system that she just lay on her back underwater and stopped, - literally stopped.

We were informed by the doctor who arrived shortly afterwards that mercifully no water had got into her lungs. Her instinctive response to the shock of finding herself without air and in freezing water was to stop breathing. Fortunately again, we were told, at that age babies are able to survive oxygen deprivation without damage for considerably longer than older children and adults might in similar circumstances. As a result she did not suffer any long term consequences of her immersion.

But, in effect, Rosie had 'died' and was resuscitated only because my wife noticed in time that she was not there. A minute or two later would have been too late. It is an incident that we will never forget and I am telling you this story in the hope that you will all be aware at

this time of year that paddling pools even with the smallest amount of water in them can be hazardous to the tinies. I now see danger everywhere. As my children grow older, I am unashamedly less adventurous than some of the parents of my children's peers. But I don't mind being branded overprotective by those who are lucky enough never to have had reason to be other than relaxed.

3rd May 2002

The dark nights are behind us. The thermal underwear is edging towards the back of the drawer, if not exactly being put in mothballs. I can even get away with turning off the central heating, without my all female household doing their impressions of Shackleton's men nearing the South Pole. It is that time when an Englishman's eyes turn to his garden.

Nothing too strenuous to begin with - the first mow. And, of course, the mower hasn't occupied a moment of my thought since it was stowed away last autumn. Amazingly, it starts first time; but instead of moving off gracefully towards the lush Baker greensward, it lurches violently to the left. Flat tyre! Spend half an hour trying to find the foot pump; locate it, eventually, under the pile of entangled old cables, ropes and wires that I have kept for decades now on the basis that they might come in useful one day. All they have done thus far is stop me finding the wretched pump. I must do something about them...later. Do my back in, pumping up the tyre; then glide off, seated astride my faithful Countax mower, creating a lovely stripy effect on what I like to refer to us "the lawn" and which others, less charitable, might describe as a moss, daisy and buttercup sanctuary, strewn with the evidence of dog ownership.

Then I remember. I read somewhere that the way you mow your lawn is very revealing about your love life. Apparently women, as a rule are more inclined to favour a lawn with a natural appearance; it is we men who like mowing in stripes and the more billiard table smooth, weed-free and precise your stripy lawn is, the less likely you are to be romantic and irresistible to the fairer sex, apparently. So I tried driving around in a random pattern this year and, of course, it took twice as long, as I covered more ground in my quest for herbiculturally induced desirability. I gazed across the newly cropped

expanse at my wife, waiting for her to be overcome by my manly, non-stripy achievement.

"That's better. You can get the garden chairs out now," she said, returning indoors, clearly struggling to deal with the sudden and unexpected virile charm of her husband. I removed the table and chairs from the shed. That needs a bit of work too – the walls are looking decidedly moribund, well the three that are still vertical. Exhausted by all that effort, I sank into one of the chairs and tried to ignore the ripping sound as the seat yielded a few more inches along the seam in its inexorable race to oblivion. Clearly the shed has infected its contents.

My wife joined me with a cup of tea. We survey the rural idyll, which was tainted within seconds by the arrival of our dogs. They were strewn around the house asleep when we slipped outside, but the promise of action aroused them all from their indolent torpor. The Jack Russell immediately began to dig a hole in my randomly mown and very sexy lawn. The Roodle, the unlikely progeny of a poodle and a Jack Russell, thought that looked like fun and started another one; the deaf Dalmatian strolled out, barked furiously (why a deaf dog would want to do that I have never understood) and relieved herself on an un-dug portion of the lawn. It's spring again.

10th April 2009

A few years ago we decided at Baker Towers that we would invest a small sum in acquiring some chickens at point of lay. We like having animals and birds around, already having a selection of domestic animals in residence not to mention the wild variety turning up in our garden for a light snack now and then (more now than then in fact). Chickens seemed a good idea, as there are six of us and we like the notion of eating our own fresh produce. And, as anyone with chickens will confirm, the home variety really do taste significantly better than shop-bought eggs. This may in part be due to the fact that our chickens have a diet that many humans would envy.

I was sharply put in my place recently when I spotted half a melon in the fridge and expressed interest. It was, apparently, 'for the chickens'. I have to say they fell upon it with the same relish as Wycombe Wanderers supporters on the away victory at Darlington this week which has hopefully halted their recent inexorable slide into

the play-offs. So, we constructed a large compound with nocturnal secure accommodation and for many months we were able to give excess eggs to friends on a regular basis and they were much appreciated. The melon had done its job, apparently. Then they gradually stop laying and you are left with five pets.

There is, of course, no question in my family of employing the more radical attitude understandably adopted by those who produce eggs for a living. All farmers warn of the danger of naming animals – and all our chickens have names. Dilys is therefore untouchable! So we have now acquired four more hens at point of lay, much to the irritation of the five incumbents.

If ever you needed a model for human behaviour, observe what happens when a Black Rock, a Speckled Star and two Amberlees are suddenly introduced into a community of Light Sussex crossbreeds who think that the spacious territory they inhabit is exclusively theirs. They don't seem to realise that we, who feed them and house them safely at night, actually own the land and there is enough melon for all.

Maybe we humans could learn something from that? We had our first eggs from the new girls yesterday, so I am about to make some soldiers and try one out in my Dalek eggcup.

4. Travelling Hopefully...

I have spent a lot of the last three decades (gosh, is it really that long?) driving around the country while taking part in theatrical tours. As is apparent from the previous selection, I like to spend as much time as I can with my family and at home, so I have over those years commuted daily distances of up to 120 miles each way, every day. Living in Buckinghamshire, as I do, it means that I can commute to places as far Wolverhampton or Leicester in the north, Bath or Malvern in the west, Brighton, Poole or Eastbourne in the south and Southend, Cambridge or Colchester in the east.

I might stay over in those places the night before a matinee but usually I find that the comfort of my own bed is infinitely preferable to the usual clinical anonymity of hotel rooms. It also frequently turned out that those of my fellow actors who voiced their amazement at my decision to spend the time and money that it takes me to commute, would actually spend even more of both in local hostelries and restaurants, rather than return to their less than salubrious lodgings. The following day I get to spend the morning at home with my wife, getting into my car early to mid-afternoon to return to the venue.

The knack, of course, is to leave enough time to cover all eventualities. There are only a handful of occasions when I have been late for the 'half' – that traditional time of arrival for actors at the theatre. Somewhat perversely it is not half an hour before the show, but thirty-five minutes, so that at the end of the countdown when 'Beginners' is called – the actor has five minutes to get himself ready for the fray. Indeed I would venture to suggest that it is the performer who is staying close to the venue that tends to be late because it is easier to lose track of time when there is no likelihood of a potential problem.

Anyway, my way does involve a lot of driving, which I don't mind – thanks to the joy of the radio.

A consequence of driving a lot tends to be that there are stories to tell about journeys, about cars and their reliability, about the road traffic laws and those who enforce them. I am no exception.

28th June 1996

I was driving down the M40 from the North recently in the wee small hours when nobody should really be anywhere other than tucked up in their beds. On a virtually empty road, I came up behind a police car doing about 60 mph in the inside lane. It is almost

impossible to drive in a relaxed way in these circumstances. The police are well aware of this.

Some years ago I was invited by the Norwich Police to attend their annual charity bash. I was given the choice of being picked up in a marked or unmarked police car. Despite, or perhaps because of, the possibility that neighbours might think I was being arrested, I thought it might be quite fun to be driven in one of the high profile, day-glo, go faster checked stripe, blue lit nee-nah nee-nah kind. It was a revelation. I learnt that, almost without exception, other drivers react in some visible way, (usually involving the application of brakes!), the moment they are aware of the presence of a police car. One unfortunate lady driver had been in front of us for some time, driving perfectly normally. As we approached some traffic lights, she spotted the panda in her rear view mirror, at the same time as the lights changed to green. She stopped. The driver of a car behind us sounded his horn. She registered that the lights were green jumped forward and stalled. By the time she got the car started again the lights had changed back to red. She then sailed through the junction and narrowly avoided being struck by vehicles coming from her left and right. She stopped the car on the other side of the lights and got out looking rather shaken, awaiting for what must have seemed inevitable, unaware that a Norfolk Policeman would have little power or inclination to deal with a traffic offence in Bedfordshire.

As we drove past her I had a flash of an uncomprehending and very relieved face. Apparently it happens all the time. On the recent occasion on the M40 I did what I had to do. As I drove past the 60 mph police car, I resisted the temptation to glance at them to convey warm reassuring feelings along the lines of:

"Yes I acknowledge that you are a police car and I am driving past you at three thirty in the morning. But I can handle that. I am sober, driving legally and wide awake (-ish!)." Such a glance could also be interpreted as "I am a cocky so and so and I challenge you to give me grief, bluebottle!" I was however only slightly surprised when the flashing blue lights behind me brought me to a standstill.

"Is this your car, sir?"

"Yes."

"Do you have any means of proving that?" For those of you who are not regular readers of this column (Shame on you!) I drive a 'D'

reg Ford Escort - my rusty steed - whose similarity to a cheetah rests more in its multiple brown spots than its speed and grace.

"If I was going to steal a car," I replied "Do you really think I'd choose this one?" They were amiable chaps and saw the humour and truth of my rhetorical question. It turned out that they had stopped me because my children's dressing up 'police hat' had been left on the rear parcel shelf. My current pony-tailed look (necessitated by successive acting jobs) suggested to them that I was patently not a police officer and therefore I might have stolen a car belonging to one. I satisfied their curiosity and went on my way.

I was stopped again in London yesterday. This time the same police hat had led them to believe that I might be an undercover drugs squad officer, affecting the hippy look and a clapped out car as a disguise. I said that if that in fact had been the case, their stopping me would have effectively blown my cover! They replied with some mirth that that was why they had stopped me - to tell me that the presence of the hat had already done precisely that! I think they were a little disappointed that the uniformed branch had not in fact scored a point over the plain clothes boys.

I am tempted to keep the hat there - it's a great conversation piece!

10th October 2008

The wielder of the fickle hobnail boot of fate was clearly delighted when, after years of being more traditional in my choice of car, I decided last autumn to buy a convertible. Not only has there only been a handful of days when driving with the wind in my hair (…alright, across my cranium) was a serious option, but my sleek Saab has proved a poisoned chariot. It replaced an elderly saloon that was starting to lose oil and water and needed a new head gasket. So, of course, as soon as it was out of warranty – new head gasket required.

Two days after I paid for that, then as I was driving back from the Oxford Playhouse with my wife last Thursday night, we were treated to the sound of spanners being pulverised in a blender and the rest of the engine committed expensive hara-kiri. As we stood on the hard shoulder watching articulated lorries getting as close as they could get without removing a wing mirror, one of those Highways Agency vehicles pulled up behind my spanner blender. These are the guys

derided by Jeremy Clarkson as 'Muppets', who drive around in 4 x 4's that look exactly like police vehicles. I have always regarded Clarkson as a champion of the driving classes (i.e. most of us), but must now take issue with his disdain for these guys, without whose cheerful assistance we would have been in a parlous state. Because the banking was vertical where we ground (and grinded) to a halt, there was nowhere other than the hard shoulder to seek refuge from the trucks. Our uniformed Samaritans put out lights and cones and stayed with us for the nigh on two hours we spent waiting for the recovery vehicle. They provided us with those silver capes handed out to marathon runners, without which we would have been even more chilled to the bone than we were.

While we waited they told us about some of the situations and crash scenes that occupy the majority of their working days. Jeremy Clarkson should spend a day with these men; I suspect that if he did, he would revise his opinion of them. I would like to thank them for preventing what was (for them, if not for us) a minor incident from turning into something worse and helping us to get through it.

18th January 2002

As I was driving along the M2 this week in my elderly Audi, I had one of those experiences that are the subject of many dark fables; the ones where a man is granted three wishes that come true, but in unpleasant ways that that the wisher had not imagined. The recent film *Bedazzled* starring Liz Hurley was based on precisely that premise. It is not my car's fault. Indeed, it has served me well, but after 205,000 miles is beginning to cost in repairs a regular sum that would be better spent in payments for a newer vehicle.

It might be a hangover from watching *Herbie* or too many episodes of *Knight Rider*, but I have always been slightly superstitious about saying anything derogatory about a car when actually in it, least of all any suggestions of disposal. But when you spend as many hours as I do driving around the country, the car does become like an extension of yourself. I did not, however, envisage that I would tempt providence by merely thinking about the advisability of finding some, shall we say, more reliable wheels for my upcoming theatrical tour, which will take me from Darlington to Taunton via Brecon and Eastbourne over the next six months. As I drove past Rochester, I

was thinking that the rather lived-in nature of the bodywork and the high mileage probably meant that potential buyers would probably not be fighting each other to take over the responsibility of Dietmar (my car's name – doesn't everyone give their car a name, or was that my first mistake?). I was also rueing the fact that the taxi that tailgated me a few months ago hadn't done a more comprehensive job.

It was at that this point that I noticed the jack-knifed lorry straddling all three lanes half a mile ahead. I was in the outside lane and there was one car between me and the lorry. Its driver slowed down and stopped. So did I and the cars in the two lanes to my left. Having stopped, I did what I suspect everyone does in a similar situation. I glanced anxiously at the rear view mirror to ensure that nothing unpleasant was about to descend on me from that direction. There was a saloon car behind me. The best adjective I can find to describe its state at that moment is 'hurtling'. As I braced myself for the seemingly inevitable and unwanted granting of my unspoken wish, the driver of the guided missile behind me rejoined the world from whatever state he had been in immediately prior and not only braked, but swerved to avoid hitting me. He ploughed into most of the cars to my left. Bonnets and boots flew up and arced through the air. Glass and bumpers shot off in unlikely directions and showered everything in sight.

Then, that moment of brief peace descended before doors started opening and drivers climbed out of the wreckage of their motor cars, most of which were much newer than mine, which had suddenly been promoted up the league of desirability as a consequence of being the only unscathed, and therefore driveable, vehicle in the immediate vicinity. A friend passed the other way an hour later and told me of a ten-mile tail back. I was the only driver behind that lorry that got to my destination on time that morning. Funny old world.

15th June 2001

Will I never learn? It is many months since I last forsook the comfort and reliability of my elderly car and took to public transport for a trip to London, but last week the previous experience was sufficiently far behind me to succumb to the temptation to try again.

I had a meeting in Victoria at the Foundation for the Study of Infant Deaths, the cot death charity of which I am chairman. After that I had to go to St Paul's, Covent Garden for a memorial service for the wonderful Jean Anderson, who has made her final exit, stage right, at the age of 93, having worked right up until this year, when she filmed a Becket play soon to be broadcast. I worked with her in the 70's when she played the doughty road-haulage matriarch, Mary Hammond, in *The Brothers*, and again a couple of years ago, in a German film shot in the isle of Man. She looked and behaved even then like a woman half her age.

Her memorial was a wonderful celebration of the life a wonderfully talented and generous lady, who will be sorely missed by colleagues and audiences alike. I was therefore going to spend Election Day in London, a city whose attractions are only slightly greater than going to a Black Sabbath Concert with Ian Paisley. Following the budgetary example of our iron chancellor – I decided it would be prudent to avoid the traffic jams on the A 40 and the exorbitant cost of parking in London. I would be green, leave the security of my polluting car behind and glide to my destination in an environmentally friendly, efficient, clean and competitively priced public transport system. Although I should have known better, I drove to Hanger Lane and entered the big city on the Piccadilly Line.

There was just enough time after my first meeting to get me to Covent Garden in time for the service. With my Rover in hand (a ticket, not a dog – or in my case cat. Yes, we have a cat called Rover. Don't ask!), I hastened to St. James Park station, only to find that the Circle Line was, like Monty Python's parrot, failing to show any discernible signs of useful life. Blackboards, showing evidence of frequent and recent use, informed the muttering, milling, malcontent crowd that there was no immediate prospect of any tube travel between Earls Court and the East End. I hastened to a bus stop only to discover there was no bus that gets me, or Dolittle, to the church on time. So I took a cab. It cost the best part of a tenner, after crawling through Central London for 15 minutes. Added to the cost of London Transport Rover this meant I was worse off than I would have been had I driven in my comfortable car, listening to England losing at cricket on Long Wave.

And now we read about the new transport agenda. As there is not the slightest likelihood of any government providing an effective, affordable public transport system to tempt us from our cars, we are going be given the stick as carrots are thin on (in?) the ground. Newer, better and more speed detection devices. An exponential rise in convictions for speeding. More and more banned drivers. More and more passengers for a deficient, unreliable and expensive public transport system.

24th April 2009

What I am about to tell you will divide you between those who are happy to cast the first stone, because they are without sin and the rest who say "There but for the grace of God..." This week I travelled up to North Yorkshire to appear in court for speeding. In October last year, a policeman with a radar gun caught me exceeding 70mph on an empty dual carriageway, on a sunny afternoon, going downhill. I was offered a fixed penalty, but because I already had nine points on my licence, I could not accept that kind offer.

So, six months later, having driven some 20,000 miles safely in the interim, I appear before three magistrates, none of whom, interestingly, ever look me in the eye once. Their chair was a lady whose demeanour made Margaret Thatcher seem positively sweet and self-effacing. My barrister described the effect on my life of a six month ban. I live in the middle of nowhere and work unsociable hours with no public transport to get me home after work in theatres all over the country. I habitually commute theatre venues up to 120 miles away and would be unable to get home without a car. He suggested that a six month ban would cause me exceptional hardship. Mrs. Granite repeatedly interrupted him and patronised him and, on my behalf, he respectfully negotiated the hectoring. He told me afterwards that he knew we were in trouble when she pronounced, meticulously, every syllable of the word 'parliament' when giving him the benefit of her knowledge of the law.

Yes, I am biased, because she referred to me as a 'serial offender' in precisely the same tone of voice as a hanging judge would refer to a mass murderer. But I will now spend the next 25 weeks (one gone already – yes, I am counting) accepting the generosity of family and friends, who will be inconvenienced much more than me and

discovering the joys of public transport. Yes, I shouldn't have broken the speed limit four times in three years (two of them were radar guns from bridges on the same Scottish Motorway on consecutive days and another was a camera on an empty underpass in Docklands at 6am on a Sunday). Like many of you, I started driving when we spent more time watching the road rather than the speedometer. Heigh ho! Anyone want to buy a used car?

18th July 2003

Ken Livingstone assumed control of the London Underground this week. Well, somebody needed to. I have spent more time down that particular hole in the ground in the last two weeks than I have in as many years. It has only served to reinforce my love affair with my car. It is a recurring theme in my travelling life. I decide that sitting in traffic jams doing half an inch an hour is ridiculous and wasteful and I sally forth once more onto the public transport system. I then find my public spiritedness evaporates in very short order.

Before I catalogue my recent disastrous journeys, I will acknowledge that many readers will have had similar experiences, or worse, a fact that serves only to highlight the parlous state of the tube. In ten days – three trains each way – (I have been working in Rotherhithe) – out of sixty trains, two have broken down. One had a most discomfiting and protracted bout of locomotive hiccups before grinding to a halt, caused (we were told by a chirpy disembodied voice) by a faulty door in carriage two that kept breaking the circuits.

An engineer arrived twenty minutes later and cured the problem sufficiently to let us limp to the next station, where we were summarily ejected. On the other occasion, there was no preamble, no discernible problem, just,

"There is a fault on this train – get off please." Then the empty train sped off with irritating ease and no sign of any problems, leaving a train-full of passengers on the platform. I have spent thirty hours on District and Piccadilly line trains, jammed together with my fellow citizens in conditions that we would rightly consider unacceptable for animals and in temperatures that are prohibited for livestock. I have been treated to a closer contact with strangers than would be considered acceptable in the average nightclub and have found myself

- 55 -

unable to raise my hand to scratch my nose without running the risk of assaulting the elderly Asian lady whose shopping was rammed against my ribs.

On one occasion, I was waiting for a District Line train to Ealing. Three Richmond line trains had passed when it was announced that the next train was Ealing bound. It entered the station. It was empty. It stayed empty, because in the age it spent taunting us, the doors resolutely refused to open. Every now and then another would-be traveller would half-heartedly push the Open Sesame button, but to no avail. It shimmied away, like a subterranean Marie Celeste to some joyous passenger free destination, and we, its frustrated rejects, glared sullenly at the two Richmond trains that followed it.

Yesterday, I made the mistake of allowing myself a brief moment of jubilation when without breaking stride, I was able to walk onto the platform and straight on to a train whose doors opened invitingly upon a half empty carriage. I sat down. We waited. And waited. Chirpy chappy number two informed us that we were being held at this station, as there had been a "breakdown on the Barking Line" (miles away) and "in order to maintain a regular service for passengers", we had to be held where we were - for ten minutes. I went by car today. It was no quicker. It was no cheaper. But there was no one shouting drivel into a mobile phone and I could scratch whenever and whatever I liked.

30th April 2004

A Councillor received 11 points on his licence and was fined £250 after being caught by a mobile speed camera four times in two hours breaking a 30mph limit in Weston super Mare. At the next council meeting he called on his own council to make speed limit signs clearer, saying the new 30mph signs were insufficient and "stupid, and there ought to be repeated signs on every other lamp post." He had an advantage that the rest of us are denied – an arena in which to air his grievances. The Metropolitan Police Commissioner Sir John Stevens, has been quoted as saying,

"I don't approve of the use of speed cameras as money making devices. The proper use for speed cameras is to lower the accident rate." He had insisted that all the Met's cameras be placed where there was a history of serious accidents. "I am not after people on the

school run exceeding the limit by five or six miles an hour. I want to target the dangerous drivers, the road hogs, and the menaces driving unlicensed and uninsured." But who protected me from the articulated lorry that tailgated me with headlights on full beam as I drove at exactly the legal limit through the 40mph roadworks on the M25 last night. Had my very real fear led me to accelerate away, I would doubtless have got a ticket and my explanation would have fallen on deaf ears.

Twice recently I have seen a police van parked just inside the 30 mph zone entering Wycombe from the west along the A40. The rear of the marked police van was on both occasions obscured by another vehicle parked (on a single yellow line) behind it, but so that the camera placed in the rear of the vehicle was still able to get a good view of the vehicles leaving the traffic signal controlled road works. Normally you would be hard pressed to muster 20mph; but drivers that had been stopped by the temporary traffic lights were released into an atypically empty stretch of road. Catching cars exceeding a 30mph limit whilst accelerating out of road works onto an empty road is the road traffic equivalent of catching wasps in a jam jar and, I would argue, guaranteed to catch those very people on the school run exceeding the limit by five or six miles an hour to whom Sir John Stephens referred.

The majority of drivers (no not you, my dear perfect reader, but all the rest of us) speed at some time or other. Every councillor, every police officer, every magistrate (and quite a few of them have been convicted, it appears) is likely to have broken the law in this respect at some time. But there is a universal reticence to acknowledge this, because it carries the implication that we don't care about the risk to human life. I am coming to the conclusion that the proliferation of speed cameras and varied approaches to speed restrictions have the potential to be more dangerous than the speeding that is being targeted. I spend much more time than I ever used to looking down at my speedometer to check that I am not marginally over the limit and as much time again checking for seemingly arbitrary alterations to the limit just for fear of being caught and deprived of my licence. I would prefer to be able to concentrate on the road and what was actually happening on it.

5. Television – from both sides

I have been working in television (off and on – it has to be said) since the early 1970's, when I was lucky enough to be cast in several of those wonderful classic series that used to be staple fare on the BBC and are now much heralded rarities.

I have however been watching it much, much longer, since the time when Muffin the Mule *and* Billy Bunter *were the highlights of the week and daytime television had simply not even been envisaged let alone desired. I will leave others to discuss whether the current multi-channel, wall to wall, twenty four hour a day output is a marked improvement on the 1950's output. I will however say that there was a lot more eager anticipation of weekly treats back then when there was so much less programming.*

But the same could be said of food, I suppose. The decades of plenty have resulted in us being blasé about eating vegetables out of season and the advent of new culinary treats, whereas the Sunday lunch of my childhood was a matter of great excitement and family co-operation. Try and tell a young person today about the excitement of shelling peas on Sunday morning!

It is, I must admit, partly because I work in the industry that I do not share the view of those who see television as a dangerous intruder into the home. There are many who decide to ration their children's access to the goggle-box, perhaps thereby making it a forbidden and therefore more attractive activity than it would otherwise be. Anyway, for whatever reason, my wife and I never laid down rules about telly watching and it is therefore our daughters who are the ones who ask if we "have to have the television on while we are eating", when supper coincides with a football match I want to see. It is perhaps, I must admit, because we had four children who therefore had each other as entertainment resources that television has never dominated their lives. It must be a very different matter for parents with only one child, or whose children were born sufficiently far apart for them not to interact as easily.

I think that perhaps the time shifting capability of modern television equipment has resulted in a lot fewer programmes being watched. There have been many programmes that I was very keen to see that were recorded and subsequently forgotten over the years, with, I cannot deny, no adverse effect.

But amongst the myriad of programmes we don't want to watch, there are still some gems and delights for the discerning and those in search of mindless entertainment alike. And I include myself in both categories.

29th November 1996

Along with many of you I watched the BBC's 60th Anniversary Awards on television a couple of weeks ago. I had been invited to attend the recording of the evening's events celebrating 'Auntie's All Time Greats' but had been prevented from doing so by a previous commitment to be in Great Yarmouth that evening. I had not felt too bad about having to decline the invitation because, although *Doctor Who* had been nominated for the Favourite Popular Drama Award, it seemed to me that the opposition was fairly heavy weight.

A short list, compiled by what the BBC referred to as 'television writers and senior industry figures', included such all time greats as *All Creatures Great and Small, The Onedin Line, When the Boat Comes In, Z Cars* and *Eastenders*. I didn't doubt for a second that the award would reside in Albert Square at the end of the evening. As I watched the awards being dished out, in common I suspect with many viewers of my generation, I was astonished at the choices of the thousands of voters who had telephoned over fourteen days at the beginning of October. Indeed, whilst I am in theory a great champion of the democratic process, whenever I am reminded that the Sun is the most popular daily newspaper, I understand the reluctance of some to rely too heavily on the referendum as a prelude to legislation.

So, Colin Firth was a model of bemused and careful gratitude when he accepted his award for the best actor in 60 years of BBC broadcasting. Indeed he beguilingly suggested that he might have just peaked, which was his suitably modest way of accepting the plaudit graciously, whilst acknowledging his understandable deference to the competition. He was as aware as many of us that even though he is a very fine actor and played Mr Darcy splendidly, his defeat of Derek Jacobi, Alec Guiness and Ian Richardson, amongst other such luminaries, owed more to being current than any other consideration. Having been starved of programmes like *Pride and Prejudice* for some years, the viewing public fell on the recent version like tabloid journalists on a royal indiscretion.

Only those of us of a certain age were able to remember the days when a Classic Serial (as they were known) was an everyday event - well, if not exactly every day, then every Sunday, repeated on BBC2 on the following Wednesday or Thursday. But a generation starved of such excellence saw this renaissance of the literary adaptation as

something new and remembered and voted for the latest good thing they had seen. Despite all their public protestations to the contrary most actors, writers and technicians within the industry, would rather have the approval of their peers and fellow artists than the popular acclaim of the viewing public, however heady and desirable the latter may be.

Most of the awards followed the same pattern, with the notable exception of the eternally unforgettable Morecambe and Wise. I think that the BBC would have died of shame if Eric and Ernie hadn't triumphed against all modern opposition. However I found myself shaking my head in disbelief, along with many of the recipients I have to admit, as all the modern programmes were feted at the expense of some incomparable classics. But then how on earth do you compare *Dad's Army, Porridge, Fawlty Towers, The Liver Birds and Butterflies* with *Men Behaving Badly* and *Absolutely Fabulous*. But *Men Behaving Badly* is current and fashionable and, indeed, very funny and well made and it received more votes than any of the other programmes. I was therefore left shell shocked when, against this trend, *Doctor Who* was voted the Favourite Popular Drama, beating even the mighty *Eastenders* and *Ballykissangel* and making me re-assess my jaundiced, elitist views on the voting habits of the British viewer. Not bad for a programme which has only had one new outing in the last seven years.

Whatever else it did, it confirmed what many of us have been telling everyone for years. There is a whole generation out there who have been deprived of the joy and terror of hiding behind that legendary sofa on a Saturday evening after the football results. All personal considerations aside, I would love my children to have their own Doctor as every generation bar this one has had for the last thirty three years.

18th October 1996

I watched Blind Date last weekend. It is one of those programmes that, in theory, I disapprove of, but which I can readily understand has a very powerful hook for its audience.

The format is designed to maintain consumer loyalty. Having watched the ritual dance of the buck and the roe, it is all but irresistible to tune in the following week to see how they got on in

Puerto del Seaside. Over the years, Blind Date has evolved from being a programme with some pretensions to spontaneity and an even-handed approach in its selection of contestants - males and females of varying ages, walks of life and attraction.

Presumably the market researchers have been beavering away and presented the programmer makers with a profile of what appeals most to their target audience and that is what we are going to get now, exclusively. The last time I watched the show, I remember feeling quite moved by the fact that two widowed, elderly people had found each other and were happily contemplating a less lonely future together.

However efficiently the programme may exploit our sentimentality, nonetheless it was inarguable that for these two people at least it had been life enhancing. Similarly, when the programme started out, I remember it not being quite so thunderingly obvious that the questions and answers were part of a carefully prepared and well rehearsed script. Worse, the questions seem to have moved away from any pretensions of subtlety into the smirkier area of innuendo. One got the feeling in the early days that, although the questioner was provided with the questions, the three candidates for cupid's sledgehammer had been allowed some personal input into their answers. Now it is inescapable to conclude that candidates are scripted, dressed and carefully chosen to fit a formula.

Boys tend to fall into the categories of sporty hunk, one of the lads m.c.p. and middle class boy next door. Girls are either kooky dipstick, tart with heart or fun loving undergraduate.

All the girls are encouraged to dress to kill with the minimum of wastage of natural resources (like cloth). It is also tempting to suggest that in most cases the producers nudge the questions and answers into a form that they hope will result in specific pairings, to achieve maximum effect in the weekly lust versus disgust competition. On my last viewing, I would say disgust is ahead on points.

But what I found most offensive about this logical extension of tabloid journalistic values into television was the behaviour of our Cilla. Cilla Black has maintained her *ordinary Scouse lass makes the big time and remains true to her roots* persona over four decades now. So presumably she feels that gives her licence to mock a male contestant who was brought up in the colonies and has what she considers to be

an upper class accent. The young victim of her relentless aping of his accent, though slightly nonplussed, remained a gentleman, to his credit, and understood his role as the seasoning for the chip on her shoulder pads. Every time he spoke, she mimicked his tones back to him and then, having eliciting the information that his parents had a bob or two, she compounded her display of bad manners by asking him why, as he was so well heeled, he needed to come on Blind Date. Clang! The inescapable implication was that Cilla believed that only impecunious no-hopers had any reason to come on her show, thereby giving the lie to the alleged ethos of the show - that it is all a bit of fun with the possibility of the odd serendipitous happy pairing. The amiable young chap was not selected by his unseen inquisitor and as he ambled off, Cilla told the girl who had rejected him that she had missed out on a chance of getting her hands on some loot.

As far as I can remember, Cilla Black has three sons, the oldest of whom is certainly of dating age. They were not brought up in Liverpool and, at a guess, were educated privately. I don't know how they speak but they are certainly part of a family where there is plenty of dosh. Would she like her sons to be treated as objects of derision and meal tickets? Or does she think her programme is beneath her own children?

30th May 2003

It seems that perennial piece of kitsch and irresistible television – the Eurovision Song Contest - has provided the nation with an 'Eddie the Eagle' moment this year. A pair of young Scousers, saddled with a below average ditty, failed to seize even that moment and their tuneless rendition secured them that grail of all Eurovision lovers (and Terry Wogan fans) – nul points.

Had they come 5th or 23rd having secured a handful of points from a neighbouring friendly state, then they could have disappeared back into grateful obscurity. In the event, they will enjoy a brief moment in the spotlight for that most enduringly British of reasons – abject failure.

They have been in demand from all the media and seized the opportunity to prove that they can sing *Bye-Bye Baby* a capella without deviating more than a semitone from the note – an improvement of half an octave over their performance in Riga. This proves only that

without the distraction of an orchestra playing, they can hold the tune, which they were unable to do in similar circumstances last Saturday. It may well be that, as they have claimed, they could not hear 'fold back' over their head sets and were therefore deprived of the opportunity to hear what the orchestra were playing. As an actor who is occasionally called upon to sing in pantomime and the odd musical, I am very dependant on being able to find my first note from the wide range offered in an orchestral accompaniment.

In this case, of course, I have to concede that the orchestra is right there in front of me, rather than some distance away and only audible through headphones, as was the case in Riga. A sensible conductor will usually ensure that something that can be heard clearly over the harmonic throng – usually the flute – will provide me with the first stepping-stone into hoped for tunefulness. Then I usually sing as loudly as I can to drown out whatever else is going on, so that I am not seduced from the tune provided for me by the composer. Darren Day discovered this to his cost when we sang a duet in the musical version Great Expectations several years ago.

This may well have been the first time that he thought, if not uttered, the words "I'm a singer get me out of here!" I had the tune and he had the harmony, thank goodness. But had I heard him, I might have been tempted at some subconscious level to edge towards the notes he was singing, on the basis that it sounded better than what I was doing. Better not to risk that! Colleagues of mine have suggested that some kind of European antipathy to the UK, based on the alleged Iraq factor, contributed to the absence of votes for our dynamic duo. Leaving aside that the song was execrable, why did Israel not then give us 12 points?

And why did the anti-war stance of France and Germany leave them also languishing well down the league table? It strikes me that precisely the people who don't vote in political elections – i.e. 60% of the population – are the ones who will vote for a song contest or to remove a celebrity candidate from the latest fly on the wall television offering.

To win Eurovision, you need a much better song and – sorry Jemini – much better singers.

10th October 2003

Everyone wants to be famous, it seems.

"Not me!" I can hear you protest dear, solitary, sane reader. Okay, not you, then; but every one else does! And television, in particular, has seized the opportunity to fill air time for a fraction of the cost of more traditional programming. The clock is unlikely to go back, I fear, unless the viewing millions tire of rubbernecking; and all the evidence suggests there is a limitless propensity for what the Germans call schadenfreude – a delight in the misfortunes of others. Even those addictive talent search programmes fill in the early weeks by parading the no-hopers, misfits and the frankly bonkers. They are, after all, more entertaining than the merely competent but unspectacular. Our daytime screens are doomed to be filled in perpetuity with misfits and attention seekers who are lured to confess all by the illusion of the 'fame' poultice which they can heat up by exposure to millions and then apply to their sad lives. And the media harpies (remember harpies – they charmed and lured the innocent to their destruction?) – they apply some temporary salve to their otherwise overloaded consciences by talking earnestly of public service and assuring us that there is a team of counsellors waiting offstage. The only truly beneficial effect is probably that it makes the rest of us feel that our lives are nothing to complain about after all. Perhaps that's the real agenda? Just as public executions were once pretty effective at achieving a largely docile population, reality TV shows are there to make us feel pretty darn normal. Now anyone can be a star. If they make a serial documentary about your airline, your driving school, your restaurant – then you may find yourself invited to appear in panto the following year. Never mind the quality, feel the fame. And fame ain't all it's cracked up to be. I entered the acting profession because I wanted to act, strangely enough. I wanted to entertain and felt that it was something that I actually could do. Public recognition was a side effect, not an objective in itself. I despair for those young hopefuls in *Pop Idol* and similar programmes who feel its okay, in response to:

"Why are you here?" to blurt out:

"Because I want to be famous." They fail to acknowledge something that is blindingly obvious to anyone who gives the matter five minutes thought. The ones who cope with that glittering bauble

fame the best are the ones for whom it is a by-product of something that they love doing, for which they have a talent and, most importantly, who are intelligent enough not to confuse the by-product with their talent that created it. Whether footballer, actor, fashion designer or chef, if fame was the only spur they would settle back at a certain point, enjoy their wealth and fame and stop doing whatever it was that first propelled them into the public eye. The ones who continue to work and strive, despite the media attention, are the survivors. The individuals for whom fame was truly the only spur - and I won't name them but you know the ones, they're famous for being famous and have done nothing significant – they soon discover that the gloss wears off and they are then subjected to the media's relentless and increasingly destructive gaze thereafter. Be careful what you wish for, someone once said, you might get it.

30th October 1999

English actors are greatly in demand throughout Europe for commercials. I have been given various explanations for this puzzling phenomenon (after all, why not cast an actor with a fighting chance of understanding the deathless prose that he will be called upon to utter on behalf of a product?). It would be pleasant to believe that the quality of the English actor is simply so immeasurably superior to our continental brethren that there is no contest. But, however beguiling that notion might be, the cold hand of reality taps me on my shoulder and, when I turn, I see a gently shaking head. The truth seems to be that our colleagues on the mainland are inclined to view the commercial with lofty disdain and as a potential career wrecker. The English actor on the other hand is perfectly happy to appear in commercials, especially if there is not the slightest possibility that they will ever turn up in our own country to blight what we like to fondly think of as our careers.

And, more tellingly perhaps, I suspect we are also cheaper! Auditions for these commercials tend to do little for the self-esteem. A U.K. casting director is hired, who invites a couple of dozen or so actors into a London studio to record the audition. Frequently this is done by an adolescent camera operator, who is keen to get the material on tape as quickly as possible so that he can nip out to get some more acne lotion.

"Right Mr Barker, just stand on the cross on the floor over there, tell us your name and..."

"Baker!"

"What?"

"My name is Baker"

"Not yet, Mr Barker, the camera's not running." You get the picture? The only plus about the whole undignified process is that the waiting room is often a reunion for mates you haven't seen since that classic serial you did together in the 70's, when the BBC was at its creative peak. The tapes of all the auditions are then despatched overseas to the producers of the commercial, who make their selection. In the couple of years that I have hawked my wares at these occasional cattle markets, I have failed to ignite the fervour of the distant unseen producers - until last week. With less than two days notice, I was despatched to Madrid to play – well, erm – God - actually! Apparently, the man in the Spanish street would accept the possibility that God might bear a resemblance to the face at the top of this column. I know, I know! Beats me too. The 25 second commercial, with another English actor playing Death, was designed to encourage investment in a pension plan. The seventeen consecutive hours taken to film it were interesting, partly because the man chosen to convey the director's instructions to us was the one with least command of English. I realised it was going to be a long day when I was asked to give

"...a big reaction of angry - but you must do it very small." Death became a very close friend quite quickly. His polite enquiry as to why they had hired a six foot three actor in his fifties to crouch at my feet rather than a younger, shorter person was not answered. After completion of the last shot, during which I had been asked to "turn the face to camera without moving the head", we learned that the huge corporate client would pay us ninety days after receipt of invoice. Just in time for Easter.

14th July 2000

You may well have noticed that some time ago the Bucks Free Press stopped carrying listings of television programmes. The decision to discontinue this service was made for the soundest of editorial and journalistic reasons. People simply got their information

about programmes elsewhere and better use could be made of the space. But in any event, the general standard of television is deteriorating alarmingly. I caught a programme hosted by Nicky Campbell and Andrew Neil this week. It was clearly setting itself up as offering a discussion of serious issues by and in front of an invited audience, liberally peppered with experts and the opinionated.

The two subjects on offer this week were topical – the controversy that surrounds the whole issue of our nation's increasing failure to succeed in sport and its connection to the evolution of 'competition' as a dirty word and secondly, the thorny one about the advisability, in terms of reducing teenage pregnancies, of giving sex education to four year olds. (Beam me up, Scotty!)

These two important issues were dealt with in a ludicrously trivial and insulting tabloid way, seemingly as a vehicle for the two presenters to score points off the motivated and variably articulate guests, who were denied the chance to say anything that didn't fit into the presenters' sound byte agenda. Anna Raeburn was so frustrated, when Mr. Neil perfunctorily cut her off in mid-sentence to go for an advert break, that she made a most eloquent gesture to his departing back. And I understood the frustration.

This is what happens when programmes with the potential for stimulating debate are given the viewing figure/advertising treatment. This is also why I believe that the BBC must resist any efforts to make it take advertising and at a stroke destroy a unique broadcasting company which has made us the envy of the world for decades. Once, single plays, *Panorama* and *Question Time* were regarded as normal BBC output.

We are now hearing that they are seen as outmoded, niche programmes, to be nudged out to pasture on BBC2 as soon as possible, leaving BBC1 free to offer wall to wall entertainment - moving inexorably from *Eastenders*, through *Celebrity Secrets* with Carol Vorderman and a cop show to a fly on the wall programme watching a gardening chef make over an animal sanctuary owner's home. And all the drama will doubtless be restricted to the convoluted relationships of yet more ill matched thirty-somethings, all totally unsuitable for family audiences. I just long to sit with the family, unembarrassed to watch a new *Planemakers, Tenko, The Organisation, Private Schultz, Vote Vote Vote for Nigel Barton* and yes, *The Brothers*– the

list is endless and I apologise only a little to the thirty-somethings and under for referring to programmes they've never even heard of – because they were all masterpieces of drama, which we all then took for granted. If only we had known...

11th October 2002

One of the plus points of being a product of the baby boomer generation is that I can remember those halcyon days when television programmes were predominantly the work of creative and talented people, rather than the result of pointing cameras at what we are learning to call 'real life' in its proliferating forms - talent shows, lifestyle programmes and flies on the ever expanding wall of British life.

All those decades ago, the BBC and ITV did, admittedly, enjoy what we can recognise now as monopolies. The BBC had the licence fee and ITV had all the advertising income. But they did, arguably, use that secure revenue to make programmes the like of which, I believe, we are unlikely to see again. Entertainment was abundant and of a very high class, but both channels recognised that, alongside the need to entertain was a responsibility to inform, stimulate and challenge the watching millions. The rot was confirmed when Margaret Thatcher decreed back in 1990 that the ITV franchises should be awarded to the highest bidders, irrespective of any other criteria, in the great sell-off that left the victorious companies with no money to make decent programmes.

With the proliferation of channels, satellites, cables etc., all the advertising revenue has now been subdivided so many times that the amount available to make each broadcast minute is a fraction of what was available when *Jewel in the Crown*, *Upstairs Downstairs* and *Brideshead Revisited* were made. The idea that any UK broadcaster could now attempt to film *War and Peace* (which they did in 1970 – and I was in it!) is as remote as the notion that what we used to take for granted - family viewing - will ever again be secure. There used not to be a watershed, because one wasn't needed. Broadcasters were not then as obsessed as they are today that every expletive and activity of an intimate nature has to be heard and seen in order to reflect 'real life'. The BBC still has the licence fee, thank goodness, but it is now competing with a horde of channels whose lack of budget compels

them to reach the highest possible number of viewers for the lowest possible cost. Thus it was that Andy Warhol's famous prediction that every one would get their 'fifteen minutes of fame' came true. The supply of willing human fodder for the *Big Brother*, survival by ordeal, pop star wannabe programmes and their clones, has thus far proved to be endless.

But there is a glimmer of light at the end of the dumbing down tunnel. *Fame Academy*, the BBC's attempt to compete with the other channels' programmes of that type, (and I wish they hadn't bothered) has failed to attract viewers, so maybe, just maybe, the public will soon be going back to the 'right' side of the camera. But it's hard to imagine the producers willingly returning to employing writers, actors and directors to the extent that we expected a quarter of a century ago. They cost money - when you only have to walk down any high street to procure willing participants for any number of programmes who do it for that bauble 'fame'. At least, when everyone who wants to be on the telly has gratified that desire, we may be left with a nation less inclined to jump up and down behind reporters and commentators while waving inanely at any visible camera.

4th August 2000

Mary Whitehouse once complained to the BBC when I manoeuvred a couple of would be assassins into the very vat of acid that they intended as my final resting place. I was quite proud at the time. This was when I was boldly going (oops - wrong cult) in my blue police box to places strange and unfriendly. These hostile places often bore a startling similarity to Wapseys Wood landfill site, near Beaconsfield, which represented many an alien planet.

The self appointed scourge of smut and violence complained because she felt the scene was too horrific for the Saturday tea-time audience. I thought it was all done in a rather tongue in cheek, nongraphic way and that she rather over reacted to a bit of deliberately larger than life cliff-hanger drama. But who's to say? But she should have saved herself for the new and murky depths of TV 2000.

Of course, occasionally, in the allegedly swinging but actually rather innocent 60's, television watching with the parents did produce those wonderful moments when everyone pretends not to have noticed that there is some minor hanky-panky of a birds and bees nature

going on. Father fiddles under chair for slippers. Mother talks loudly to cat. Teenage son goes bright red and feigns avid interest in the lettering on side of HB pencil, until the, ahem, funny business was over. Recently, I found myself standing in front of the telly talking loudly and at length about the fact that wall tiles were metric now and not in rods, poles or perches, during a bed scene in some well pre-watershed soap, which would have had my father eating his slippers, mother hurling the cat at the telly and me exploding with embarrassment. This was to prevent my eight year old daughter from feeling obliged to express an interest in things that she has plenty of time to find out about.

Then I read the watershed is to go the way of good programmes, taste and drama. Thank heavens for radio. We are living in a world where the lunatics, who seem to have bought all the shares in the asylum, are talking about instructing four year olds in the finer detail of activities of a connubial nature. A world where we have television programmes hosted by grinning Americans, who trumpet freedom of speech and dress a sorry gladiatorial combat up as some sort of therapy session for the fame junkies who are lured onto their shows. There they act out their inadequacies, real or imagined, for the entertainment of the similarly sad voyeurs in the studio, who get their six seconds of fame by competing to praise the clever, cynical and very rich ex politician, who smugly and oh so compassionately sums up the whole tacky charade with a naff, moralistic homily at the end. And they're all so surprised when emotions spill off the screen and cause a very real death. A strange blurring of reality is taking place. An Aeroflot customer care employee is now a media star and appearing in panto this Christmas.

A talented actor of my acquaintance who co-starred in a successful BBC sitcom less than ten years ago is running a B & B in Bournemouth. The proliferation of docusoaps is gradually easing drama into oblivion. I predict a day when the only audience for television will be out of work actors.

Everyone else will be trying to get on the telly.

26th October 2007
Here's a thought for you. Buckingham Palace is to be demolished and the site redeveloped as an Olde Englande theme park. Nelson is

to be removed from his column to adapt it for use as an abseiling and bungee jumping platform and Westminster Abbey is to be converted into a multiple entertainment centre with cinemas, bowling alley and designer outlet centre.

Yes, okay – completely ridiculous, even though London Bridge was once sold to a millionaire who rebuilt it in Texas. However, the news this week that the BBC Television Centre is to be sold off sent a chill through this columnist's heart no different to that I would have experienced had those other unthinkables been true. The news is particularly bizarre as, to the best of my knowledge, the TV Centre has comparatively recently undergone an expensive internal refit. I was there a month ago to record a commentary for a DVD version of one of my *Doctor Who* stories which I filmed there in the 80's. The place was alive and buzzing.

To sell it to provide heaven knows what – more intensive housing, offices, a retail park - is quite simply the secular equivalent of sacrilegious. I know change is inevitable, but the buildings I mentioned above could similarly have been plundered and vandalised if the desirability of change was the sole criterion. The BBC Television Centre has been an iconic image for several generations in the UK and overseas and was so for me long before I worked there for the first time in 1970.

In 1971, I was hurled across Studio 1 by Anthony Hopkins in *War and Peace*; in the 1980's, I battled the Daleks and Cybermen in Studio 6. During those wonderful creative days one could pop into the viewing gallery next door to the studio you were in and watch *The Two Ronnies* or *Morecambe and Wise* recording their shows. My first ever photo shoot took place in the *Blue Peter* garden – which will presumably be under several tons of concrete quite soon.

For many people the Television Centre represents broadcast in its purest public service form and to sacrifice it for the podcast, phone-in and reality television generation in order to make a point about reduced public funding is quite simply an act of wilful vandalism. Keep your hands firmly on the keys to Buckingham Palace, Windsor and Balmoral, ma'am – or they may be next.

8th September 2006

Fortunately, there are still enough people who buy The Independent, The Guardian, The Telegraph and The Times to justify continuing to print those newspapers, despite the lowest common denominator, circulation grabbing content of the tabloids widely referred to as Red Tops. Red Topitis is now creeping into television. And sadly the BBC has gradually succumbed, at least partially, to employing ratings as a criterion instead of excellence. It loses the moral and artistic high ground every time it attempts to compete on that basis with the ever-proliferating number of commercial channels, most of which have to please advertisers and sponsors with ever dwindling budgets.

The pie is not getting any bigger, so the slices have to get smaller, and rely on income-generating alleged 'quizzes' and pandering to the seemingly endless number of people who want to be humiliated on television. Yes, the world has moved on from *Andy Pandy*, *Billy Cotton's Band Show*, *Wacko*, *Dixon of Dock Green* and *Crackerjack*. Whether that is for the better or not, I will leave to you. When the career accountants moved in to television, numbers became everything, rendering obsolete the notion that a smaller number really enjoying a programme is preferable to lot of people not minding it. Never mind the quality; feel the viewing figures. And it is for this reason that the broadcasters continue to ruin our complete enjoyment of programmes by split-screening the picture at the end and allowing continuity announcers to trail what's coming next, very often in a tone and mood that cuts right across any involvement one might have had in the outgoing programme. And we may just want to read the cast list!

How many times have you had to rush right up to the screen to discover who 'that actor' was, because the upward scrolling credits have been reduced to a tiny fraction of the screen to allow them to demonstrate the dubious delights of what's coming next? We can wait; we really can. We know what we want to watch – for heaven's sake let us enjoy it!

6. That Was the Year That Was

Some of my writing defies easy categorisation, so Tim has selected a few items here from the year of publication of this book. It is an eclectic selection which answers very neatly the question "What do Bruce Grobelaar, Johnny Depp, Ben Fogle, Winston Churchill and Captain Mainwaring have in common?"
I know that is a question that has been occupying your minds for aeons.

Well, they all appear, in varying contexts, in the next few articles, all written in 2009.

23rd January 2009

Yet another pantomime season draws to a close for me this week. One of the opportunities offered to panto performers is to visit hospitals with the aim of bringing some festive cheer into the lives of those for whom Christmas has been marred by illness or incident. It is usually the very young and the very old that we inflict ourselves upon, perhaps because unlike the in between ages they usually seem prepared to find the experience tolerable and even uplifting.

There are of course the odd individuals (like the one Catherine Tate based her 'Gran' character on), who are appalled by the sight of fairies, principal boys and assorted kings and genies bearing down upon them with intent to charm and make their distaste apparent. This year, I was invited to visit a hospice on the outskirts of Bath and share with them stories of my life and times, which they seemed to enjoy. But really I was the main beneficiary. I was quite honestly unsure what I could possibly offer to people who were coming to terms with their own mortality in such a final way.

But I have never had a more interested, friendly and warm reception. I sat next to a young lady in her thirties who, it turned out, was not only a great *Doctor Who* fan, but was particularly fond of my version of the great man. It was humbling to be able to give so much pleasure, simply by talking to someone whose life expectancy was apparently short. Her greater joy, however, was in having survived, against her original prognosis, long enough to attend her daughter's 18th birthday party the following week. She had for many months been preparing gifts for her daughter in the expectation that she would not be able to present them herself.

The fact that she would be able to do so irradiated her with so much pleasure that you would think she had just won the lottery. And in her eyes she had. I will doubtless moan and whinge again about all sorts of trivial things in my life, because we all too frequently forget to count our blessings.

But I will also do my best to remember what really matters more often, as I did when my daughter skidded and wrote her car off two days before Christmas. My best Christmas present was that she was unhurt.

1st May 2009

My wife and I were invited last week to join the diners in Hell's Kitchen, a television programme that I might otherwise not have watched, being more a fan of eating than I am of cooking. However, in view of the fact that we were about to be whisked off to the distant reaches of East London to sample the fare of Marco Pierre White's trainee celebrity chefs, I thought it would be polite to familiarise myself with the process.

Firstly I have to concede that my prejudices about the all-round nastiness and brutal autocracy of the chef as a species were dispelled. Yes, the man with names from three cultures, can adopt that particular persona when necessary to get a service out to the customers, but as the saga unfurled he showed himself to be a man certainly capable of giving credit where it is due and of empathising with the trainees in the very artificial circumstances in which they had to assimilate in days, or even hours, what his usual employees might expect to learn over years of burnt fingers and dropped soufflés.

I think with only a couple of exceptions this bunch of celebrities rose to the challenge superbly – and in several cases, surprised even themselves with their level of commitment to preparing mashed potatoes (sorry – 'pommes purées') or asparagus.

Other commentators may have things to say about what 'list' these famous (or not so famous in their eyes) people may belong to. It's easy to mock – and indeed they may have had a variety of reasons for offering themselves up for potential – career advancement, money, curiosity. Who cares? Must we always snipe when people raise their heads over the parapet? All of them have a living to earn and we should judge them by how well they did what they did – and not by

some yardstick imposed by the 'knocking' media. Anyway, I suppose we were lucky to attend in the second week, when the trainees had improved their culinary skills under the eagle eye of Marco. I had perhaps the best meal that I have ever had (that wasn't cooked by my wife) in years, possibly since I sampled the fare of his namesake Raymond Blanc (do you have to be 'White' to be a chef?) and we derived even greater satisfaction when we learned that our 'pommes purées' had been prepared by the great Bruce Grobelaar.

17th April 2009

I read it in a newspaper (not this one, I hasten to add) – so it must be true. Tesco, it is reported, have instructed Silver Fern Farms in New Zealand who supply the retail giant with lamb for the British table, that they must stop using sheepdogs to round up their sheep (the clue is in the name folks!), unless the dogs can be trained to be gentler, more considerate and more sheep user-friendly.

How you train a dog to send a written invitation to a flock of sheep to join him at the south-eastern corner of the 10,000 acre field, Tesco have not to date offered to explain. They have, it is alleged, suggested that it will be less stressful for the sheep if the shepherds – wait for it – 'flail their arms, beat sticks or wave flags' to persuade the recalcitrant, grass chomping flock to toddle, unstressed, somewhere else. Maybe we could export teams of Morris Dancers to assist the sheep farmers of New Zealand?

Some would say that that would rather elegantly kill two birds with one stone. Not I, however, dear reader. I spent a happy half hour, in Nottingham of all places, one evening last year watching a team of the jovial jingling jumpers strut their stuff for an appreciative audience outside a town centre hostelry. Great fun!

Back to the sheep! I know the supermarkets are trying to improve their act in every area, from phasing out battery chickens to introducing us to cholesterol reducing spreads – but isn't this directive just a tad on the going too far to plain barmy side? Or is that baaa-rmy?

One of the shepherds is quoted, rather restrainedly in my opinion, as judging this edict from Tesco as 'absolute baloney'. Clearly, New Zealanders are less forthright than their Ozzie neighbours. For those of us who used to love watching *One Man and His Dog* and enjoy the

occasional forays into shepherding seen on another personal favourite *Country File* (long may the great John Craven present it too) – this is incomprehensible. I long to hear that, for once, the great British press have actually got it wrong. Perhaps it was an April Fool? Please? You know along the lines of offering counselling and compensation to prisoners who are traumatised by their incarceration when they are prevented from watching *Hollyoaks* or ordering Indian take-aways. Titter ye not. It will happen.

30th January 2009

Anyone who watches those home makeover, how to sell your house or try before you buy programmes will know that marketing has changed over the last few decades. When my wife and I were last house-hunting twenty-five years ago, we loved finding places that were cluttered, poorly decorated or unfashionable, because we could see the potential to create something that reflected our needs and tastes.

Houses that showed too much evidence of recent updating and decoration generated a disincentive to buy because, although well presented, they might not be to our taste, however neutral and up to the minute. That has apparently all changed. Prospective purchasers want to see your house devoid of all character, without all your personal possessions, books, paintings and all those things that families accumulate over a lifetime.

I don't begin to understand that, but have to acknowledge that if ever we vacate Baker Towers, we will have to ship out the animals, the books, the stuff of our lives that others would call clutter, paint everything in one of those innumerable varieties of shades of white and remove all evidence that we eat, drink or wear clothes.

Let's hope that by the time we move again, if we do, things have reverted to those less regimented days when the interior designer's scorn had not been heaped upon us. And speaking of marketing, may I put out a plea to anyone in the shower gel or shampoo manufacturing industries.

Given that more than half of the population need spectacles, could you please put the words SHAMPOO, CONDITIONER, SHOWER GEL in bigger letters on your products? The same font size as your brand name – which is always legible – would be good. I am fed up

with getting out of the shower to get my glasses to discover which of the many plastic bottles is which. I live with a wife and four daughters, so the 'products' are everywhere. And the man who invents an easy clip on label for leads for electrical equipment will make a fortune. With mobile phones, cameras, MP3 players and laptop computers to be charged, it would save hours rummaging through the wilderness that assorted cables can easily become. And there's all that knitting at the back of the computer too, and assorted USB leads and Sat Nav connectors that seem to entwine around each other, like teenagers, the moment you leave the room.

6th February 2009

I was heartened to learn this week that even in these dark and depressing times of recession and financial uncertainty, there are still people who are prepared to go the extra mile to put aside their own problems and help out those less fortunate than themselves.

Our troubles, for instance, are minuscule compared to citizens of many other countries around the world and it would do us good to remember that.

The citizens of Reykjavik have set a good example to us this week. A radio programme in Iceland highlighted the parlous condition of elderly people overseas and the good citizens of that country's capital organised a national appeal and, as a result, are sending a ship load of warm clothing to relieve their plight.

This is the more admirable given the collapse of their country's financial systems and economy. So, the first consignment of clothing and blankets will soon arrive in Grimsby for distribution to the shivering pensioners of England. Are we perhaps in danger of over-egging the hardships facing our nation when we still remain pretty darn wealthy in relation to the majority of the world?

It was apparently press reports of the terrible crisis hitting Britain that convinced the generous Icelanders that we were in need of their charity. I suppose the next thing they do will be to send snow ploughs and huskies to us. After all the weather conditions we are currently enduring are worse than anything they have ever experienced in Iceland and probably worse than those endured by Ben Fogle and James Cracknell in their recent race to the South Pole. At least if the media reporting is to be believed.

The Norwegian team against whom they were competing, it seems, didn't share the Icelanders' compassion for our current miserable state and weren't fooled into thinking we were deserving of any pity. Just as Amundsen did a century ago, they beat us into second place.

Mind you, the snow is bad enough at the moment to make me think about forsaking my habitual rubber crocs and putting on more sensible footwear. I have compromised by wearing them with socks. Don't say the British bulldog spirit is dead. That survives. It is just common sense that is facing the grim reaper, as is evidenced by the fact that UK coastguards are now obliged to fill in a risk assessment form before responding to an emergency call out, stating 'Reason for Journey.'

5th June 2009

The debate over politicians' expenses rumbles on fuelled by the gleeful media. The whole farrago started when the government of the day lacked the courage to present to the public salary increases for MPs that might appear excessive to the man on the Clapham omnibus but which, in the world of business, would have been considered modest. It is pointless to compare the salary of your elected MP with that of a nurse or teacher, however tempting it can be to highlight the difference in their perceived contribution to society. The blunt truth is that an MP does have to maintain an office with staff and in many cases does have to run two homes in order to function in both constituency and Parliament.

However, in a pusillanimous attempt to disguise what was intended to be a salary increase, an expenses system was constructed with 'nod and a wink' encouragement to claim expenses up to an amount that made the total salary acceptable. A culture then developed in which as long as you had a bit of paper with proof of expenditure on it that fitted the jigsaw of the claimant's intended total payment expectation, then you just chucked it at the appropriate office and waited for the money.

Some, but not all, of the utterly preposterous were rejected.

It may well be that any reluctance to appear dishonest was quietened by the belief that they were merely receiving their proper salary via a different mechanism, but if a better honey trap could ever be set up, I don't know what it is. And the thing that this ludicrous

bait threw up with clarity beyond the greatest anarchist's possible expectation is just how stupid these people are whom we have elected to represent us in Parliament. No one thought about the possible reaction of a citizen whose tax office had disallowed as an expense the newspaper on his hotel bill. No one said (loudly enough anyway),

"Hang on not only is this ridiculous, it is suicidal". And if they weren't bright enough to see the potential electoral meltdown ahead of them, then they simply aren't the right people for the job.

Maybe this self inflicted cull will leave us with the MPs who have that winning combination of intelligence, dignity, principles and scruples. The inner London ones are just lucky, despite what they may have thought originally, as the gravy train chugged by!

27th March 2009

Baker Towers is a cottage and storage space is a luxury beyond our tamest dreams. As a result, over two decades cardboard boxes of old files, photographs and 'stuff that may come in useful again one day' have been jammed up into the available roof spaces. As spring approaches, the urge to cleanse the nest has provoked me to haul them all back down again to purge or recycle.

As anyone who has done this will attest, it is a great time-waster and memory provoker. My daughters' school exercise books are apparently too precious to discard. Four times eight subjects times ten or so years represents a lot of paperwork. We are in negotiation and the boxes currently sit awaiting a decision and edging closer to the front door. I am hesitant to override their desire to keep them, as I clearly remember my reaction when, in my mid twenties, and not having thought about him for more than a decade, I asked my mother where my old teddy bear was, only to be told,

"Oh, I gave him away years ago." This trauma is probably responsible for every bad thing I have ever done. Judging by current attitudes to crime and sentencing, had I discovered this horror when still a child, I could easily have embarked on a criminal rampage in a world full of other peoples' teddy bears and been sent on a recuperative holiday by a sympathetic judicial system.

But I have for now been reunited, briefly I suppose, with those 78s and LP's I cannot bring myself to chuck away but which nobody else wants, the newspaper reviews that failed to mention that I was even

in the play although I was playing the lead, the boxes of wires that fit heaven only knows what or why, the framed theatre posters bearing my name in tiny print at the bottom, which meant a lot in 1970 and I still can't just jettison. And all that 'stuff' that we liked once but would appal those omnipresent style gurus on the telly.

One item I thought might be worth a bob or two. I checked on eBay. There were fifteen similar items without a single bid between them. And no-one wants all those old videos in the age of the DVD either. No wonder storage facilities are springing up like daffodils along the A40 into London. I must investigate!

31st July 2009

For the last ten years I have been recording *Doctor Who* audio plays for a BBC licensed company, Big Finish. The joy of audio is that I look the same as I did in the 80's, the sets are stunning, the actresses gorgeous and the monsters really scary. They are limited only by the listener's imagination. Between the end of Sylvester McCoy's reign as Doctor on TV in 1989 and the renaissance of 'new Who' in 2005, these stories, recorded by me or the Davison, McCoy or McGann versions of the Doctor kept the deprived fans ticking over during the 'wilderness years'.

The audios are now proving popular in the States too and the American distributors invited me over to their stand at Comic Con in San Diego last week to join in the high tech, dazzling lunacy of the biggest sci-fi/fantasy convention in the world, attended by around 130,000 people, most of whom are there on all five days. That is a lot of people when you are trying to enter or leave the building!

The stars attending the event range all the way from Johnny Depp to – well – me, I suppose. I saw the casts of Dexter (one of favourite programmes), Fringe and Heroes as well the familiar faces of the Star Trek and Star Wars oldies.

The way to differentiate between them and the countless Jack Sparrows, Mr. Spocks, Supermen and Buffies wandering around is that the real ones aren't in costume, are surrounded by minders and (in most cases) looked a lot better in their costumes when they used to wear them.

Someone came up and asked me the time at one point; I was told afterwards that he was Richard Dreyfuss. This seems to happen to

me every time I go to the States. I fail to recognise someone famous. When I was in Los Angeles in February it was Pamela Anderson. But my abiding feeling after witnessing all that adulation and hype is of slight embarrassment. There are very few other jobs that attract the kind of adulatory attention that actors receive, although for the likes of Johnny Depp or Robert Downey Jr. it must be restricting and overwhelming. It is undeniable that there are many jobs that deserve our praise more. I would start with nurses, doctors, teachers ... I am sure you can add to that list.

Just reading the Bucks Free Press letters page is enough to bring me back to Earth!

12th June 2009

Isn't it interesting that the nanny state has no trouble at all in getting pointless rules and regulations enacted and enforced, but drags her inelegant heels when it comes to the ones we all want enforced? Heaven help me, if I ask for more than a handful of painkillers to stock up our medicine cupboard. You used to be able to buy them in bottles of a hundred. Now in order to get sufficient quantities for a family of six, I have to visit half a dozen shops in quick succession, which anyone with an IQ that was measurable wanting to take an overdose would be similarly able to do. But no. As usual the majority must suffer for the hypothetical acts of a few who can still do whatever they're trying to prevent without significant impediment.

Another example? I take pills, the same four every day. But because the local Primary Care Trust is one of the 40% who advise doctors not to prescribe more than month's supply at a time, I have to traipse back and forth, bothering the doctor and pharmacist regularly, as they all run out at different times.

The reason I cannot get more than one month's supply? Not my health, but a hypothetical loss of money. Were I to shuffle off this mortal coil, there might be more pills wasted. At least, 60% of P.C.T.s have a little more sense. Sadly, not ours. What about the hours of wasted time for surgeries, pharmacies and the poor patients – many of whom have to travel considerable distances without the benefit of convenient public transport?

What about our time? In May a new swerve test was introduced for motorcyclists as part of their driving test – to reduce accidents. There have already been 15 incidents of crashes and broken bones during the test! And with all the regulations about who can use ladders and when, the jokes about how many people it takes to change a light bulb are now being eclipsed by jobsworth reality.

But they still can't stop cyclists riding on the pavement, or rogue clampers luring motorists into parking on waste ground and then blackmailing them (with legal authority) into buying their own cars back. And they can't construct a system of government that encourages the best MPs to stay in post. Mr.Goodman – you will be sorely missed – a proper, decent, constituency MP!

An endangered species.

10th July 2009

One of the few pluses of my driving ban is that I am repeatedly experiencing the generosity of friends who repeatedly offer lifts when it means going out of their way and when I might otherwise be stranded. But then there are the minuses. I was working in Birmingham this week recording an episode of the lunchtime drama *Doctors*. This necessitated travelling on the Chiltern Line. No, my complaint is not about that service; the trains were on time and comfortable. But sadly not everyone who travelled with me made ideal companions.

Returning home on the first night a group of young people got on and promptly turned on their 'boom box' or 'ghetto blaster' – a large piece of equipment balanced on the perpetrator's shoulder and turned up full volume – on a train full of people trying to read their books or papers or doze. The railway children 2009 style sprawled on the seats bellowing dreary obscenities at each other and the world at large. I looked round the carriage only to see the more practised and hardened travellers studiously avoiding eye contact and giving very good impressions of so many wise monkeys. I realised that were I to challenge this behaviour, which I ached to do, I might find myself alone in doing so and, these days, I could have been offering myself for some desultory knife practice, so reluctantly but probably sensibly I suppressed my desire to remonstrate and kept my gaze on my crossword. It was hard.

The following night a young woman shared with her mother every detail of a conversation with a friend about their planned holiday in Malaga – for fifteen minutes – loudly enough to be heard in the next carriage. I caught the eye of a lady sitting opposite. We exchanged silent indications of the desire to kill.

When Malaga Mary finally finished a friend joined her, having got on at the next station, and we heard the whole story again, just as loudly. When they finally got off my thitherto silent friend looked at me and said,

"What a truly ghastly young woman." We discussed some fairly terminal sanctions we would like to impose and returned to our reading material, until the next moron with a phone got on. We didn't have long to wait. This one discussed the birthday present he was giving his girl friend that night. Riveting stuff. Three months to go...

14th February 2009

For this week only I am the Bucks Free Press American correspondent reporting to you from New York. I hope you are suitably impressed – and no, it is not an expenses paid trip, as anyone who knows this paper's august editor, will only too readily believe. My visit did not start auspiciously. By chance, my daughter is here at the same time, on a trip with friends. We had agreed to meet up and she was to ring my mobile when she got there. She did and left a message. A text told me that I had a message, so I accessed my message box to pick it up. I listened to a recorded voice asking me for a pin number – which I was unable to supply, never having needed one before.

At vast expense I rang Vodafone UK to ask why I was suddenly, after ten or more years blissfully pin-less I now suddenly needed one. It was to avoid naughty phone-jacking foreigners accessing my fascinating messages, I gathered. Okay. Can you give me the code please? No, you can only be given that if you are phoning from England. But it is because I am not in England that I need it and you have just taken me through a series of security checks before you gave me that infuriating answer! Sorry – those are the rules.

But my daughter is looking for me in New York and has left me a message telling me her whereabouts in the reasonable expectation that I will pick it up, but you are telling me I can't access it for a week

until I return home. Yes. Guess which phone service I will not be using when my contract runs out?

The next joy was that my daughter rang my wife in the UK to check which hotel I was in. She went there and was told that I wasn't a resident – despite the fact that they had photocopied my passport when I checked in. Because another person had made my booking, his name was on the computer.

It took me 24 hours of phone calls, all routed via England, to finally meet up. But - I did get to see the musical Chicago on Broadway on the same night that "Sully" Sullenberger (the Hudson River hero pilot) and his crew were there as honoured guests and received a standing ovation. And quite right too.

13th March 2009

When Manchester United played Newcastle last week there was apparently an incident of verbal 'handbags' in the tunnel at half time. We are told that the Ferrari crashing, Portuguese winker and European footballer of the year, Christiano Ronaldo felt compelled to tell Newcastle defender Steven Taylor that he was a rubbish footballer after the latter had tackled side-stepping Christiano a little too vigorously during the first half.

Taylor responded that whether that was true or not, at least he wasn't ugly – like Ronaldo. The pair had to be pulled apart, apparently. In the list of witty rejoinders,

"Yeah, but at least I'm not ugly like you" doesn't really make it very far out of the Primary School playground – and even there some seven year olds might even feel a little bit embarrassed afterwards at the predictable nature of the riposte. It was certainly not up with the likes of Winston Churchill's famous reply when Lady Astor said to him,

"Winston, if I were your wife I'd put poison in your coffee." He replied,

"Nancy, if I were your husband I'd drink it." But then I suppose footballers don't spend a lot of time working out their one-liner ripostes in the same way that (one suspects) politicians and media personalities do. It is hard to imagine Lee Bowyer or Ashley Cole (...and what on earth is that nice Cheryl doing with him for Heaven's

sake?) summoning up anything like Churchill's response when accused by a woman of being drunk,

"That may be so madam, but you are ugly and in the morning I shall be sober." Yes, it is a variation on Taylor's "You are ugly" riff but, at least it has value added, that important quality, much favoured these days. If looking for a good put down, unless you have the wit of a Wilde or Blackadder, the best option is simplicity. You can't beat Capt. Mainwairing's

"You stupid boy!" The reason the exchange sparked my interest was that Steven Taylor played six matches on loan at Wycombe Wanderers at the beginning of 2004. Loan players come and go and are easily forgotten, but Taylor impressed the fans both as a player and as a person.

He was particularly liked because without fail, win or lose, he came over to the fans at the end of every match and applauded and thanked us. That goes down very well with supporters.

7. The Age of Chaos

It would probably be possible to fill an entire volume with my railing ineffectually against the 21ˢᵗ Century plague of political correctness and the general jobsworth mentality that pervades public life today. I have yet to meet anyone who views the worst excesses (some of which you are about to read) as reasonable or even sane – and yet lurking in our midst there are creatures – I can't believe they are actually people – who enact and enforce these most inane rules and regulations designed principally to protect <u>them</u> from criticism by minorities who are as baffled as the rest of us by the logic that drives the enactors.

Kafka and George Orwell would feel they had been understating their distorted visions of a bureaucratic world gone mad if they were alive today to witness the worst excesses of the pettifogging legislators who blight our lives in every arena.

If you were looking for evidence of alien invasion – this could well be it.

21st July 2000

It is five years ago today that my first column appeared in this august (or should that be July?) weekly. To those of you who have taken the trouble to follow me all the way from the froth and fun of Freetime, (tucked tantalisingly in the motor section), to the dangerous cutting edge of journalism on this page, I say thank you and welcome. To anyone who was hoping to find the wise words of Arthur Church in this, his usual space in the paper, I apologise for any disappointment and hope that you will find my musings, ramblings, diatribes and rants go some way to filling the gap that his retirement has undoubtedly left. Elsewhere in this paper you will see a photograph of a visit I made this week to Hughenden First School, where I met the children of Year Two, who apparently thought my King Rat at the Wycombe Swan last Christmas was "well bad", although one young stalwart asserted that I wasn't that scary when I was on my own without my rats to back me up, so there!

For the purposes of the photograph I put my arms around several children to gather them in for the camera. Then, the following day, I read in the paper that a lollipop man in Kent, who is so popular with the children that they all line up to slap palms with him and do 'high fives', has been told by Kent County Council to stop the

practice, as any physical contact with the children is forbidden under council regulations. Political correctness and fear of opportunist legal action are making us all afraid of our own shadows. However good the Samaritan might be, today he would check the EC Code of Practice on Administering Care and Unguents to Strangers in a Public Place (Para 2a (iv) Appendix J, before helping anyone who had been set upon by thieves. Even then he would probably get into trouble for using cotton wool to bathe his wounds or when the removal of plasters pulled all the victim's hairs off. I heard that there was genuine concern this week at a local school over the advisability of removing a splinter from a child's foot, even though it was protruding from the boy's sole.

At a recent Health and Safety training session, a teacher had been warned of the possible legal ramifications of any form of physical intervention, in the event, I presume, of a politically incorrect alien life form entering the resultant hole in the lad's foot and turning him into something from the X-files. A nine year old boy in Virginia was charged with aggravated sexual battery, handcuffed and finger printed for brushing past a girl in the school cafeteria.

Of the many imports from America, the paralysis and fear created by deranged or greedy litigation are even less welcome than The Jerry Springer Show, films that show Americans winning the battle of Agincourt and Mike Tyson. In New Jersey recently a six year old boy was forbidden to hand out party invitations to his friends, who were all male, because the school principal deemed it sexist and discriminatory. Those of us who have not had a common sense bypass can only keep shouting that the emperor is not only naked but his skin is peeling off too – and hope that sanity is restored before we all retire to our politically impregnable individual survival pods.

24th May 2002

As acronyms go, P.C. seems to have attracted more than its fair share of meanings. Police Constable, Personal Computer, Privy Councillor instantly spring to mind and there are probably more.

The one that I suspect provokes the most chills down the spine is Political Correctness. What started out as a fairly laudable aim – the elimination of the overtly offensive from everyday activities and communication - has been hi-jacked by series of bodies which, it

seems to me, have little better to do than play Hunt the Obscure Insult. I count myself extremely lucky to work in a profession where political correctness is about as common as permanent employment. Actors habitually demonstrate their ease with each other by being what others might perceive as politically incorrect after very short acquaintance. It is a function of the job that we explore relationships and sensitivities, so it is perhaps a shorthand way of saying that we trust each other enough to separate affectionate humour from inappropriate insults. And sexism and racism are virtually non-existent in the acting profession (and I am not referring to job opportunities here, just attitudes).

If a part is written from a plump, middle-aged white bloke then I am more likely to get it than a thin, young black woman – and ditto contrariwise. That makes life much simpler. Would it were so in other areas. The news that John Denham the Police Minister was castigated for using the hyphenated word 'nitty-gritty' at a Police Conference first of all perplexed and then appalled me.

It appears that Metropolitan Police have banned the use of the expression on the basis that it was used to describe the detritus left after a slave ship was emptied. Of my many reference books, none offers that as a derivation, so I would presume, reluctantly, to question the detective work of the Met on this occasion. Apparently the officers of the Met are also banned from using the expression:

"You're a good egg." We will leave aside the delightful notion that the Met is awash with Bertie Woosters who take tea with Aunt Agatha at Claridges and then pop into their panda for a spiffing tour of duty alongside PC Poffy Fortescue. Even if that scenario had any credibility, what on earth, I hear you agreeing, is objectionable about being referred to as 'a good egg'? Well, gather round my little innocents. Egg is a very clear abbreviation of the expression 'egg and spoon' which is cockney rhyming slang for 'coon'. Beam me up Scotty! The latter is clearly an unacceptable word, but to connect to it an obscure and debatable patois unknown to utterers and listeners alike is clearly, and quite simply, bonkers. Oops, shouldn't say 'bonkers' should I? That refers to – oh never mind!

We use scores of words and expressions on a daily basis whose obscure and long forgotten origins may well be dubious, blasphemous or crude. It is the way that they are used and heard now

that is relevant. Do we really need an etymological task force to trawl ancient dictionaries for obscure meanings in order subsequently to proscribe the use of words thitherto completely inoffensive?

Perhaps now is not the time to point out that the word 'police' is arguable derived from the words 'po' and 'lice'. To 'mar' something is to spoil it. Add that to 'low' and… Marlow becomes less attractive. Here's another one for 'P.C.' – 'Preposterous clap-trap!'

26th October 2001

We are lucky to live in a tolerant society; one that acknowledges the differences between people and, to a greater extent than most other countries, one that allows the possibility of dissent, protest and freedom of worship and political belief. However, it begins to tax the tolerance of even the most saintly, when (alright -alleged) members of terror networks can play our legal system like a penny whistle to their advantage (and, even worse, at our expense), and delay, for three years, extradition to a country that wishes to put them on trial on charges of planting explosives, murder and terrorism.

The knowledge that the countries that spawn, train and fund the terrorist psychopaths allow no dissent or deviation from their particular narrow restrictive vision of the world makes it even less pleasant to stomach their cynical exploitation of the very freedom that they so hate and desire to destroy. And all the while, this lover of British Justice is living on Social Security and benefiting from Legal Aid the cost of which will certainly be measured in hundreds of thousands of pounds. And instead of taking steps to ensure that the spirit rather than the letter of the law is upheld, we march firmly forward down the path of tolerance, which would be commendable if everyone else were playing by our rules. Alas, they are not.

And still the desire to be seen to be politically correct pervades western society at all administrative levels. Primary school teachers who have objections of principle (and they exist apparently) to using the events and aftermath of World War 2 to illustrate the social and technological changes in Britain since 1930, have been offered an interesting alternative.

The Department for Education and Skills' guidelines suggest that classes should listen to the John Lennon song *Imagine* and discuss the lyrics.

"It's a way of bringing history more up to date", said a spokesman for the Curriculum and Qualifications Authority. Now call me reactionary, but it defeats me how the words of a pop musician, however talented he undoubtedly was, can lead to a greater understanding of post-war Britain than might be arrived at by more conventional history teaching. But political correctness remains the wholly (insane) grail.

A French tourist, who slapped his 8 year old on the bottom outside an Edinburgh restaurant, after the child had behaved abominably inside, was reported to the police and held in custody for 48 hours. He will have to return in February to stand trial. And the Institute of Management recently warned its members that that they might be in breach of the Human Rights Act if they phone employees at home. Unless a contract of employment stipulates that the employee has an obligation to be available outside normal working hours, an employer has no right to ask for their home phone number or to call them. They could be sued for invasion of privacy. And it's not just in the UK. In Denmark, IKEA, have decreed the end of Christmas parties for fear of offending the non-religious and the teetotal. Also banned are wedding and birthday presents, (they might offend the unmarried and Jehovah's Witnesses respectively).

In Madison, Wisconsin no religious items are to be attached to the merry seasonal 'Holiday' tree, as it is "totally inappropriate for the state to be promoting religious beliefs." Tell that to the Taliban. But don't phone them at home!

17th July 2009

Being healthy and safe are evidently both desirable aims. But the quest for Health and Safety – the capital letters elevate the notion into something almost like the Holy Grail - seems to have the potential to bring hitherto normal activities to a shuddering halt.

I was recently handed a thirty page document by a stage manager at a theatre I was visiting on tour. It was a risk assessment, which he had been obliged to compile in order to satisfy the requirements of the insurance policy covering the production company. It was full of references to 'stairs – danger of tripping', 'blackouts – danger of walking into things' 'water in cups – danger of spillage' and even 'bright lights – danger of dazzling!' I wanted to add – 'Irritating and

pointless documents – danger of apoplexy.' By writing these no-brainer things down and giving me a copy of them, he had satisfied the requirements of the tick-box form sent to him by the Insurers. I had been warned; therefore, if any of those things happened to me, they were in the clear at least.

In this context, it is no surprise to read that a sixty year old man in Morden, South London recently died while a paramedic stood outside his house conducting a sixteen minute risk assessment; because when he arrived the door of the flat was open and he feared the place might be being burgled. I don't blame the poor, hapless paramedic but the strictures under which he has doubtless been instructed to operate by his litigation-averse employers.

We really cannot allow the cotton wool, fear of litigation culture to stifle us any more. Can you imagine where the human race would be now if risk assessment had existed a few centuries ago? America would still be the land of the Cherokee and Sioux, there would be no air or rail travel, no cars …

Hmmm – maybe I am destroying my own argument here. But, it is appalling to hear this week that parents were banned from attending their children's' sports day in East Bedfordshire because "it would be impossible to guard against paedophiles." A spokesman said,

"All unsupervised adults must be kept away from children." Wow! Leaving aside the question "Who supervises the supervisors?" – We are once again allowing an evil minority to blight the lives of the majority by characterising us all as potential monsters. It must stop.

21st July 2006

A married clergyman and chair of Governors helps out with reading in class and kisses a ten-year-old girl on the forehead when she achieves some success. The girl's mother complains and he is obliged to resign his governorship. He may have been naïve to believe that the values of an innocent age might pertain today; his action may have been ill-advised, given the paedophile hysteria that pervades education now.

But what a sad indictment of a world where suspicion and automatic prurient outrage hold sway. I am a school governor. I would probably know not to kiss a child on the forehead, however well he or she had performed in a class activity, but I might very

easily have patted them on the back, literally as well as metaphorically. I might have given a shoulder a squeeze, naturally and instinctively. I once put my arm around a child that was crying, to ask what the problem was, in much the same way as I would want a kindly adult to have done for one of my children when they were smaller. I was told that my action was inappropriate. Indeed, teaching staff are instructed not to touch children at all, unless another adult is there to witness the innocence of the contact.

I'm not sure that we are constructing a world where genuine kindness and affection can ever thrive again. We have allowed the evil behaviour of a tiny fraction of one percentage of the population to dictate how the rest of us behave, in a way that is almost Orwellian in its awfulness.

One of my daughters spent her first term in primary education holding the hand of her male teacher while sucking her thumb. Being a kindly, gentle man he recognised her need and vulnerability and tolerated this constant appendage until she felt brave enough to let go. He shared the problem with us, smilingly, and we felt lucky to have had such a caring man to ease her through those first difficult weeks. Today they would doubtless castigate the perceptive nun who befriended and advised me in my first weeks in secondary school, when I was struggling to socialise.

I want to live in a world where that can happen, because changing that world into the cold, calculating, legally defensive environment we are heading for, will rob us of so much and, I strongly suspect, diminish the incidence of real abuse not a jot.

24th August 2007

Anyone who has any doubt at all that the lunatics are now running the asylum need only scan the daily papers for a few moments. And I am aware that those key words in the last sentence will probably attract the attention of the PC PCs.

In the last few weeks alone the following incidents have taken place in the UK. A clerk working for the RAF has been awarded £484,000 for straining her thumb while inputting data on her computer. Compare this with the £57,000 awarded to a serviceman who loses a leg in action. How much would we get for strained credulity?

A pensioner in Wiltshire has been told she can no longer tend a small flowerbed in Urchfont, where she lives, unless she puts out three warning signs, wears a fluorescent jacket and employs a look-out. Bournemouth Council has banned its swimming pool employees from loaning armbands to children in case they catch something nasty while blowing them up.

A Jamaican born dustman has been ordered not to wear a St. George's Cross headband at work on the grounds that it is racist. He now sports a skull and crossbones headband which is considered acceptable by his worryingly blinkered employers. I like his style.

In the same as we read of the appalling behaviour of a minority, but a sizeable minority, of young people, there is a story of a mother in Bedfordshire who was being investigated by the police for inappropriate parenting. When her child had a tantrum in a shop she took her outside, put her in the car, closed the car door and stood a few feet away watching until the toddler calmed down. To me that sounds a rather good strategy.

And, unbelievably, an 18 year old science student from Bedfordshire has been banned from applying for an Environment Agency flood management training course because she is English. She was told that only applicants from ethnic minorities could apply. Apparently Irish, Welsh and Scottish would be acceptable. In an age when most local authorities and government departments are struggling with diminishing budgets, may I suggest that a very good way to save a shed load of money would be to release onto the job market the bureaucrats who make all these ridiculous and irritating decisions? Though, heaven knows, I would be hard pressed to think of any useful contribution they could make in any capacity for anyone else.

18th June 2004

However much we all rail against its ludicrous excesses, there seems to be no stopping the juggernaut of political correctness. So forgive me for revisiting this theme again. Until someone applies for a job in local government (perhaps the area producing the worst excesses) who shares the opinion of everyone else I have ever met, then seemingly the March Hare and the Mad Hatter will continue to dominate our lives.

Everyone is so scared of being blamed for anything that they construct a wall of absurdity around them that will eventually bring this country to its knees, I fear. The days when a man of inspiration and talent could revolutionise an organisation are now largely over. Almost every television programme you see now is the result not of a talented producer or director having the courage to do something new and exciting, but of the endless deliberations of a committee of the cautious who don't want to stick their necks above the parapet individually, while the really creative and talented people are sidelined in case they do something dangerous like succeed or fail.

When I started acting in television a few decades ago, I would meet a director and read for him and he would, on the basis of his experience and judgement, cast me (or not). Today when I meet a director, he films my chat with him and my reading for the role and that film is watched by the producer, the executive producer, the departmental head, the head of programmes, the deputy assistant head of paper clips and his dog. The actor who offends the least number of those people gets the job. In my book, that does not contribute to the creation of exciting television.

We are being bludgeoned into submission in every area of life by careful and risk avoiding practitioners of the art of not making waves and edging up the greasy pole of life without being noticed or frightening the horses. Every week the news media bring forth fresh examples of pottiness. Schools seem particularly prone to providing examples of sledgehammer/nut syndrome. You can't blame them; the poor beleaguered teachers are proscribed by regulation at every turn. The ghastly spectre of paedophilia casts its shadow over all our lives and a sick minority are setting the agenda for the largely decent majority. Just as does fear of litigation from parents that want schools to bring their children up for them as well as teach them and will sue at the drop of a SAT.

Some bright spark at Derbyshire County Council has come up with the wheeze of instructing teachers accompanying children on school trips in the summer to take spray-on sunscreen with them. Spray on? Yes, of course. Mustn't run the risk of being accused of being a sun cream rubber-on fetishist. No physical contact! A school in Wiltshire has issued an interdict banning home made cakes from its summer fete. Shop cakes are okay, full of all those healthy nourishing additives

that we all crave, because anyone made ill by eating them can sue the manufacturer, not the school. The nut is now barely visible beneath the incessant pounding of the sledgehammer. But wait – there's more. The rule even applies to children bringing in a cake for their birthdays to share with their classmates. I am surprised that reason wasn't in case other children, whose birthday it wasn't, felt discriminated against and might sue!

18th April 2003

Future historians will perhaps look back at this era and marvel at the steady erosion of common sense. The more every human activity is codified, described, proscribed and reduced to policies, codes of conduct and computer programmes, then the further away we seem to move from that bastion of previous generations - common sense.

Fear of exposure to blame and subsequent litigation has paralysed human interaction in all areas of life. In primary schools, many teachers dare not risk giving a hug to a crying child for fear of subsequent misinterpretation and they can't apply a plaster to a graze in case the child has an allergy. Every activity is the subject of a policy; and the Health and Safety folder on my shelf is giving an inferiority complex to its smaller neighbour the complete works of Shakespeare. Aside from the accumulated tedium of all these publications, with their appendices and addenda, the more risible of which attract deserved criticism, the knock on effect is that they induce a kind of paralysis. Even if an activity is not subject to specific regulations, the defensive mode switches in and rather than be blamed for some yet unknown transgression – a masterly inactivity is deemed preferable. If you don't do it – then you can't be blamed. Better still write a computer programme that avoids all predictable pitfalls for the service provider. Then defend that provider with a multiple option pre-recorded help line and whilst the customers may have steam coming out of their ears, at least they can't sue.

The letter written to the widow of a Royal Marine killed in action in Iraq asking her for a refund of her late husband's salary and indicating that her home would soon no longer be available to her was, it appears, written by a human being who could perhaps find no regulation to cover the case and prevent such crass and cruel insensitivity. Those of us who still rely principally on good old

common sense would perhaps have been composing a quite different letter to the widow and mother of the son of a man who had died on active service for his country - a letter offering support and reassurance perhaps?

There was no common sense programmed into the computer of the bank that sent my mother an invitation to secure a better life by raising money against her home. The bank was the same one at which an executors account had been opened a month earlier when she had died.

There is no common sense in a legal system that allows a convicted killer to sue his former employers for wrongful dismissal after attacking a man with an axe. The Preston Council had apparently failed to follow proper procedures in depriving the killer of his job as a health inspector. The £8,000 cost of the hearing will be borne by the tax payer.

And common sense has left the building when the surviving thief shot by farmer Tony Martin is allowed to sue the incarcerated defender of his home for loss of earnings. After serving his term for breaking into Martin's home, the burglar claimed to have post-traumatic stress disorder. He lost his case mercifully, but again we paid his legal aid expenses of £5,000. Meanwhile Tony Martin remains in jail after a parole board claimed he "was living in the 1950's". Ahh! Before any of those policies and codes of practice were written?

Lucky Tony.

8. An Actor's Life For Me

There are very few professions, if any, that do not have the potential to throw up incidents and scenarios worth re-telling to a wider audience. The difference for an actor is that usually the other people in the story and the subject of their work are known to a wider circle of people than might be true in less high profile professions.

There seems to be an insatiable appetite for tales of the doings of the famous – hence the proliferation of those glossy magazines with names like 'Hi' and 'Wotcha' or 'Hotstuff' and 'Right-oh'. Although, I must confess, that at least half of the people who are featured so heavily in those magazines are completely unknown to me, which is not all that surprising given that their fame is for doing things that are of no interest whatsoever to anyone other than themselves and the readers of those magazines.

But I am being grumpy again – move on, Colin, move on…

As a young man, the possibility of my ever earning a living as an actor was dazzlingly attractive at the same time as being seemingly unattainable. Inevitably, the actuality of an actor's life is more about hard work, persistence and luck than it is about stardust and tinsel. It is a beguiling, frustrating, endlessly challenging and tantalisingly uncertain way of earning a living. And uncertainty <u>can</u> be tantalising when anyone can be plucked from obscurity at any time and turned into a star – for however short a time.

The next phone call may just be the one.

14th March 2008

I am lucky to work in a profession where 'taking a sicky' is as unattractive to the employee as it is to the employer. Not only do I enjoy my work but 'The show must go on' is etched through my generation's bones like Blackpool rock. But I have had to bow out of performing twice already this year. I missed the last two days of my pantomime in Norwich because a respiratory virus finally defeated me and attacked my vocal chords; and I arrived at the theatre in Eastbourne on Friday and opened my mouth to produce only an inaudible croak. I had been battling a cold and clearly had not completely mended after the last bout.

My determination to battle on may have been a mistake, as I am now still voiceless (in any way that would enable me to perform) even

after three days of silence and prescription drugs for the chest infection I am now harbouring.. And boy have I been taking stuff! Every member of the cast has suggested and generously provided different wonder remedies. I am rattling with herbal remedies, vitamins, coated in miracle honies, awash with linctuses, hot lemony drinks with whisky (no complaints there), reeking of balms and unctions rubbed into chest and forehead. I have steamed and gargled and slept upright.

But I still sound like the kind of person you don't want to receive a phone call from late at night. But I won't be making any. Were I not working I would take it in my stride, but for an actor 'being off' is a bit like being the walking dead. I know my understudy is excellent and they all assure me they are coping and are even kind enough to say they are all missing me, but I should be with them to open in Cardiff this week and as I write this it looks unlikely. I suppose eleven days sick leave in forty years isn't bad (I missed a week when I put my back out leaping onto a bed in one of 'those' farces twenty years ago) – but at the moment I feel a fraud, particularly when I should have been doing a matinee and was watching the FA quarter finals on TV, which I would have enjoyed much more had I been rushing offstage to the crew room to catch up on the scores. I must really be sick!

1st October 2004

For the first time in many years, last week I appeared on BBC1 on a Saturday evening, just after the football results and the news, in the hallowed time slot once reserved for *Doctor Who*. But last weekend, I faced a foe more implacable than the Cybermen, more lethal than the Daleks and probably more highly paid than all the actors who have ever played those enemies of the Doctor, encased in their unwieldy suits. The mistress of the arched eyebrow and the even archer barb, Anne Robinson, was on sparkling form in *The Weakest Link*, when she encountered a phalanx of Doctors, without a regeneration in sight. What you as the viewer, if you had watched the programme, would not have seen was that I was twice responsible for delaying the start of the recording because I failed to spot the red light on the camera and introduce myself into it at the appropriate moment. This meant that they had to re-start a long complicated tracking shot twice, because the contestant at the end of the line was

having trouble with his varifocals! This was, of course, manna to our velveteen inquisitor who, like a shark scenting blood in the water, needed no prompting to slowly turn her gimlet eye onto your hapless columnist. Unlike the usual contestants on that programme, most of us had previous experience of working in television studios and in front of cameras, so certainly the chatting element should have come as no surprise; although I was amazed that some of my fellow guests were clearly unprepared for the level of personal abuse to which they were subjected. If they had not actually seen the programme before (and the Barefoot Doctor told me that he hadn't) then surely some kindly family member or friend could have marked their cards. I am so used to total strangers telling me that I am both older and bulkier than I was twenty years ago when I played Doctor Who, that it came as no surprise when Anne also latched onto that fact.

Interestingly, I thought that the actors handled their moments in the hot seat better than the genuine Doctors, who perhaps tend to dish out uncomfortable truths more frequently than they receive them. Actors are exposed to rejection, criticism and personal comments on a depressingly regular basis. If it's not directors and producers, it's reviewers that remind us of our many deficiencies. Doctors in their workplaces are generally treated with great respect and deference; GPs and psychiatrists may occasionally be criticised professionally, but rarely personally – and it is the personal that provides the sting for most of Ms. Robinson's barbs. Maybe I am a masochist, but I rather enjoyed the sparring.

I was concerned that the editing process might have resulted in some adjustment to make the host look better at the expense of the guests, which certainly happens on other programmes, but I am happy to report that this was not the case on *The Weakest Link*. I am, of course, mortified that having survived to the last round, that the tension of the moment – and here none my previous TV experience prepared me for the onset of brain paralysis – left me unable to remember that Barcelona was the previous European host for the Olympics or the name of Damien Hirst.

And so, my charity did not get its £21,000. But, hey, MacMillan Nurses did – and, boy, do they deserve it.

7th September 2007

I compèred an orchestral concert in Durham last weekend, at which my daughter made her live debut as a singer. Afterwards she was asked for her first ever autograph by a young girl. I should, I suppose, remember my first autograph, but I don't and am somewhat embarrassed to say that I now take the business of signing autographs as a routine part of my job, in the same way as hairdressers accept that clients chat to them about things they wouldn't tell their friends and family. My lifetime haul is three autographs. The first was Violet Carson – before she became Ena Sharples in *Coronation Street* and was 'Aunty Vi' on Children's Hour on the radio. Then Harry Secombe, perhaps the most universally loved celebrity ever. Finally, Emil Zatopek, who won the 5,000, the 10,000 and the marathon at the 1952 Olympic Games in Helsinki. I was lucky enough to see him run at Crystal Palace in the 50s.

The only times I have ever asked for an autograph since have been on behalf of friends or Charity events. I was castigated by a particularly avid collector friend when I failed to ask Kylie Minogue for her autograph when I met her recently; but not only did it not occur to me, but if it had I most certainly would have resisted the temptation. Sadly, some members of the public do not have similar reticence. Eric Morecambe told a story of being asked for his as he was being wheeled into hospital after his first heart attack. Other actors tell of autograph books being pushed under cubicle doors in toilets. I was once asked for mine while standing in a urinal. I suggested that I should perhaps wash my hands before complying? Oblivious, the gentleman agreed to wait.

On occasion, autograph seekers have thought I was someone else and I must confess that I usually sign the name of the person they thought me to be. I have signed as Tom Baker occasionally (a common request!) and on one occasion as Tim Brooke-Taylor – yes, I don't see it either! A favourite moment outside the stage door of the Wimbledon theatre twenty odd years ago was being asked if I was 'Colin Baker' by two attractive young ladies.

"Yes" I replied, with a modest smile. They jumped up and down with delight.

"Can you get us Dennis Waterman's autograph?"

10th January 2003

"Don't you know who I am?" has always seemed to me a rather redundant question, whatever the answer. It is usually uttered by people who think that what they see as their fame should be blindingly obvious to all but the meanest intelligence. I once heard it used by a Coronation Street actor with whom I had the misfortune to appear in panto. A bouncer had refused him admission to a night-club, as a private party was in progress. The soap nonentity demanded that the host of the party be brought to the door. The man came and mini-brain demanded admission. The man politely declined and was then treated to the Redundant Question.

"Yes I know who you are," he replied. He then delighted all within earshot by telling him precisely what he was too, and where he should hurry away quickly to. I try to tread quite carefully in handling the fact that my face may be known as a result of appearing on tellies in a squillion front rooms. I was once stopped by an imperious lady in Hampstead, demanding to know how she knew me. I was then appearing in a television series called *The Brothers*. As self-effacingly as I could, I suggested that she might have seen me on the television.

"I don't have one," she said dismissively. "Weren't you at my grandson's Bar Mitzvah?" But excessive coyness can be similarly fraught with pitfalls. In order to avoid Bar Mitzvah moments, I have entered into lengthy discussions about where someone might have met me, only to have them realise that they had seen me on the telly and then get irritated because I had made a fool of them by failing to say so. I succumbed to temptation this week and paid the price.

On receiving a new Marks and Spencer account card, you have to have the card validated in store before use. I attempted to do so at their Swindon store and was told I had to provide evidence of identity. My other credit cards were not good enough. They needed a driving licence or passport. As I walked away, an employee came up and said,

"It's Colin Baker, isn't it? Doctor Who?" I modestly admitted that I was indeed he. The irony of the situation hit me. I took the young man to the service counter. He confirmed my identity. But they remained adamant. People are no good, apparently. Bits of paper with your photo on are. I went downstairs and used another credit card pay for my purchases. A mischievous fate decreed that the lady

behind me in the queue recognised me and we chatted. I explained to her the irony of my being recognised by her and others but not able to convince M&S, although, somewhat inconsistently, they would take payment on the card which they wouldn't accept as confirmation of my identity. A passing supervisor overhead our conversation, said,

"Oh that's silly, I'll sort it out. Wait there." She returned five minutes later with an air of defeat – and the manager. He knew who I was too, he said, but the rules were for my protection and had to be adhered to. So, rather than go to the hassle of trying to remember to take my passport with me to Marks and Sparks, I shall use my credit card in future and deprive them of the extra profit. Don't they know who I am?

11th September 1999

I have just returned from playing Captain Hook in Cornwall, as part of a summer community initiative for local young people. They were all Peter Pan's lost boys, Indians, pirates etc., and were joined by professional actors in the principal roles, creating a show designed to appeal to as wide an audience as possible. The production attracted the extended families of all those young cast members, in addition to the normal audience seeking summer entertainment. This extra box office revenue, in turn, helps the theatre balance its books and remain open. No mean feat these days, alas.

It is always quite difficult for me to plan to take a holiday. Being a jobbing, and therefore only intermittently employed, actor means that I rarely know in advance what I will be doing when or where I will be doing it. So the added attraction for me was the opportunity for my family to spend two weeks in Cornwall with me. They sunned, surfed, sanded and sea'd while I strutted, scowled, shouted and skullduggeried. I did manage, courtesy of some helpful rehearsal scheduling, to spend a few mornings and one evening frolicking in the foaming brine in the sandy cove we discovered and immediately annexed as our own exclusive property. The production coincided with the hottest week Cornwall had experienced this summer. Of course.

The joys of leaping around the Jolly Roger wearing ruffs, waistcoat, heavy embroidered jacket and thick black curled wig twice daily in a theatre without air conditioning are roughly comparable to the

boundless pleasure to be derived from having a sauna whilst wearing an overcoat, woolly scarf and balaclava. My make-up descended inelegantly down my face and streamed around each end of my mascara'd moustache. I was in fact more Alice Cooper than James Hook. I subsequently discovered that the theatre did actually have air conditioning, but it was too noisy to use during a show. That being the only time that it would ever be needed, it seemed to me a masterly stroke of ineptitude and profligacy to go to the expense of installing it. 'Twas ever thus.

Those who design theatres seem pathologically averse to asking advice from those who will be working in them. When a famous south coast theatre opened, the actors arrived for the inaugural production to find that during the design and building process, it had not occurred to anyone that the inclusion of dressing rooms might be a good idea. After the hasty acquisition of a couple of caravans, the show went on. Dressing rooms were subsequently built on, as a very visible architectural afterthought, at the back of the theatre. A flagship theatre in Surrey was constructed with a fly tower (the tall bit into which the scenery gets hoisted up) which was several feet too short to enable it to fulfil that purpose. Flats could not be raised without the lower extremities remaining very visible to the audience. And the Fairfield Hall in Croydon has dressing rooms three floors up from the stage, accessed by a lift, the breakdown of which once resulted in an unscheduled performance of *Snow White and the Four Dwarves*. Consequently, actors are no longer permitted to use the lift to access the stage.

Another theatre I have played has a plumbing system whose waste pipe passes through the auditorium. Actors are therefore exhorted not to use, and certainly not to flush, during a show, unless, presumably the sound could be explained away in the context of the show. The storm scenes in *King Lear* or *Moby Dick*? It's such a glamorous job!

25th May 2001

It might be tempting to view with little sympathy the actors' and writers' strike in the US. The screenplay writers are looking for a share in the huge profits being made by the producers as a result of the huge new market for their films created by DVD and other

electronic means of distribution. The actors over there are due to join in the withdrawal of labour at the end of June. Acting and writing are widely seen as soft jobs practised by primadonnas who haven't done an honest day's work in their lives.

Yet, as a profession, we labour under the shadow of two quite unusual handicaps. Firstly, unlike almost any other job, we have a tiny but very high profile percentage of the workforce, doing what is in essence precisely the same job as the rest of us, who command salaries immeasurably beyond the reach of the bulk of humanity. It is arguable that if there were high profile nurses and teachers, owning several palatial homes and being photographed by paparazzi living in the Bahamas on nectar and ambrosia (the celestial version – not rice pudding), then the rest of their beleaguered professions would have even less likelihood of their getting the recompense for their work that they deserve. So what chance is there for actors and writers who, understandably, are not seen to be quite as deserving?

Secondly, unlike any other job apart from coronation programme sellers and unicorn keepers, more than 85% of the workforce is unemployed at any given time. And even though the job opportunities may seem to have increased with the proliferation of cable, satellite and other channels, nonetheless the overall size of the financial pie remains resolutely the same. As a result, even though minimum wages may have risen, in practice salaries offered to actors today are, for the majority of the profession, actually less than would have been offered for comparable work ten years ago.

British actors are in a worse position than their striking American counterparts. Equity – the Actors trade union - has given six months' notice on its cinema and films agreement in an attempt to get fair payments for actors when their films are shown on television or sold on video or DVD, for which they currently receive nothing. The producers have so far refused to even talk about this.

In the UK, actors are paid a flat fee for their work, which covers all future usage like television broadcast, video and DVD sales. They get nothing extra, unlike their American colleagues, if a film is a success and rakes in megabucks. The difference between America and the UK is so stark that British actors working alongside Americans on the same UK feature film, such as Mission Impossible, could be tens of thousands of pounds worse off. To date, $1.8 million has been

distributed to American actors as a result of the success of Mission Impossible, but not one penny has been paid to the British performers who worked alongside them.

Whilst what we do is clearly not essential in the same sense that the teaching and caring professions would rightly claim for themselves, nonetheless what we do creates something that the majority of the population consumes voraciously. In a profession where there is no such thing as a steady job or a pension, should the creators not benefit as well as the bosses?

9th August 2002

I am currently in final throes of rehearsal for a play called *Corpse!* – (the exclamation mark is a major feature). It will be at a theatre near you at some point in the next four months (well, the tour ends in Milton Keynes in December). Between now and then we will be visiting venues as diverse as Edinburgh, Manchester, Bath and Richmond, some of which will involve my finding accommodation for a week. Nowadays that involves either an hotel or flat, but only a few decades ago actors would be predominantly reliant upon theatrical digs when on the road.

Alas, the theatrical landlady has now been consigned to the leather bound annals of acting history along with greasepaint and weekly repertory. They were a breed apart. The most famous perhaps is the legendary Birmingham landlady who sported a violent red wig that shifted precariously around her head as the day progressed and her intake increased. They only catered for theatricals and, despite a reputation for fierceness and parsimony, they understood the peculiar needs of those who work and eat at unsociable times. Very often they had an uncompromising attitude to the use of their toilet facilities. Although I never actually encountered it myself, I have met many actors who have endured a proscriptive notice on the loo door declaring variations of 'No solids after 10 pm.'

Notices encountered by fellow actors include 'All foreign coins found in the gas meter will be prosecuted.', 'No politics, no religion or friends in after 11pm.' And the wonderful 'Please note – there is a chamber pot under the bed. If used during the night do not replace, as the steam rusts the bed springs.' Norman Wisdom tells of finding a dead body under his bed, when during the night he searched

underneath for something more usually found under the mattress. The landlady's husband had apparently died that day (of natural causes, mercifully) and rather than lose a booking she had found a temporary home for his cadaver pending the undertaker's arrival the following day. Very often actors, unable to face the inedible food on offer at their digs, particularly during post-war rationing, would bring food back for their landladies to cook.

One young actor, in the 1950's, returned to his digs one afternoon to find that his doting mother, anxious for his welfare, had called and left him a succulent sirloin steak and a bunch of asparagus. He was greeted by his landlady with the words,

"Yer mam came this afternoon and left something for you. I've cooked your steak and put your bluebells in water." My all time favourite tale is of the great theatrical knight who returned to theatrical digs he had vacated suddenly during the night decades earlier. Having, he thought, knocked over a glass of water, he groped his way round the room to find the light switch to clear it up. In fact, he had knocked over a bottle of ink, and the wall and furnishings were literally covered with the inky remnants of his groping in the dark. Unable to face the wrath of his landlady he had bolted into the night. Years later in the same town, he felt the need to return and apologise to the landlady for his youthful folly. He was ushered into the parlour, where he sat down – on the landlady's pet Chihuahua – and broke its leg.

24th November 1995

Acting has always been an insecure profession. But I always knew that. I feel great sympathy for those who thought, with good reason, that their steady rise through their chosen trade or profession would result in - at least - job security and a pension. Job security now is a rarity. Middle aged men and women across the whole spectrum of employment are having their hopes of a comfortable retirement after a lifetime's work shattered by redundancy.

People who haven't compiled a CV or attended an interview for thirty years, are being forced to acquire those talents and learn to conceal their true feelings when facing an interviewer who may have the social skills of a dung beetle and the intellect of its staple diet. Once I was interviewed for a role in a public information film. After

an encouraging chat with the director and producer, a 'suit' who had been sitting quietly behind them suddenly said,

"How tall are you?"

"Six feet." I replied.

"No you're not!" he said, somewhat rudely, I thought. We had a brief exchange on the "Yes I am!" and "No you're not!" theme familiar to all parents of small children. Then I had a brainwave.

"How tall are you?" I said to the man.

"Five foot eleven." he replied.

"Come and stand beside me." I invited cordially. He complied. I towered above him - well, by an inch, anyway. I suppose it was a tactical error to add, "Satisfied now Shorty?" But it made the others snigger. He was the man from the Ministry. I didn't get the job.

Age is another hurdle for actors. Unlike the rest of the work force, where age is related to pay and retirement - with actors, age is exclusively relevant to the part on offer. If the film script says "The squinting axe murderer is in his late thirties" then Hiram J Schlockenburger III won't see you if he believes you are 41. Moreover, you would be well advised to enter the room with eyes, as well as fingers, crossed and some agents would go so far as to urge you to take an axe. This tendency is a major reason for the actor's resistance to that question beloved by the press after an interview. You may have been asked,

"What do you think of people who intimidate householders by confronting them on their doorsteps and demanding signatures on petitions that support their particular NIMBY ('Not in my backyard!') obsessions?" You have probably replied

"I find such people beneath the contempt of decent folk. They should be put in the stocks and pelted with rotting vegetables". The journalist is then trained to ask "And how old are you Mr. Baker?" - a question as relevant to the opinion expressed in the preceding interview as,

"What is your inside leg measurement?" or "Do you think Gameboys are politically correct?" ("33 inches" and "Who cares!" respectively, incidentally). I cannot be the only reader who is only interested in the age of the subject of a story if it is relevant (e.g. a seven year old Pulitzer Prizewinner, or a children's TV presenter over the age of twenty.) Whilst I have no desire for reasons of vanity

to conceal my age from the world at large, in a profession where preconceptions restrict employment it can be dangerous to let it all hang out! I was once being interviewed by a producer for a part in *The Onedin Line.* (Now that dates me!) The interview went well, I thought, until the producer suddenly said,

"How old are you?" I temporised by asking him how old the part was, giving what I hoped was an ingenuous, disarming grin. It patently wasn't and he persisted. I then tried another tack.

"How old do I look?" He repeated his question. With the benefit of decades of hindsight, I realise that the next ploy was doomed to failure. I suggested that I could easily try to second guess his requirements, lie to him and get it wrong and that really it was what I looked like that mattered, surely? His demeanour convinced me to reply. I told him the truth. He said I was too old, and the interview ended. By that time, however, I doubt if any answer would have produced a favourable reaction. (Colin Baker is 31).

6th June 1997

When I left Drama School and had received my first job offer, I was then able to apply to join the Actors' Union - Equity. In those days, certainly, that was every aspiring actor's holy grail - to be able to call oneself an Equity member meant that you were an actor my son, mixing freely and swapping anecdotes in that exclusive club that also contained Laurence Olivier and Richard Burton. Obviously one's store of anecdotes tended to be limited to,

"We did a really great improvisation in class last week - we all really believed that Fiona was utterly repelled by David... it was terrifying!" (This of course is somewhat diminished as a coup de theatre, when one is privy to the fact that the opportunity to voice her loathing of David was one for which Fiona had been yearning for nearly three years). The other moment of truth as an actor comes when Equity tells you whether or not your name is free. It would obviously be a potential cause for confusion, and some would say undesirable, to have two Colin Bakers acting their socks off all over the place. I was told, however, that my name was available, if I wanted it. Not a choice offered too many in life! One then has to try and be objective about something as personal and subjective as one's own given name. I had no strong feelings on the subject. My name had been a distinct

handicap in my youth, when in the Eagle comic in a weekly series about three thoroughly decent sporty coves, all called John and known as the three 'J's, there was a swot and thoroughly unsporty, bespectacled weed called - Colin Baker. I am sure there are many Chris Evanses and Jeremy Beadles out there too, who rue the fickle sledgehammer of coincidence. But having that ordeal I felt I had earned the right to carry my own name with dignity at least, if not overweening pride. And the coincidence was unlikely to happen again. I hesitated briefly when a friend suggested that if I wanted to be a film star - and dreams seem more substantial when you're young - then Colin Baker didn't have quite the manly resonance say - Dirk Bogarde, Clint Eastwood or Kirk Douglas. He suggested that Turk Thrust or Randy Stallion might be names to help me to climb the greasy pole to international stardom. I read the runes and saw therein that I might regret these beguiling new identities and that they might not appear quite as desirable thirty years down the line. Even though Rip Torn had a perfectly good career and starred in many films, he was the exception rather than the rule.

So I remained Colin Baker in real and public life. Perhaps I did make a mistake. First of all it is a quirk of fate that there should be another Doctor Who called Baker. I only hope that he gets half as many people calling him Colin as I do vice versa - usually press photographers who call out,

"Nice big smile now Tom - over here" which is guaranteed of course to produce exactly the opposite effect to that intended.

The other pit-fall manifested itself some years ago when I received a phone call from the office of Denis Norden's *It'll be Alright on the Night*. They asked me if I would choose my all time favourites of the outake tapes they would send me. I was flattered and agreed, saying I could already tell them; it was the one that went "Colin Baker, News at Ten, wife and two children and large mortgage, at Westminster, fed up, soaking wet, freezing etc. etc." - or words to that effect.

The researcher laughed and agreed it was jolly good, ha-ha-ha. We both missed the clues in that conversation. I arrived at LWT to record the programme to be greeted by a polite researcher who kept popping outside the room returning with increasingly senior colleagues who peered at me, nodded amiably and swiftly withdraw.

They had of course been under the impression that they had been booking Colin Baker, the newscaster and perpetrator of the very out-take I had considered so funny. I wonder if he is troubled by correspondents asking for his autograph "even though my real favourite was Jon Pertwee" or asking how to become a Dalek.

15th November 1996

All estate agents are called Nigel and smell of aftershave. All plumbers promise faithfully that they will turn up and fail to do so. All doctors are patronising and treat us like an inferior species. All female shop assistants would rather talk to their colleagues than serve us. All male shop assistants say, "Can I help you at all sir?" every 30 seconds whether there's anyone there or not. All car mechanics suck air through their teeth and shake their heads. All lawyers are more interested in their charges than your case. All journalists are heartless door-steppers who make it all up. All footballers are alcoholic thugs. All politicians are self serving hypocrites intent on lining their own pockets. All people who work with computers are nerds. Scots are mean. The Irish are fey. The Welsh are dour. Northerners call a spade a spade. And all actors are 'luvvies'.

Yes, all the above statements are ludicrous generalisations and defame the groups concerned -with the exception, of course, of... (Better not! - Ed). I'll let the others look after themselves - but on behalf of all other non-luvvie actors I'd like to take issue with the luvvie stereotype which has been perpetuated by the media as a result of the behaviour of a handful of performers whose modesty and sensitivity are in inverse proportion to their fame. Indeed the media are to a large extent responsible for giving exposure to that handful of actors who talk a load of pretentious twaddle about their work. I am eternally grateful that the best actor of our generation, the wonderful, self effacing Sir Anthony Hopkins refuses to get drawn into any pretentious discussions about his work. He opts for the infinitely more attractive technique of shrugging off the praise rightfully heaped on him with disarming remarks about the make up department having given him a wonderful moustache, which virtually did all the work for him.

He compensates wonderfully for the actor (and I swear this is true) who paid some passing thugs to beat him up, so that he "really, but

really, knew what it felt like, you know?" I am sure they would have done it for nothing. I'd have been sorely tempted.

But the self indulgent nutters exist in all professions. It's just that well known actors, like royalty, have their every shriek, whoop and excess recorded by an ever present media throng who know exactly which are the right actors to target in order to confirm the luvvie image and enrage the rest of society. In its alternative spelling of 'lovey', the word becomes a less powerful emetic. It is a word I remember being common in the North, from which I hail, as an all purpose term of affection to the world at large -as in,

"I don't know your name but I want to be friendly". It is a shame that it has now been hi-jacked in its newer form to express contempt for the members of the profession to which I belong. 'Luvvie' carries with it connotations of galloping insincerity, of exaggerated outpourings of suspect bonhomie followed swiftly by the glazed eye as the vacuous perpetrator gazes over your shoulder at the infinitely more important person at the other end of the room -darling!

They exist, of course they do. The acting profession encompasses, like any other, a wide range of characters that also includes emphatic non-luvvies like Jimmy Nail, John Thaw and Dame Judi Dench as well as the handful, that I shall not name who make the rest of the theatrical profession cringe.

One of our faults as a nation is that we have a tendency to push people to the top of the heap solely in order to then hound them into oblivion at the merest whiff of fallibility. Naturally enough if the bulk of the populace are giving certain performers plaudits and prizes for simply doing their job, it is almost inevitable that the less (shall we say) objective and self aware of them will be tempted to take themselves too seriously. A fatal mistake.

They then indulge in the theatrical excesses to which one or two recipients of Oscars and other awards have succumbed, failing to recognise the values of the infinitely more attractive qualities of modesty and understatement. But then usually their performances have often shown precisely those characteristics too.

19th April 1997

I have just returned from hosting a three day sales and marketing conference in Bournemouth for a large brewing company. My job

was to interview the key executives and marketing managers in front of a couple of hundred of their middle managers and salesman, with the intention of keeping them au fait with the company strategy and position, motivating them and giving them what, from the profit levels they were describing, appeared to be a well deserved corporate pat on the back. I also had to run and adjudicate the afternoon sessions, which comprised team challenges in the form of those games that encourage teamwork and initiative.

It was quite salutary for an actor and occasional writer to witness the levels of intense pressure to achieve that salesmen endure. It was also staggering to see how they could function at all after massive self inflicted sleep deprivation and how much of their own excellent product they were able to consume with no apparent ill effect. The event was marred slightly for me when I was told only a couple of days beforehand, that I would be expected to give an after dinner speech on both evenings (there were two separate sales forces involved). Now I have made occasional visits to village halls, universities, retirement homes and the like to give a light-hearted and decidedly not risqué ramble through what I like to call my career. This I am pleased to say has usually been politely received and not unappreciated. I have not however ever considered myself a likely candidate as after dinner speaker for a banqueting room full of rugby playing beer salesman from Cardiff, Southampton, Bristol and Swindon. However, as the saying goes, there is no such thing as a problem, there are just opportunities.

This was to be my opportunity to see if I could muster any mirth by recalling many of the genuinely funny things which have happened in my career on stage and television. I spent a fair few hours making copious notes and knocking them into some shape.

I was introduced by the area MD who told the well oiled masses that their special treat of the evening was that a casino had been set up for them in the ball-room and they would all be given a pile of chips to go and gamble. The first salesman to make a million would receive an indecently gargantuan bottle of champagne. He then continued, "But before you all go off and enjoy yourselves, Colin Baker is going to give us an after dinner speech". There's nothing like a big build up! He handed me the microphone which chose that moment to decide to self-destruct. Much fiddling with electrical

equipment. Technicians running across with new microphone, attaching the wires.

"Testing - One Two. One Two". After a long minute of doom laden silence, I was handed a functioning mike. I have to be fair, they gave me a polite hearing and laughed when they realised that they were supposed to. But many of my anecdotes describing what would in my world have been hilarious rib ticklers went down with them as well as their stories did with me later in the bar - like the one about how Jim Jenkins in sales got his major multiple off sales leading brand discount margins confused with the credit scheme on sale tied house tariff. That got the best laugh of the night. I joined in of course. He who pays the piper and all that. I learned my lesson.

Back to the drawing board. I chopped out every story that had had provoked a confused half hearted ripple and substituted some material which I cannot, I'm afraid, claim was entirely free of the kind of innuendo that I would normally consider unsuitable for a mixed audience. I was introduced. I put my hand into my breast pocket for the notes for my new speech and found that I had left them upstairs in my room. Alas, this time the microphone was working. There was nothing for it. Running from the room crying "I want my mummy" was not on. Thank heaven for adrenalin.

Because I knew I hadn't got the notes I went for broke and somehow got away with it. I celebrated by consuming large quantities of their product and retired at 1 a.m. At 4-55 the fire alarm went off. But that's another story.

26th April 1997

Regular readers will no doubt be anxious to know what happened when the fire alarm went off. For those - shame on you - who do not regularly and automatically turn to this column, last week I recounted my experiences at a company conference and my narrative ended when at 4-55 a.m. the fire alarm went off. Those of you concerned for my health and reputation will be happy to learn that I was, at the moment of the great awakening, sleeping the deep, untroubled sleep of one who had sampled well the extensive and splendid wares of the brewing company whose conference I was attending. In fact, I was a mere four hours into my well earned slumber. My first reaction to the shrill siren, which perversely appeared to emanate from

somewhere inside my bed head, was that the early morning call I had requested was being delivered to me in a remarkably unsubtle way. I groped around for some means of turning it off, battering blindly at the wall in search of knobs, switches - anything to blot out the cacophony. As I turned on the light, the noise suddenly stopped.

It was only four hours before I had to leave the hotel, so I turned the light off again and sank rapidly back into my dream - in which, incidentally, there were no politicians of any hue slagging each other off interminably, quoting dodgy statistics and evading questions. A blissful state. A few seconds later the wretched din started up again. I picked up the phone to the night porter and complained rather forcibly that there was a dreadful noise in my room. He replied,

"It is the fire alarm sir, would you please come down to the assembly point straight away?" Ah! Apparently I was not the only person who then staggered across to the door to read the fire drill instructions. I then staggered back to the bedside table to get my glasses. I returned to the door, saw where I was in the hotel and learned that I had to leave my possessions in the room and head straight for the assembly point. I am appalled to relate that I then took a swift mental inventory of how I looked at that moment and what I had with me. I looked much as a naked, overweight, middle aged man might look in the middle of the night and took steps to remedy that, putting on the clothes I did not want to have to replace as a result of their consumption in a conflagration. I seized my laptop computer which contained a lot of work for which I had no back up. I flung some other personal possessions into a bag and cautiously opened the door.

I have watched *London's Burning* and know that opening doors can be a risky business in the middle of a fire. An empty and quiet passageway. I took a fleeting look at my room strewn with last night's discarded suit, shirt and tie, nipped back and picked up my unread daily paper (it could be a long night after all) and clutching my precious lap top went downstairs to the lounge. There was already a large number of people assembled. Most unlike me were sensible and valued their lives more highly than their literary output and clothing. One or two were actually wrapped in towels. Most were in

dressing gowns - which hitherto I have never taken to an hotel, but may well in future. Some were like me, fully dressed.

Only a very few had brought anything with them other than their hangover and that desperate matey humour that is *de rigueur* and invaluable in these situations. I was amazed by my apparent refusal to allow for the possibility of my own immolation.

In retrospect, my disinclination to believe that something as inconvenient as a fire could interrupt my sleep and life could easily have contributed to my early demise.

I learned the following day that other residents had gone further down this path and actually ignored the alarm on the basis that they had experienced previous false alarms, which this in fact turned out to be. Someone had been sufficiently be-fuddled by alcohol, presumably, to find it entertaining to smash the glass of a fire alarm to waken up those boring wimps who had retired early.Irritating though it was - it was preferable to the alternative reason for a fire alarm being set off.

9. Flights of Fancy

Hotels, as you will gather, have played and continue to play a large part in my life as a strolling player. Despite my tendency to commute where possible, Aberdeen, Truro and Newcastle frequently appear on my tour lists and then there is no choice – I have to stay there for the duration of the week. There is a great difference however between the star rating of the hotels that one is booked into by the organisers of corporate shindigs and TV companies and those that I frequent when I am paying for myself.

Theatrical tours invariably mean trawling through 'Digs Lists' maintained by most theatres to assist visiting companies in finding somewhere to stay that doesn't negate the purpose of doing the job financially.

Employers pay a touring allowance that was set many years ago at way too low a level and has never got anywhere close to compensating actors or technicians for the actual cost of living away from a home that has still to be maintained in addition to finding accommodation on the road. And they also pay travel based on the cheapest advance tickets they can find from venue to venue, when of course most of us try to go home for that one day off on Sunday, when trains are notoriously scarce.

Many people are inured to the vagaries and variable reliability of public transport. I have experimented with it from time and fled back to the comparative reliability of my car every time. Not very planet friendly, I know, but it does help to preserve my equilibrium.

Sometimes of course, oceans intervene and there is no choice.

12th August 2005

When people say that they love travelling, I suspect that what they really mean is that they love the experience of being in other countries, rather than the process of getting there. Having been on twenty different aeroplanes in the last month – a total of 74 hours spent in airports or on planes, I can proclaim myself cured of any vestigial delusion that the process of travel broadens anything other than the posterior. Until "Beam me up, Scotty" technology is available, I would like to offer a few tips to those whose job it is to transport us, in the unlikely event than any of them really do care about our "comfort and convenience" – a mantra they trot out every time they announce something that is demonstrably for other

reasons. Immigration first. They know roughly how many people will be coming through an airport at any given time. It is certainly not for our comfort and convenience that we shuffle forward in a queue for 40 minutes after enduring a fourteen-hour flight. Obviously demand fluctuates but staffing could be flexible if other aspects of immigration work were located at airports and the extra staff could be drawn on at peak times. In Australia, an otherwise hospitable and user-friendly country, when you arrive the trolley you need for your luggage requires prepayment of three dollars in coins. Who, other than resident, arrives in a country with coins in their pockets? If they need the money then add the three dollars to the airport taxes for pity's sake! It is not for nothing that they are called airport "terminals". They really are the end. And the security questions!

"Did you pack your bag yourself?" No sane passenger is going to reply,

"No, my wife did it for me."

"Are you carrying any flammable materials?" Duh? Of course, – stick this lot on a fire and, woof, up it would go. Shirts and trousers burn. Or am I missing something? (Incidentally why do flammable and inflammable mean the same thing, when visible and invisible don't?) And does anyone ever depart from or arrive at an airport gate that doesn't require a twenty-minute walk? I think all the empty gates you trudge past are just dummies, designed to impress the gullible traveller. The real reason is that they are saving aviation fuel.

"If they walk the first couple of miles, over a year we'll save millions!" Next week; carousels and passengers.

5th December 2008

It felt like Groundhog Day not Thanksgiving Day when I travelled to America over last weekend. Each time I fly I think:

"This time… maybe this time, my flight will be unworthy of comment. Maybe it is not just me. Maybe everybody has less than perfect travel experiences." And, if that really is the case, then we are all paying too much for the privilege. My journey out to Chicago to attend a Sci-Fi convention was marred by the fact that the aeroplane's entertainment system 'went down'. Okay, rather that than the plane itself, of course. But it is amazing how much longer nine hours seems when all you have to take your mind off the Liverpudlian to

your left, who wants to have sole control of the shared armrest, is the one newspaper you bought before boarding and the airline's flight magazine. Not only did my neighbour want that armrest, but in between arguing with his wife, his lack of that 'no touchy' imperative, that drives the majority of us, ensured that his legs and body went pretty much wherever he wanted too. Add to that the fact that I had coffee spilt down my front when a flight attendant bashed my elbow from behind as I raised the drink to my lips, then another one poured water over me instead into my proffered cup – and you will get the measure of my in-flight experience.

The return journey couldn't be as bad, surely? First of all it is around an hour quicker. Then on embarkation I discovered to my joy that the entertainment system was fully functioning and was showing movies I hadn't already seen. I was on the end of an aisle and the seats next to me were empty. Oh joy! Had the malevolent sky goblin finally turned his attention elsewhere? Then just as they were about to close the doors, a couple with two young babies struggled up the aisle into my little oasis of promised calm. While the six-month old slept, the eighteen-month old screamed and vice versa. The couple were appropriately apologetic, unlike my outward bound neighbour, and of course one sympathises with parents of babies when travelling. Then the man sitting in front suddenly propelled his seat backwards with such force that my apple juice toppled off my fold down tray leaving me looking more incontinent than intercontinental.

It's good to be back!

22nd November 1996

I have just returned from ten days filming in Tangier for a television series. I was the object of much envy when I told friends that, like Webster's Dictionary, I was Morocco bound. The grey middle weeks of November with all that Winter gloom ahead seem the ideal time to head for North Africa and its temperate blue skies. Oh that fickle finger of fate has a sense of timing, doesn't it? The trip started ominously when I left at home the digital mobile phone that I had acquired specifically in order to keep me contactable in emergencies during my absence.

I could not bear wasting all the effort of getting it, so I got the hire car to turn around on the Marlow by-pass and go back for it. I just

managed to check in on time and was even able to change my seat allocation from the middle of a rank of three - (hell on wings for a six foot burly like myself) - to a window seat at the front of steerage. This afforded me an excellent view of the lucky handful who could, while swigging complimentary champagne, swing a slightly larger cat in their seats than I could, assuming I were able to move my arms in the first place.

A Moroccan gentleman sat in the aisle seat. We smiled that wary traveller's smile at each other that tacitly agreed that we are well disposed to one another but had no need of idle chat. We arranged our papers and books neatly on the empty centre seat and settled back for the four hour trip to Casablanca.

As soon as we were airborne a stewardess approached my companion and whispered in his ear. He shrugged, nodded, gathered his things together, glanced at me guiltily and slunk off to the rear of the plane, to be replaced immediately by a young Arab lady and her toddler, whom she popped onto the middle seat beside me. The little chap was about one year old and found me every bit as fascinating as one of my children would have done had they been placed next to an exotic foreigner in similar circumstances. He pointed at me with glee and gurgled at his mother who looked relieved at my apparently benevolent acceptance of his fascination. He stood up in his seat and prodded me. Mother smiled apologetically and sat him down again. This process was repeated many times and became a game. Gradually young Genghis' mother became less concerned for my welfare and drifted into conversation with another Moroccan family across the aisle. My gurgling, dribbling companion tried to feed me with his jar of creamed rice baby food. (Some things are universal.) He threw his toys at me. He plucked my bread roll from my tray and hurled to the floor with joy. His mother picked it up and gave it back to me.   I manfully declined to accept it, indicating that he could have it now - honestly. In fact I hadn't really wanted to eat it in the first place.

By the time we landed, he was belabouring his long suffering mother with my newspaper, there was more creamed rice on my clothing than in Genghis and all his toys were thrust on my lap. His mother continued to interpret my fixed, probably rather manic, smile as evidence of my genuine adoration of my new little playmate. But at least I had managed to give a good impression of western men, who

by comparison with most other nationalities could be accused of being naturally far from well disposed to babies. Indeed I was amazed at one point to see the first officer pluck Ghenghis from his mother's arms and give him an affectionate series of kisses upon the moist food smeared lips. I arrived in Morocco at the same time as the worst weather since 1973 (apparently). Four inches of rain fell the first day. The next ten days were spent dodging the torrents and gales. What we managed to record on film could perhaps have been achieved with a little ingenuity among the palm trees in Torquay and at Brighton Pavilion. On the journey back someone knocked a can of coke over on my lap. I will pass over affairs of an internal digestive nature. It's nice to go wandering - but oh! So much nicer to come home!

23rd November 2001

In the 1980's, when *Doctor Who* was at the crest of its popularity, I was invited to attend a convention somewhere in the USA. On exiting my hotel room one morning I nearly tripped over the recumbent form of a young woman dressed in battle fatigues lying asleep across the threshold of my door. It appeared that she had been charged with my safety by the organisers of the convention. She was wearing camouflage fatigues and a name badge that identified her as Captain Yates, a character from the Jon Pertwee days when the Doctor worked with the Brigadier and 'Unit'.

The principal difference between her and the male actor who played the role on television was that she, as an army reservist in a country where the right to bear arms is enshrined in a written constitution, had cradled in her arms a rifle with live ammunition in it. I was unsure what the threat was to my well-being that resulted in this young lady deeming it necessary to lie in wait in this dramatic way, but I could not honestly say that I would have slept as soundly knowing what was on the other side of the door. I assured my well meaning but deluded guardian that I would be much happier to take my chances with assassins and autograph hunters and be secure in the knowledge that she and her arsenal were safely stowed elsewhere. The next time I saw a similar gun was last weekend. I was invited to Boston to attend a Science Fiction convention when another guest dropped out at the last minute due partly to a reluctance to fly in the

aftermath of the recent hi-jacking of aeroplanes from the same city. It struck me that if there was one airport in the world that would now be trouble free, it would have to be Logan Airport, Boston.

The security at Heathrow was painstaking and confidence inspiring. Baggage was x-rayed, metal detectors deployed and I endured stoically a rather thorough frisk by somewhat embarrassed male security guards. On the return journey from Boston, however, the only additional security to that in force before September was the addition of a number of uniformed soldiers, carrying what I must assume were guns with live ammunition – otherwise why carry them. One of them, who could have been no more than a teenager, approached me and fired a staccato burst of unintelligible words at me while gazing at the floor. It sounded remarkably like something he had learned by rote and was regurgitating in precisely the same way as those chants that accompany triple paced marching in movies where chisel faced sergeants put rookies through hell to make soldiers of them.

Sadly, I couldn't understand a word. I begged his pardon. He repeated his indecipherable mantra. On the third repetition, I understood that he was asking me if I was carrying any sharp implements, knives, hypodermic syringes etc. I reassured him that I wasn't and he ushered me past him. No-one offered to frisk or pat search me.

Call me cynical, but surely even a terrorist who has a passionate regard for the holy books of whatever religion he has contorted to support his manic urge for mayhem might just cross his fingers behind his back and lie about the ice pick secreted in his beard.

29th February 2008

Having been working in Northern Ireland and Scotland for the last four weeks, I have been flying up and down from Heathrow each weekend. On seven of the eight journeys I took my small wheelie case onto the plane and stowed it happily in the overhead locker.

I travel light because it saves around forty minutes waiting for checked-in luggage on arrival. Over the four weeks, that's more than five valuable hours not spent standing in a baggage hall watching an empty belt go round. Last week, however, a young lady who clearly didn't like the cut of my jib, asked me to prove that my case was

within the current size limitation guidelines stipulated for carry-on luggage. Confident that it was, as I had checked the BAA website and measured the case carefully, I lowered it into the stainless steel frame used to check luggage. The handle on the end stopped it from going in smoothly. As I flattened the handle and pushed the case down, my inquisitor (who spoke English as a third language and was only eventually comprehensible) told me squashing was not allowed and I would have to check the bag in.

I explained that I had travelled into Heathrow two days earlier with same bag which fitted effortlessly into the overhead locker. It is not about the overhead locker, I was told, it is a security issue. I suppose it was pointless to attempt to deflect the heavy hand of officialdom when it is in motion, but I enquired as politely as I could why the projecting handle of my wheelie bag presented a security issue.

She explained that any further discussion on the subject was pointless and that burly men with automatic weapons, who were not averse to casual torture, were willing and anxious to practice their techniques on me if I did not immediately trot off to the check-in counter. Well - words to that effect, as far as I could deduce through her impenetrable accent. Naturally, the Glasgow baggage carousel broke down and it was nearly an hour before I emerged, blinking, into a world of glazed and defeated fellow travellers.

This week I have crammed my smalls into a case so tiny that, even if my tormentor is on the gate again and has a good memory, she will be hard pressed to disqualify it for travel in the overhead locker to Aberdeen. Wish me luck.

27th January 1998

I have never entered Britain as an alien (no *Doctor Who* jokes please) and therefore do not know how, say, Americans are greeted when they pass through immigration control at Heathrow. My suspicion however, based partly on observation as I pass through the UK residents channel, is that they are not subjected to the same indignities and frankly absurd questioning which non-USA residents have to endure in the States.

One is herded rather than shepherded through roped off passages where uniformed officers bark out instructions like,

"Stay close the right wall" and "Don't cross the yellow line." Then one queue of two hundred travellers files through one control point as the US residents are dealt with by half a dozen officials who then go off duty. Experience earned the hard way has taught me to suppress my habitually overactive desire to confront bureaucracy. I learned this lesson on a previous visit when I was unable to fill in the immigration form correctly because I had failed to make a note of the name of the Hotel at which I would be staying.

So for my address in the States, I honestly wrote "Don't Know". First mistake. I explained to Mr. Suspicious Granite that my hosts would be meeting me and whisking me off to wherever it was, so he needn't worry. It appeared my comfort was not his main concern. He then asked me if I had any US currency with me. As it happens I did not and said so. Second mistake. How then could I convince him that I was not attempting to gain entry to the land of opportunity, the hamburger and Ronald Reagan purely in order to remain there for as long as possible as an illegal immigrant? I replied.

"But I am English. What possible reason could I have for wishing to live in America?" I thought that would put his mind at rest and speed me through immigration. Third mistake. I was delayed for some time as enquiries were made as to the validity of my claim that I was the guest of a Science Fiction Convention. But I must share with anyone who has not recently seen it, the contents of the Green Visa Waiver form issued by the U.S. Department of Justice, which visitors must fill in order to gain entry. It says "Welcome to the United States" and then tells to you answer Yes or No to seven questions. Some are understandable and ask, for instance, whether you are intending to seek work. But others are baffling.

"Have you ever been arrested or convicted for an offence or crime involving moral turpitude... or been a controlled substance trafficker... or are you seeking entry to engage in criminal or immoral activities?

"Have you ever been or are you now involved in espionage or sabotage; or in terrorist activities; or genocide; or between 1933 and 1945 were you involved, in any way, in persecutions associated with Nazi Germany or its allies?" An acquaintance of mine made the mistake of writing "Express purpose of visit" under the last bit and spent several uncomfortable hours explaining his sense of humour to

several burly gentlemen to whom mirth and irony were not a familiar concepts. But the notion that a genocidal drug trafficker is going to find himself thwarted in his ungodly aims by the intervention of this form is beguiling.

"Curses, here I am a 72 year old ex-Nazi and I was so near to triggering my thermo- nuclear device full of controlled substances under ze United Nations, but zey gave me zis green form. Being an honest and principled terrorist, I ticked the Yes box and zey sent me back to South America." If ever they encounter a terrorist or drug trafficker who is also an inveterate liar - there goes the neighbourhood!

25th June 2004

I was due to fly to Prague next week for a costume fitting for a French film to which I will be contributing a small role at the end of August. The film company is currently based in the Czech Republic – a country for which I have an inordinate fondness since they summarily despatched our old footballing foes, the Germans, from the European Cup. Apparently, it makes more sense for them to fly me across Europe for the day than to find any other method of kitting me out for the part of an English aristocrat in the latest cinematic version of Les Trois Mousquetaires. No complaints there; Prague is a beautiful city. The production company asked for details of my passport and, like probably hundreds of other would-be travellers a month, I discovered that the wretched thing ran out last week. A year or so had passed since I had last used it and it is tricky to remember to renew something that lasts ten years, unless you have a ten-year diary. I don't.

I suppose it is too much to ask the authorities to remind every passport holder when their passport is about to expire, although by adding a pound or two to the cost of each new passport, such a measure could easily be funded. But it is not too much to expect them to offer a means of effecting a renewal within the six days that existed between the time of my unwelcome discovery and the scheduled departure. Being a silver-ish surfer, I logged on to the Passport Office web site and discovered that there were three different processes on offer for renewal under the category of 'Urgent applications': travelling in over two weeks, travelling within

two weeks and, yes, travelling within 48 hours. That's the one for me, I thought. So I telephoned the Helpline number specified on the website. A very pleasant lady told me that the option I wanted – the 48 hour one - was no longer available. In fact she didn't know they were still showing that one on the website – it shouldn't be there! We do a four hour one now. Phew! Cancel anxiety attack; all systems back on line. I would have to make an appointment to go into one of the half dozen passport offices around the country, give them the completed form, photos etc – and four hours later – new passport in my pocket – Prague here I come! Would I like to make an appointment now? Yes, please! It was Wednesday. No appointments at the London office today, I'm afraid. That's all right – tomorrow will be fine. Ah – none tomorrow either eh? Or Friday? In fact you don't have any appointments before next Wednesday – the day after I am supposed to fly. Could you check Peterborough office then? None before next Wednesday there either. Or in Newport or Liverpool or Durham. So let me get this clear. You used to have a guaranteed 48 hour service which you replaced with a new improved 4 hour service, the catch being that the 4 hours doesn't start until a week from now? No-one can just give me a swift temporary two week extension somewhere if I come laden with birth certificates, back copies of the Bucks Free Press and a bevy of solicitors and clergymen who know me? No!? Great! And there was I thinking we were all one big happy European family!

30th June 2007

If Ken Livingstone's intention is to stop people wanting to go to London, he has succeeded in my case. I have been working in Richmond in the evenings this week and have also been obliged to travel up respectively to Westbourne Park, Putney and Soho on three days to do other work in assorted studios. I am not complaining, I insist, before saying that work for actors is like the proverbial buses, there is none for what seems an interminable time and then everyone wants you at once. Ken's extension of the Congestion zone further west has resulted in an exponential rise in the volume of traffic attempting to avoid entering the payment zone resulting in a mind numbing one and a half hour journey from Chiswick to Putney – some four miles – for no reason that I could discern other than sheer

volume of traffic. A journey from the BBC to Richmond – six miles – took an hour and a half. Were there a viable public transport alternative that would enable me to get home in less time, for less money and at the times I needed to get there, then I would have seized that with both white knuckled hands.

What is going to happen when millions of sports loving tourists descend upon the capital in 2012, unless the transport infrastructure is radically overhauled and improved, heaven only knows. Then I had the joy of visiting Westbourne Grove to record a *Doctor Who* audio adventure – yes I still get to use the Tardis from time to time – not in vision mercifully – as the infamous multicoloured coat would probably be unable to take the strain. A joy that was intensified when I returned to my car to find it clamped. I had bought a parking ticket for five pounds that covered the period for which I was parking but my mistake was clearly popping a spotted dog dashboard magnetic toy on top of it to hold it down. In any event the attendant, doubtless ticketing me in the torrential rain, failed to spot it. One hundred and fifteen pounds and ninety minutes after discovering my first ever yellow boot, I was released and made it to the theatre for my evening show by the skin of my teeth.

24th August 2001

I had always thought that the premise of the film *Home Alone* was a little far fetched, the notion that a family might accidentally go on holiday leaving their son behind. Recent information about the sudden rush of blood that hits many of us when we make our annual pilgrimage in search of sun, fun and bankruptcy, has made me revise my opinion.

Holidaymakers do apparently forget family members when they go on holiday, according to research carried out by an online travel service. Three quarters of travellers surveyed admitted there is so much to do before a holiday that they often overlook major things. The researchers also discovered that as the summer holiday exodus gets under way, £425m is wasted on household expenses and replacement goods due to simple forgetfulness. That is more than £28 for every one of the 14,942,000 Britons who take a foreign holiday each year. The research also revealed that 12% of people have turned up at the wrong airport or on the wrong date, 5% of travellers

have forgotten their passport, tickets or luggage and 2% have arrived at their destination without having booked accommodation.

One traveller in 100 has actually forgotten to pick up a member of their own family before heading to the airport, the study found. That's an awful of 'Home Alones'.

The millions spent unnecessarily arise from a variety of reasons. 40% of the adults questioned across the country are forced to buy replacement toiletries, sunglasses and swimming costumes because they have left them behind. Food goes off in one in five fridges around the country, dead plants can be found in 22% of households on return from holiday and one in 10 have milk and newspapers on the doorstep and discover that their radiators have been pumping out heat for the duration of their absence, perhaps in a subconscious desire to duplicate the excessive temperatures they have been enduring whilst away. I can confirm too that the organisation of an overseas holiday in particular can be sufficiently stressful to create the need for a further holiday in order to recover from the first one.

A generous friend having offered us her house on Majorca was too good an opportunity to miss for a self employed, vagabond actor, whose year thus far has been somewhat unproductive.

Aeroplane seats from Stansted, costing less per person than my last trip up to Edinburgh, made the dream even more possible. But there are all those other things to think about aren't there? Car hire, driving licenses, car insurance, holiday insurance, medical insurance, foreign currency, house, dog and cat sitters and the reams of detailed instructions to them about the idiosyncrasies of our house and its contents including the treacherous loo seat that we know and love but that is a trap for the unwary.

Then there are passports, suitcases, travel to airports, remembering the half a kilo of bits of paper that someone with a uniform and a grudge against stressed pale-skinned people in shorts might ask us to produce at some point. And all the while the children are agog because I am not up there on the ceiling with them singing the Cliff Richard countdown song from Summer Holiday "X days to our Holiday!" I'd like to think that I won't be one of those statistical amnesiacs or terminally disorganised travellers revealed by the research. But all bets are off.

10. Issues of the 90s

My natural position in relation to party politics can best be summed up as 'a plague on all their houses' or 'none of the above'. Whoever holds the temporary reins of power contrives to do some things well and others not so well or abominably. And whoever is not in power takes the word 'opposition' literally and opposes everything more or less automatically. I am generalising I know, but you must admit that the tendency towards the default position is pretty compelling in politics.

However, there are some issues and events that transcend the need-to-be-elected imperative of the political parties and get all of us involved in the political (with a small 'p') process. Issues like racism, the gun culture, fox hunting, ID cards and GM crops provoked heated debate throughout the 90's and I felt that as a columnist it would pusillanimous of me, if I didn't allow myself occasionally to risk provoking some readers to bombard the letters column the following week with outraged reactions to my opinions.

But it is sometimes too tempting to try to dodge controversial issues in order to keep all the readers happy.

23rd March 1996

I am sure that every person reading this article has, like me, been devastated and appalled by the events in Dunblane last week. I cannot recall, amongst the many atrocities we can all call far too easily to mind over the last few decades in the British Isles, anything to match the horror, the inhumanity and the evil bloody pointlessness of that slaughter of those most innocent, open and vulnerable infants and their teacher. I have not spoken to a parent of a child of that age who has not felt that horror even more poignantly every time they look at their own child and imagine even a thousandth of what those parents and families must be enduring now.

If we could somehow ease their pain by sharing it, we would all do so willingly. But whatever we say and do, they are going to wake up every morning for years and re-live that dreadful realisation that it did actually happen to their child. The pain may never diminish. At best the resilience of the human spirit may enable them to learn to live with the loss of their precious little ones, who were in fact scarcely more than babies. Whenever these tragedies occur there is an

understandable desperate attempt to see some glimmer of hope amid the wanton destruction. Indeed it was salutary and encouraging to see our political leaders as the human beings they undoubtedly are. I found myself wishing that it didn't always take something as unthinkable as what happened in that Primary School to re-focus our society on the very real benefits of a dogma free cooperation based on the certainty that we all breathe the same air and, deep down, want the same things.

When I was a young man, I was, for a brief time, a member of a gun club. I shot at targets and thought little about the real purpose of the creation of the rifle that I held in my hands. In later years I owned a shotgun and enjoyed the challenge and competition of clay pigeon shooting. At no time did I feel that any of the people with whom I was associating were predisposed to an obsessive and unstable attachment to the weapons they were using. Both these activities seemed acceptable hobbies.

In the last week it has been suggested that guns used for sport or competition should not be allowed to be taken or kept at home, but be kept only in secure storage at the clubs. I have heard Gun Club officials countering this with the argument that this agglomeration of weaponry would provide a very tempting target for criminals and terrorist organisations. I say that if those clubs cannot provide the same kind of security as that provided, say, by the army, then they simply should not exist. If people wish to own and fire guns for sport then they must bear the cost of rendering them incapable of use outside the sporting environment.

With the exception perhaps of shotguns, which it can be argued are legitimately used by farmers to protect their stock and control predators, no other weapons of any kind should be allowed to be owned by individual citizens - and certainly not any handgun or weapon capable of being rapidly fired. And it is not like suggesting the banning of knives.

We need knives in everyday life to prepare food and for countless other legitimate purposes at home and in the workplace. Guns however are designed for and can do only one thing. They dispatch a chunk or several chunks of metal at high velocity in order to violently disrupt the material they strike, whether it be a target or another human being. We must sacrifice the right of the citizen to go

about his currently legal business of enjoying the hobby of sporting shooting in order to prevent the depraved, the evil and the inadequate from acquiring the kind of skills and weaponry that was able last week to destroy so many lives. No recreational activity that is capable of such abuse is worth keeping in the face of the actuality of what happened in Dunblane. There are freedoms which a civilised and democratic society must voluntarily surrender in order to prevent the innocent and the defenceless once again, as always, paying the price for other people's selfishness and our inertia.

30th August 1996

The question of whether we should or should not be asked to carry identity cards has hit the headlines again. It is unfortunate that its current proponent is a man whose smile has all the warmth of an iguana waiting until the juicy fly is just a few inches closer to the full extension of his tongue. It is almost as if he has entered into some sort of competition with Michael Portillo, he of the manic rictus, to see which of them can in the words of Hamlet

"Smile and smile and be a villain." I've got my money on Portillo! It is, of course, not Mr Howard's fault that his face irritates me most when he is being oh so patient with an irritating journalist, who is persisting in asking the wrong question (i.e. one that does not neatly cue the answer he wishes to give and indeed is going to give).

And in case I am accused of political bias here, let me say that Robin Cook from the Labour party front bench provokes a very similar reaction, but without the smile. But leaving aside Mr Howard's saintly contempt and his infuriating inability to perform a glottal stop properly, hence his pronunciation of 'people' as 'peepell', - leaving, as I say, these minor and petty observations behind, do we really want a national identity card? Well, yes, I suppose we do, unfortunately.

I have never been convinced by the well meaning occupants of the fabled land of clouds and cuckoos who fulminate about the erosion of our civil liberties. The only liberties eroded, it seems to me, are the liberties of the criminally intent, who are precisely the ones we need to deprive of their liberty for varying lengths of time.

Yes it would undoubtedly be a drag to have to produce a document on the whim of a uniformed representative of Her Majesties

Government. But we already submit to that minor indignity every time we travel abroad or have to produce our licences and insurance within seven days of being stopped in our cars. And, although I have never yet forgotten to take my passport with me to the airport when travelling overseas, my main and only concern would be that I might forget or lose the darn thing.

However, the current initiative of the Home Secretary seems to be that he wishes us to voluntarily pay twenty or twenty-five pounds for a combined ID card and Driving Licence. This would have to be renewed at a similar cost every time the holder changes address (which could prove prohibitively expensive for families with several children who have to move around a lot). The sad aspect of the whole manoeuvre is of course that the 'peepell' who would be most inconvenienced by the requirement to carry an I.D. card are precisely the same ones who will most certainly not be spending the twenty or so pounds to get one, and if the cards ever become mandatory will spend considerably more than that to get a fake one. And despite any security precautions in the manufacture of the cards there will undoubtedly be bogus versions available before you can say,

"You are not obliged to say anything but..." Therefore aside from the well heeled and the curious, I don't suppose there will be a great rush to be the first to pay for the privilege of being a card carrying, fully paid up member of the United Kingdom.

And thereby hangs another controversy. Do we have the Union Flag on the card? Well I would like to float the idea that we use the opportunity not to appease those, of a republican or other disposition, who wish to detach themselves from the rest of us, but rather to allow those who are unashamed inhabitants of their corner of these islands to indicate so publicly. Why can't those of us who are proud to hail from England, Scotland, Wales or Ireland have respectively a crowned Tudor Rose, Thistle, Dragon or Harp on our cards?

This would simultaneously avoid the potential use of the card as yet another missile in the Northern Irish internecine impasse and allow all of us to be what we know we are - Irish, Welsh, Scottish or English.

20th June 1997

There are many reasons why Prince Charles should be allowed, and indeed encouraged, to pluck Mrs. Parker-Bowles from the uncomfortable notoriety of the shadows and, if that is what both parties wish, spend their lives together. Whatever an ungenerous press has consistently thrown at Camilla Parker-Bowles, it cannot be denied that she has maintained an impressive and dignified silence others might usefully emulate.

History has repeatedly demonstrated that the beneficial effect of rulers is in inverse proportion to their domestic happiness. Henry the Eighth and Edward the Eighth are cases in point. The prospect of a Charles the Second feeling constrained by his traditional, but now surely nominal, role as head of the Church to conduct an intimate relationship via mobile phone and risk nocturnal collisions in country lanes is not a beguiling one.

I have never understood why it is considered more acceptable for the heir to the throne to conduct first an adulterous and then a possibly extra-marital relationship than it is to divorce and re-marry. It is suggested that the public will not accept Queen Camilla. That is arguable, but there is absolutely no reason why the future King's consort should not be as high or low profile as the country will tolerate. Indeed, one has every reason to suspect that the lady herself has no personal ambition other than to be with Charles. And there really is no accounting for taste, thank goodness; otherwise I myself wouldn't have won the heart of the finest lady in Christendom.

It cannot be beyond the wit of the country's constitutional power brokers to construct a situation whereby country, state, church and public opinion can be satisfied with an arrangement that enables those two people to live together openly, if that is what they wish. One is led to believe that the marriage of Charles and Diana would not have happened, had Charles not been conditioned to believe that his choice of a life partner was severely restricted. Then the glossy magazines would never have found poor Diana and played their part in removing her forever from a world where she might have reached her thirties via a less stressful route.

Similarly poor Charles, when asked if he was in love with his teenage intended might not have felt the need to express a public (and tragically prophetic) uncertainty as to what love was. Diana was

the something borrowed and he was the something blue. And blue he remains, although she has, in a sense, been given back, albeit transmogrified into something quite other.

Of the Queen's four children, three have married and divorced. The fourth is very sensibly biding his time. The only one of the three divorcees who displays every sign of being a fulfilled, balanced and useful member of the family is Princess Anne, who is happily remarried and commands universal respect because of her manifest common sense and good humour. Only a curmudgeon or the constitutionally constipated could now deny Charles his human right to seek their personal fulfilment and happiness within the law of the land, which should apply equally to all, without fear or favour.

A desirable side effect of a more personally fulfilled Charles would be that he may have better things to do than to pronounce on the teaching profession in the way that he did last week. His expensive education at Cheam Preparatory School and Gordonstoun (at which he was reportedly very unhappy), was delivered by what might be designated the very 'old fashioned teaching methods' that he espouses. They left him with a modest 5 O levels and 2 A levels. His personal contact with the State Education system is minimal and restricted to the odd inauguration of a new building, where he sees a temporarily cleaned up version of the one that the rest of us have to use. The advent of Royalty of course demands an expensive face lift at the expense of the local tax payer and the installation of sanitary and Windsor friendly loos.

Neither Charles' qualifications, nor his experience entitle him to attribute to the teaching profession blame for the alleged deficiencies of a generation, the pieces of which he claims to be picking up through the undoubtedly excellent offices of The Princes' Trust. In a war it is the foot-soldiers that take the bullets: the teachers are taking the flak that should be aimed much further up the chain of command. No wonder 40% of Secondary teachers want out.

7th November 1997

Thirty years ago, I had the misfortune to drive through a Police radar trap in Blackburn at 42mph in a 30 mph limit. It had been set up a few yards past a 30 mph sign after a long stretch of derestricted road; and at a time when derestricted meant you could go as fast you

liked. When I saw the sign I slowed down but not quickly enough to escape the net of the Lancashire Constabulary. I was studying law at that time; and with the frightening confidence of youth and a measure of righteous indignation, I decided to represent myself at the hearing. The case immediately before mine concerned two young men who had systematically stripped the lead off their village church roof and then sold it. They were truculent and rather less than grovellingly repentant. Having listened to the catalogue of their felonies and misdemeanours unfold, the magistrates bound them over to keep the peace. No fine, no suspended sentence, no probation, just,

"Off you go lads, and don't be naughty again!" I was surprised, but optimistic that my tale of woe would receive a sympathetic hearing. I spoke movingly of my respect for the law. I said that I had slowed down as soon as I saw the 30 mph sign, which was partially obscured by the same trees that concealed the police officer and his radar gun; and that had the trap been a mere dozen or so yards past the sign, I would undoubtedly have been driving legally.

Giving me a fixed and baleful stare, the chairman of the magistrates proclaimed in a very strong Blackburn accent,

"I am fed up with young hooligans driving round 't countryside endangering life and limb. You will be fined £40 and your licence will be endorsed." Forty pounds represented twenty weeks of my salary as an articled clerk. I have no desire to trivialise what is happening in Massachusetts, in telling my little story to illustrate that justice is a very elusive notion. Inevitably, every case is passed through the subjective filters of other people's prejudices and doubts and their fears of the prejudices and doubts of a watching and critical world.

It is a combination of these ingredients that has resulted in the palpable injustice of the verdict in the case of Louise Woodward. No-one has ever suggested that this girl wilfully and with malice aforethought set out to murder Matthew Eapen.

Yet many ingredients - the television circus, an adversarial legal system whose central players are all too aware of the intense media interest, a phalanx of medical and forensic experts who are all equally certain of the correctness of only their own interpretation of the evidence, the extraordinary convergence of what seems to be the only twelve people in the world prepared to convict for murder in this

case - all these factors seem to have unhappily combined to result in the possible incarceration, for upwards of fifteen years, of a teenage nanny, little more than a child herself. We are the nation whose legal system took a decade or more to right the injustices meted out on the Guildford Four and the Birmingham Six.

We are also the nation that still hasn't acknowledged other injustices of the past like the grotesque execution of Derek Bentley, as an accessory to a murder committed by his accomplice, who was too young to hang. But the fact that our legal system is similarly imperfect should not prevent us from campaigning on behalf of Louise, who is caught up in a system more about winning and losing than discovering the truth - and against whom there is, by any standard, only the most flimsy and circumstantial evidence of guilt. I hope the American Courts don't take as long as we have in the past to rectify the injustice.

13th March 1998

Any regular reader of this column will know that I am not a fan of fox hunting. I will not however provoke the time honoured tirade of personal invective from the usual suspects by setting out yet again my reasons for being embarrassed to belong to a species that purports to have moral values, that can build great churches to the glory of God, that can write poetry, compose music and create great Art and at the same time make a sport out of the mass pursuit and inelegant destruction of one small mammal.

Too late, I think. I've already said enough to waken the red in coat, tooth and claw. Parliament is demonstrably still capable of being hijacked by powerful interest groups. It was clear that in common with the majority of the electorate, most MPs would have voted for an end to hunting with hounds. Yet the will of the majority was bulldozed aside by the use of bully boy tactics in the Commons. Did we really elect these baying, whooping overgrown schoolboys so that they could thwart legislation only by means of the captious amendment and the filibuster? What price democracy?

Given my antipathy to hunting, I am sorry that the Countryside March was so strongly associated with the pro-hunting lobby. As a result the March attracted practically every single person in the country who wanted to retain the right to participate in what are

euphemistically called country sports. About a hundred and twenty thousand of them, according to the Independent, - despite claims of double that numbers. The marchers included many other citizens, who may or may not have had strong opinions about hunting, but who do care about the inexorable destruction of our farming base, about the disenfranchisement and disillusion of rural communities, about virtually non-existent rural transport which necessitates dependency on the increasingly punitively taxed private car, about the vanishing village schools and post offices and the insidious threat of the encroaching urban sprawl.

There are also a vast number of people who feel strongly, as I do, that the countryside is getting a raw deal but who stayed away from the March because they felt unable to be seen to support hunting. I suppose one should recognise the campaigning skills of the pro-hunting lobby for their hi-jacking of these other more fundamental and worthwhile rural issues to support their unspeakable pursuit of the uneatable.

It is perhaps an indication that they see all too clearly that, despite that nice Mr Blair's onset of political timidity at the sight of the red-faced shires, the days of hunting are nearly over. At the heart of the whole question of rural England is the apparent willingness of successive Governments to allow the farmers to go under. I had at one time been inclined to share.

The opinion of some that it was hardly equitable to support farming with massive subsidies in the face of cheap imports from abroad, when other industries like coal and steel have been decimated without similar financial aid being offered. This argument appears to have some merit until one reflects how vulnerable we would be in the event that any of the four apocalyptic horsemen should visit our little islands.

During the last war we were able to survive blockade and isolation in the face of a Nazi dominated Europe, as a result of being able to feed ourselves from our own land. I know it is no longer fashionable to think of small national concerns in the face of increasing globalisation, but we only need to cast the briefest of glances at the former Yugoslavia, to realise that we have not reached anything resembling a mutually co-operative Europe yet or indeed to ponder

the future effects of El Nino or global warming. We sacrifice our traditional agricultural base at our peril.

21st August 1999

It seems that now the Duke of Edinburgh has lined his sights up on his own foot, he is determined to let himself have it with both barrels. Perhaps it could become the first ever royalty-only blood sport. Blue in hounds-tooth and claw? I have been puzzling over his completely baffling remarks about an Indian being responsible for a piece of shoddy workmanship. Had there ever been an expression in popular use, (along the lines of 'Jerry built'), which, however inaccurately, connected poor craftsmanship with Indians, then I suppose the Duke would be guilty of only bad taste and racism, by casually repeating and lending royal authority to an existing stereotype.

However that has never been the case. To the contrary, the Indian and Pakistani stereotype is quite different. They are universally acknowledged to be collectively diligent and hardworking, frequently putting in hours which the white work community might envy. Their reputation for industry in building up and maintaining businesses is probably second to none. So Philip's casual remark, presumably intended by him, (however ludicrously), to be seen as amusing, was not only in execrable taste and racist, but also evidence of his arrogance and complete detachment from the world in which the rest of us live - in short, his stupidity.

Fortunately, his previous serial gaffes, which have caused offence to the Chinese, the deaf, black women – the list is seemingly endless – have alerted us to his boorishness and to the fact that his privileged life has not brought with it the humility and common touch that might make the anachronism of a hereditary ruling family acceptable at the dawn of a new millennium. Nor has he the sense to pretend to have those qualities. In 1985, I appeared in the Royal Variety Show. Robert Hardy, Derek Waring, Ronald Allen, Simon Williams and I, complete with top hats and canes, performed a Jack Buchanan number - *I guess I'll have to change my plan.*

In the line up after the show, we were presented to the Royal Family. The Duke stopped before us and noted that we were the chaps who did the Jack Buchanan number. He asked me if we had had much rehearsal for it. I replied that we had all had a few sessions

with the choreographer but had only all rehearsed together that very morning. HRH seized his opportunity with relish,

"Yeah, bloody looked like it too!" he laughed. We all dutifully joined in. But I suspect had we jocularly put him down, the temperature might have dropped considerably. The politeness of others and their desire not to rock the boat, cushion him from any real understanding that his treatment of others might just be unacceptable. But perhaps the Emperor might, even at this late stage in his career, benefit from being made aware of his excessive inadequacy in the clothing department. The crassness of his remark in that electronics factory gives another weapon to those who favour republicanism. And despite my reluctance to espouse the dry, civic functionalism of a politically appointed president, at the cost of generations of tradition, it is getting harder to defend resistance of the notion. I did wonder whether he had confused cowboys with Indians. Clearly he wouldn't wish to offend anyone who rides horses, fences off land and shoots things, so he wouldn't be able to comprehend the implications of a cowboy builder.

But an Indian electrician might be considered fair game. He would have no reservations about brave-ing their wrath. Perhaps they'll Sioux.

8th October 1999

The politicians have excelled themselves during the last week. The Really Bad Idea count has increased dramatically on both sides of whatever shifting dividing line still exists between the two major parties. That said, the Mekon is trying his darnedest to drag the one-nation Tory old guard off to the right, encouraged doubtless by the worrying success enjoyed by the Schicklegruber fan club in Austria this week. (Post baby boomers ask a friendly old fogey who the Mekon is – and indeed Adolf!) And as that plain-speakin' Yorkshire lad gets progressively greener, with envy no doubt of all those politicians who do have a chance of being Prime Minister one day – his resemblance to Dan Dare's enemy from Venus gets closer.

The bad idea from Blackpool is the proposal that parents dissatisfied with a headteacher could force the 'SATSfinder Generals' at OFSTED to visit a school and, if they agreed with the parents'

assessment of the situation, order the Local Authority to replace the head and put in a new board of Governors.

We will leave aside for a moment the fact that only on another planet (perhaps William's planet of origin - Venus?) are there stacks of willing volunteers to be school governors, all ready to dedicate hours of their time to the unpaid business of overseeing the running of the sophisticated, regulation stifled businesses that schools have necessarily become over the last decade. I suppose for a politician to be able to wring hands like Pontius Pilate and pass the buck to us is a very attractive notion. They take no responsibility themselves but still get the credit for appearing to empower parents. It begs the question that the Inspector of Schools, so beloved by both Governments, should have his expert finger on the pulse of education without the need to wait for concerned parents to ring alarm bells. It is political posturing which is no substitute for good management and proper funding.

The bad idea from that nice Mr. Blair's lot is one that touches uncomfortably on my area of employment. Culture Secretary, Chris Smith, has decreed that every film made in the UK will have to contribute 0.5% of its budget into a fund to provide training for new technicians and production staff. Why pick on the film industry, which is already struggling financially? If young film-makers are worth training, why shouldn't the costs of that training be funded in the same way as other professions? And given that only a small percentage of films do more than cover the costs incurred in the making of that film, if New 'Clean right round the U-bend' Labour are determined that the film industry should be singled out for such a levy, why not take it from the profits of successful films? I feel strongly about this because I know that the squeeze on the budget of a film will be felt at the sharp end. The actors who try to earn a living in a profession where more than 85% are out of work at any one time will be invited to work for yet smaller fees – 'take it or leave it'. This very week I turned down a nice part in a very low budget film, made by an award winning team of film makers, because over six weeks I would earn less than I earned twenty years ago for a week! It's bad enough already without your bright ideas, Chris. One dictionary definition of 'culture' is the 'production of bacteria'!

4th September 1999

The Government has stated that it is committed to the thorough testing of Genetically Modified crops before they will give approval for full scale commercial growing in the UK. To give them the benefit of the doubt, it might be because they, like the rest of us, are unclear as to the long-term effects of tinkering with the building blocks of nature. And if that truly is the reason, then how can they possibly justify conducting those trials in an open and uncontrolled environment?

If we have learnt anything about nature over the last few hundred years, we should have learnt that once unleashed, it will not be contained by us. If a virus, spore or bacterium exists anywhere on the planet, then within a very short time it will exist everywhere that has an environment favourable to it. GM crops, whose characteristics and potential are as yet not fully understood, are being grown and cultivated, not in a controlled laboratory environment, but in farmers' fields from which material and seeds can be carried by birds, animals and the winds to the four corners of the earth.

This does not seem a very sensible idea. Some very chilling films have been made about the unwanted consequences of the innovative zeal of rogue scientists whose quest for knowledge of and power over nature have clouded their vision. Yes, alright, that is the stuff of fiction.

But think of all the things that we are now discovering about foods and products that we have thitherto considered to be safe. High factor sun creams are now pronounced not a good thing. They filter out the rays that cause sunburn, thereby allowing the wearer to believe they can stay in the sun longer. We have now learnt however that the carcinogenic elements of those rays are not filtered out. We have known for years that those E numbers, added to our food to make them look more appetising in order to increase sales, are bad for us.

Tikka masalas and baltis simply wouldn't appeal, apparently, unless their colour was enhanced by the addition of tartrazine, sunset yellow and ponceau 4R. These additives have the potential to provoke allergic reactions, boils, migraine and asthma. A bacterium called MAP carried by cattle and linked to Crohn's disease, could be contaminating our drinking water, it was revealed back in April. Our

consumption of salt, considered safe for years, is beginning to cause concern. Artificial light sources are now considered to be a causative factor in breast cancer, a fact that was indicated by the significantly lower incidence of that cancer in blind women.

The 24 hour society where electric lighting extends our days has resulted in the inhibition of the production of melanin, which is believed to regulate the production of oestrogen. The list of things formerly considered acceptable, or even desirable, which have subsequently proved to be otherwise, is lengthy.

For years we were encouraged to sleep babies on their tummies. Cot Death figures have more than halved since that practice has been reversed after the *Back to Sleep* campaign, as a result of years of research.

But we have never had the power before to get down amongst the tiniest ingredients of life itself. Now we do, we should be telling the Governments and the Monsantos that we demand that they exercise a lot more caution. We are not just biological Luddites, if we insist that genetic modification of food is too new a science to be casually dumped in the fields of England. And it is greed not idealism that has put it there.

20th November 1999

When anyone starts a sentence with, "Now don't get me wrong, I am not a racist but...," there is usually one thing that you can safely bet on. They are about to say something racist.

However, they genuinely believe that their particular brand of outrageous prejudice is based on some universal truth which they, being superior to the object of their lofty disdain, are entitled to broadcast. It is, therefore, with no pride that I admit to harbouring an antipathy to the French nation that has been confirmed by recent events. It is the French en masse I mean, because, I confess, I have never met a French individual to whom I could honestly have ever taken the slightest personal exception. But, despite the fact that after hundreds of years of enmity, the French have been our allies in both world wars this century, our national psyche does seem imprinted with the kind of instinctive dislike that characterises cats and dogs, (until they're forced to live together and discover that each other isn't quite as irredeemably vile as they had thitherto supposed).

And it seems that the European Union is not sufficiently powerful a unifying glue to provide that effect. The position taken up by the French Government, presumably with a careful eye on its own powerful agricultural lobby, is quite simply disgraceful. However when Britain is roused, it has historically proved resolute and implacable. I will be surprised if the majority of the British public feel inclined to purchase anything French until their blatantly illegal ban on the import of British beef has been long lifted and forgotten. It is the sheer hypocrisy of their attitude that appals, particularly in the context of the recent discovery that French livestock are routinely fed on human excrement.

The French attitude to the European community is cynical and self-serving and is summed up by a story told to me this week by a friend who lives just outside High Wycombe in a village that has for years had a small garage with a single petrol pump. But the family who own the garage have been forced to give up selling petrol because their pump was too close to the road and failed in that and several other ways to satisfy EEC regulations. To comply with those regulations would have cost more money than they could afford or justify. My friend also spends time living in a village in France, where there is another small, family run garage, whose petrol pump is actually on the kerb of the road. The owners sell fruit and vegetables in baskets around the pump and the owner serves petrol puffing vigorously on a cigarette dangling out of the corner of his mouth.

You see, the French don't take the EEC bit quite as seriously as we British do. We are by nature law abiding. We queue. The French nation is to a man those people who are unembarrassed to go up the outside lane of the motorway, when the two inside lanes are queuing politely to go through road-works. I prefer the polite way, but then I would wouldn't I? I'm British. So I am very hopeful that we will politely register our protest by declining in our thousands to knowingly purchase anything French. Wine lovers need not panic. Spanish and New World wines are much better value for money anyway. And our own struggling farmers may just benefit in the future if we consumers use the power, that we undoubtedly have, to demand that Britain moves towards becoming more agriculturally self sufficient.

11. Words, Words, Words

My British-ness also manifests itself in the fact that while I have always been fascinated by all languages in general, I am particularly fascinated by our own wonderfully rich language. I have yet to be persuaded that there has ever been a language so complex, so subtle, so abundant in its vocabulary or so varied in its construction. In those halcyon days when grammar was taught as a part of a separate subject 'English Language' in our secondary schools, I loved discovering how our language worked and as a result found the learning of other languages considerably less arduous.

I am delighted to hear that after years of neglect in the National Curriculum English Language is making its way back onto the curriculum. The words 'preposition', 'conjunction' and 'participle' will no longer be meaningless gobbledegook to the upcoming generation.

During my spell as Doctor Who in the 1980's I was allowed occasionally to slip in words into my dialogue that demonstrated my Doctor's corresponding love of language. I called a character in Timelash *a 'microcephalic apostate' when we agreed that the existing insult in the script was too prosaic and simply not 'Doctor'- ish enough.*

That said, I fully support the various campaigns for plain English. The legal documents of my youth were incomprehensible to the very people who were signing them, even though the lawyers who drafted them, it is to be hoped, understood the gist and import of them.

But at the same time English must always be a living language and be allowed to assimilate the new way of speaking of each generation. But it would be tragic, in my opinion, if in our quest for simplicity, we were to lose forever the ability to enjoy the complexity and joy of the writing of Jane Austen or Dickens.

Once we have a generation who can appreciate the complexities of grammar again, rather than shy away from them, our written language might once again produce sentences with series of interlinked clauses, adjectival phrases and dare to tiptoe into a subjunctive mood. Oh I do go on don't I? As you will see if you read on....

17th March 2000

English is arguably the richest language in the world, having been shaped by fifteen hundred or more years of assimilating the tongues of a succession of conquerors, invaders and immigrants and then by

the importation of thousands of words from the vast empire that these small islands improbably dominated for a couple of centuries.

Clearly, it would be absurd to freeze a language at any point of time and say this is how it should and must be used. Latin has suffered that indignity only because it has been a dead language for so long that we can only conjecture how it might have sounded. So I am by no means suggesting that English should be preserved in aspic. It is alive and must be allowed to grow.

But that inevitable development should not, I believe, stem from laziness, neglect or ignorance. So, the abduction of the word 'wicked' by a generation that chooses to give it a meaning entirely other than that which it had before, is a natural process, however much it may confuse the old guard.

The loss of that charming word 'gay' to describe a light hearted, carefree mood, whilst undoubtedly sad, is nonetheless an indication of a changing world. Not only has 'light hearted carefree' – ness itself become a thing of the past, but the change of use of that word helped to nudge a whole section of the community into an acceptability it had not enjoyed before. But there are certain tendencies that I would suggest are unacceptable; and I would urge you all to fight to the last cliché to prevent their becoming acceptable.

The sloppy use of 'should of' instead of 'should have' occurs more and more frequently and, if not strangled at birth, will poison our language, which is already in danger of dwindling into tabloid speak - a style of writing which owes more to pidgin than a real language. Many today might regard the works of Dickens as being reader unfriendly and over-complicated in terms of sentence structure.

The fact is, however, that he wrote for a readership of ordinary people, who avidly awaited each new instalment of his stories. Now any eagerness is for the next episode of an Australian soap, where sheilas are beaut but might just chuck a mental and men take a sicky at the drop of a cork festooned hat. There's language on the move for you. And on this side of the tower of Babylon, Mr Darcy would no longer be a man of probity and distinction, but 'a well sorted geezer'. A current bugbear is the perplexing misuse of the words 'amateur' and 'professional'. I fail to understand why the former should be regarded as derogatory and the latter complimentary. An amateur is someone who does something for the love of the activity;

a professional does it for a living. That is the only difference. In terms of acting, an amateur may work diligently and be utterly compelling in a role, but cannot, as a result, ever be described as professional.

A professional may fail to learn his lines, turn up drunk at the theatre, kick the stage doorman's dog and be sick over the audience; but to call him an amateur, as a result of these failings, would only serve as a gross slur on all those amateurs who perform for love alone. And as for the doctor on TV this week who commented on something or other,

"This is an abnormal deviation from the actual norm" – well words fail us both!

9th March 2007

I consider myself to be a literate and reasonably numerate person and rarely find myself in a position where I am incapable of, at least eventually, understanding the reams of paperwork and forms that are currently the inevitable result of living and owning a home in Britain, 2007. I even spent eight years as the chairman of a national charity, which meant I had to sign the annual accounts, which with a little help from our advisers I was usually able to do without fear of being asked to explain them.

However, this week I received from the Inland Revenue a communication that purported to explain my indebtedness to them (naturally) and I spent half an hour trying to make sense of it, before giving up and telephoning my accountant. In the same post, came my electricity statement from British Gas. (I have never quite adjusted to the fact that I live in an area where piped gas is not available, but my electricity comes from a gas supplier.) With the bill came a leaflet proudly explaining my 'new, easy-to-understand energy statement.' As soon as I read that I knew what was in store, in exactly the same way as when any organisation purports to have made changes to "improve service to their customers" you know that the real reason is almost invariably entirely the opposite.

Firstly, what I received bore little resemblance to the example in the glossy accompanying leaflet, which I had to use a magnifying glass to read; and secondly, what it did contain was less easily comprehensible than the previous statements. Doubtless, they paid some advisory

company vast sums of money to research, advise and design the wretched thing. They should ask for their money back. Maybe it was the same company whose fees resulted in the recent increases in postal charges when they came up with the brilliant notion of renaming the Royal Mail, 'Consignia' Or painting the tails of BA's fleet of planes with ethnic designs. Or the BBC re-branding themselves by scrapping the familiar, calm and easily identified BBC globe in favour of a variety of frenetic dancers whose noisy gyrations wore thin and irritated within a few short weeks.

If it works don't fix it is a maxim sadly ignored by upwardly mobile executives who, like tomcats on the prowl, feel they have to make a mark.

27th September 2002

I took my teenage daughter and her friend to Peterborough this week, to see the play in which I am currently performing. In conversation with another actor after the play, he chose to use some rather colourful language during the course of a story he was telling about some badly behaved 8 or 9-year-old boys.

In his defence, he was actually quoting what the young thugs had said to him, when he chastised them for stealing some chocolate from the lady stage doorkeeper at the venue we were performing at in Cheltenham last week. My colleague was then clearly taken aback when I said to him that it was probably the first time that anyone had used those particular words, conversationally, when I was in the presence of any of my children. He asked my daughter how old she was. On learning that she was 17, he turned to me, somewhat perplexed, and suggested that there should be no problem in that case in his having used swear words, given that they must have heard them on a daily basis from their contemporaries at school.

I know that the actor concerned has a daughter a few years older than mine, and therefore has been through the process of bringing up children himself. Interestingly, my daughter and her friend told me that they too were surprised and slightly shocked themselves that an adult had used swear words in front of them; and they were unsurprised that I had implicitly remonstrated with my fellow actor by bringing the matter up.

They told me I looked apoplectic, which I hope was a slight exaggeration and contributed to partially by the fact that I was still perspiring from the effort involved in rushing up and down stairs under theatrical lighting while engaged in a strenuous sword fight.

We all know that swearing exists. We all, sadly, hear it on a daily basis. Yet I doubt that the unfortunate perpetrator would have told that particular story had I been with, say, an elderly relative instead of my teenage daughter. What that says about attitudes to what is acceptable behaviour, I'm not sure, but I hope it doesn't mean that our language is going to descend even further into the habitual unnecessary use of adjectives that many find still unacceptable in everyday conversation.

My parents never swore in front of me, nor did I in front of them. My memory is poor about what I did at school now, but I recall experimenting with using the forbidden and shocking expletives with my friends, until as an adult I saw swear words for what they are – verbal aggression employed by the inarticulate to assert themselves over others. By chance, a good friend who is going through a tough time at the moment told me that she was mortified because, for the first time in her life, she had sworn at her mother on the telephone. Despite the fact that she realises that it was her current situation that provoked the lapse of her customary decorum, she felt that an ingrained parent/child taboo had been shattered and feels very uncomfortable about it.

Our language has such a wonderfully diverse vocabulary that it is a terrible waste to use words that offend many, when there are some perfectly good words that fit the bill better. But then,

"Depart forthwith, you miscreant!" would probably not achieve the same effect.

7th February 2003

Mobile phones and their users are easy targets for vilification. I share most people's irritation at the apparent conviction by some that their conversations are of interest to the rest of us. I refer to the "I'm on the train" syndrome, as uttered by (usually) men, many of whom could probably be heard by the other party without electronic assistance.

But the aspect that bothers me more is the steady erosion of our language, which is already suffering body blows from casual daily misuse in all forms of the media. I am not being a linguistic Luddite here. I acknowledge that language must evolve. I have no objection to the inclusion in dictionaries of words like 'minging', or the re-definition of words that originally meant one thing and have been commandeered by a new generation who have decided that, for instance, 'bad' should also be capable of meaning 'good'.

That's evidence of the fact that English, unlike Latin or Sanskrit, is alive and well and living in the street as well as the schoolroom. What the mobile phone is doing, via texting, is encouraging randomness in spelling, invited by the small screen and comparatively laborious process of inputting messages.

"R U in 2nite? I need to C U." is clearly easier to write one letter at a time, while rushing from one lesson to another than "Are you in tonight? I need to see you."

But I cannot bring myself to do it. If language is about communication, and the abbreviation communicates exactly the same meaning, why does it matter? All I can say is that I truly believe we will lose something rather special if we don't guard our language with the same zeal that speakers of Cornish are displaying in their attempts to restore their ancient language to more common use in Cornwall. In English, we have the most versatile, rich and widely used language in the world.

A brief trawl through Roget's Thesaurus is enough to convince even the most sceptical that the sheer volume of words that have evolved to convey the subtlest of shifts in meaning is matched perhaps only by the Eskimos' alleged legions of words for snow. When the written word was the only means of communication of ideas, we saw the greatest growth of the everyday use of vocabulary and subtlety of construction that Britain has ever seen.

A few pages of Jane Austen or Charles Dickens are all you need to read to acknowledge that. A shift to the spoken rather than written word as the predominant means of conveying ideas and drama has already had the effect of reducing the number of words in everyday use. It has also resulted in a casual attitude to grammar and the construction of sentences.

But the text message has a greater potential to erode our language, particularly as it is predominantly being used by the very generation that we should be trying to enthuse with a knowledge and love of the richness and diversity of language. When the most powerful man in the world has a tenuous grasp of his own language, the rest of us should all do what we can to preserve it. His latest utterance?

"The war on terror involves Saddam Hussein because of the nature of Saddam Hussein, the history of Saddam Hussein, and his willingness to terrorize himself." —George W. Bush, Grand Rapids, Mich., Jan. 29, 2003. C U in Baghdad?

23rd June 2006

Chris Moyles, a Radio One DJ, recently sparked a minor brouhaha in the media when he used the word 'gay' in the recently evolved sense of 'naff' or 'a bit rubbish' to describe a mobile phone ring tone. As a minor student of language and its evolution, I cannot be the only one to spot the irony of the homosexual community complaining that a word that they purloined to describe themselves has now evolved yet again to mean something else.

When I was young 'gay' simply meant 'light hearted' and since its shift in meaning there has been a gap in our vocabularies of a word to describe the particular mood that is subtly different from 'happy' or 'joyous.' It is undoubtedly true that a word was needed to replace 'queer', which, despite being originally coined by the gay community itself, needed a rethink when it started to be coined as a term of abuse. So even though nostalgia for a more innocent age of dance bands and picnics might lead us to wish otherwise, we cannot really complain when a word evolves. Nor can there be any complaints when it evolves yet again.

I imagine that Satan probably views with disfavour the metamorphosis of the words 'bad' and 'wicked' to mean the exact opposite of their original meanings; and trouser manufacturers are doubtless perplexed when their products are rejected because they're 'pants'.

However much we linguistic conservatives might wish it were otherwise, language will continue to evolve. The only plus point perhaps is that as soon as adults (and I believe Chris Moyles is one) start using words coined by the young, then they instantly fall out of

favour, something I learned to my cost when I described something as 'cool' to my daughter recently. I had not realised that it was possible to adopt a facial expression that could simultaneously register disgust, pity, incomprehension and weary embarrassment so vividly. What is unforgivable is the casual mangling of our language through ignorance and sloppy thinking. Twice recently, on Radio 5 admittedly, I have heard BBC reporters use the word 'grevious' to describe bodily harm, importing the same gratuitous letter 'i' that is often inserted into the word 'mischievous'. And the use of "should of" instead of "should have" is increasing at an alarming rate among presenters and reporters alike. One presenter suggested that a politician's argument was a 'mute' point. I wish more politicians made mute points.

6th February 2004

I studied Latin and Greek at school and have never regretted it. I did so because I enjoyed studying languages and they were the only ones available apart from French, which I also studied to 'A' level. And although there are now several other modern languages available for budding linguists to study at school, I am delighted to learn that Latin, in particular, is still holding its own, despite not being of immediately obvious everyday use to the student. Interestingly, once a student starts to learn a classical language they tend to stick with it, which is not as frequently the case with modern languages.

The reason, I would suggest, is perhaps that the themes that are dealt with are written in a much grander and dynamic scale. The French we learn at school tends to be very useful everyday stuff about going to the library with Jacques or playing 'le football' with Thierry. Whereas, given the source material available, most of the texts and vocabulary used to teach Latin and Greek concern the doings of kings, emperors and armies. There are poisonings, battles, treachery and abductions of fair (and not so fair) maidens and most of these activities are a direct result of a bunch of gods whose behaviour was far from exemplary.

A modern language scholar will learn how to go shopping, converse in urban society and navigate the transport system in the country of choice.

A classics scholar is inculcated in the finer points of war, murder, betrayal and political chicanery. Small wonder then that once the stories of Vergil, Tacitus and Homer have been experienced they exercise a stronger grip on the reader than tales of driving on the autobahn with Helmut. The other attractive characteristic of Latin is that once you've learned the rules then you're up and running, there are very few exceptions – and there's no one to give you grief about the finer points of pronunciation either.

There is yet another reason for encouraging the inclusion of Latin in the syllabus. For a couple of generations now the teaching of English grammar has been perfunctory at best, to the extent that a teenager of my acquaintance looked blank when I spoke recently of prepositions, participles and clauses.

However, the teaching of Latin demands a familiarity with the roles of words within the sentence and an understanding of the building blocks of language that I was taught when I was ten years old but which baffles postgraduate students today. And it seems self-evident to me that the more one knows about the workings of a thing, the easier it is to put it to efficient use, whether it be a car, a mobile phone or a language.

As far as modern languages are concerned, I wish that more were available in schools. Clearly the lack of suitably qualified teaching staff and the unpredictability of demand make it impossible at the moment to offer Chinese, Portuguese and Japanese in every school in the country, but a strategy that enabled schools to pool resources might over a decade or so produce a new generation of students able to communicate with nations whose citizens form a much larger proportion of the world's population than our immediate European neighbours.

When China really does open up to the rest of the world, those who can converse and communicate effectively with that vast market will literally have the world at their feet.

2nd April 2004

I have been trying to justify to myself my admittedly uncompromising attitude to the speaking and writing of the English language. I am sometimes made to feel unnecessarily pedantic when

I point out what seems to me to be a glaring error or use of a word in entirely the wrong sense in a written document.

More recently, particularly in primary education, the tendency has been to overlook inexact spelling and grammatical errors in order to encourage the child to communicate freely without being restrained by fear of potential criticism of the language used (or abused) in the expression of their ideas. But I believe that that attitude, (and I have seen signs that it is slowly beginning to change), has ultimately failed to do even that which it was intended to do - i.e. free children up to be thinking and creative.

My upbringing and education were conducted in an age when grammar, punctuation and vocabulary were highly valued. Indeed, in examinations, marks were deducted for inaccuracies in any of those areas.

Later, five years of legal training reinforced my previous education. In a legal document, a comma wrongly placed or a word whose meaning is imperfectly understood can lead to litigation in the future; and the lawyer who drafted the ambiguous or misleading document can find himself in trouble.

Just as in mathematics the ability to know that nine times nine is eighty-one, without resource to fingers and toes and bits of paper, so the easy and instinctive use of words and punctuation is an asset in later life, irrespective of the way that the individual ultimately earns his or her living.

As that excellent programme *That'll Teach 'em* demonstrated, the 1950's educational ethos (so despised by the educational 'theorists' of the last decades) of teaching the building blocks of times tables, spelling, grammar and punctuation early and meticulously was not only more empowering to the child but ultimately preferred by the child too.

The incidence of 'should of' in everyday speech (two words that have no business adjacent to each other in any construction of the English language that I can conceive) has multiplied exponentially since content has been allowed to dominate form; as have 'me and my friend', 'I didn't do nothing' and the omnipresent intrusive 'like' that seems to have replaced 'sort of' as a redundant conversational intrusion.

It is a hundred and ninety one years since Jane Austen wrote Pride and Prejudice, which came second to Lord of the Rings in the BBC's search for the best novel. I don't believe that many people would contend that the teaching and understanding of English has benefited from the passing years.

Jane Austen and her readers knew the difference between 'that' and 'which'. It is subtle but important. Nobody cares much now.

"And why bother?" I hear some say. "As long as we understand each other…" We should bother because just as Turner would never have painted those moody pictures of misty light at sea had he not first thoroughly understood the rudiments of artistic creation, so a good knowledge of the building blocks of language opens up limitless possibilities.

But what hope is there when a chair of school governors in Kent received the following official notification:

"The LEA or governing body must provide facilities for pupils not taking school meals to eat meals what they bring to school." They should of written it, like, more careful.

12. A Selection of Early Articles

As I mentioned earlier in these pages, my contributions to the Bucks Free Press have dwindled in length as the paper has evolved over the years from broadsheet to tabloid shape,(if not style, thank goodness), and my column has migrated from its original position across the whole of a page laterally to its current position down the length of a tabloid page vertically. As a result, the items in Tim's next selection, being from the early days of my tenure as columnist, are longer than some of those that have preceded them in this book. These were the days when it was rarely hard to think of something to write about, when I was writing for the first time about many topics that have subsequently been revisited. I realised gradually that I should keep some of my powder dry, if I wanted to have any longevity as a regular columnist.

You will find some themes that overlap with bugbears aired earlier in the book but the difference is that the freedom accorded by the longer length allows me to wander off the point occasionally if something ensnares me along the way.

The first item is about travel (yet again!) but served to remind me of a strange but beguiling play written by Richard Digeance. It concerned the malcontent owner of a fish and chip shop and his affection for a piece of haddock that he couldn't bring himself to sell – and with which he conversed. There was nothing untoward, I assure you; the fish was female -Henrietta, as I recall. It strayed into surreal waters (sic), but was nonetheless fun to do and could have done well, I believe, had the author not lost confidence in the piece after the first week and ended the planned tour abruptly and permanently. All I have to remember the show by is the prop bottle of tomato sauce made lovingly, in foam rubber, by our stage manager. It sits on a shelf in my office, next to the cross I carried as Van Helsing in Dracula *and the garter I wore in* Corpse! *in 1987.*

3rd May 1996

I am currently rehearsing a play called *Fear of Frying* by Richard Digance which will open next week in Epsom. On my journey to Surrey this morning, I found myself in the wrong lane of a contra-flow on the M25 which took me some ten miles past my intended turn off. Rather than trek the ten miles back again down the other side of that same stretch of diabolical road, I compounded my folly by attempting to cut across country from Reigate in the general direction of what I hoped would be Epsom. In my desperate

meanderings, I found myself driving along a road which was disturbingly familiar. A floodgate of memory was suddenly opened and took me back some thirty years to a time when as a young actor I had bought myself my first car - a pale blue frog eye Austin Healey Sprite. It was my absolute pride and joy.

At the same time there was a young lady of some 19 summers that had caught my attention. She lived in leafy Surrey suburbia with her parents. I had driven down from my less salubrious Balham home to take her out for the evening. In retrospect I freely acknowledge that I was utterly stupid to succumb to her insistent requests to drive my car. Although she had a learner's licence, my car was not insured for any other driver.

There floated in the air an unspoken promise that she would consider me a worthy escort on subsequent occasions if I did let her drive my lovely car along this particular straight and quiet lane just for a teensy weensy few seconds. Flutter, flutter, pout with blue eyes peering up at me entreatingly from the mass of freckles under blonde curls.

She drove quite competently for a full five seconds. Then a car appeared coming from the opposite direction, whereupon she jammed her foot on the accelerator instead of the brake and drove straight into a tree.

If that wasn't bad enough, she begged me not to tell her parents that she was driving. They would be frightfully cross and never let her see me again. And I did want to see her again didn't I? I told everyone that I had swerved to avoid a deer. They refused to allow her to associate with such a palpably dangerous driver and I had to pay for the extensive repairs myself.

Obviously, I couldn't claim on my insurance and she had no money, not that any was ever offered. It was just as well she was forbidden to see me because I couldn't afford to take anyone out for the next six months anyway.

A salutary lesson. But I suppose in many ways cheap at the price! Young men - be warned! A Sprite in the hand and all that.

17th July 1996

A lot of fuss was made recently when Take That decided that they had taken quite enough of that - and probably this and the other, for

that matter. Girls from the age of five to fifteen got into quite a state about it and although thankfully it didn't provoke the mass hysteria and occasional suicide that was inspired by the untimely demise of, say, Rudolph Valentino, it was sufficiently momentous, we are asked to believe, as to justify the destruction of a small drizzle forest of newsprint.

What will happen to the boys now? Will Robbie make it without the creative genius of Gary to provide the songs? Can Gary survive the loss of Robbie's iconoclastic sex appeal? And what about thingy, whatsit and doodah? Frankly my dear...!

Other idols have passed with less fanfare - usually because they have run their natural course of popularity. It is actually beneficial to the acquisition of legendary status to go early.

Would Marilyn and Elvis have been as desirable and marketable if they had survived to be seen in their 1996 decrepitude? Would their posters still be available in every High Street? However talented and undoubtedly special they both were, I somehow doubt it. Sinatra was every bit as charismatic as either of them but we have had to witness the diminution and waning of his prodigious talent. So while he still lives - and long may he do so - he is unlikely to stand on the same pedestal as that upon which we have placed Monroe and Presley, whose status not only survives but is enhanced by every book that attempts to debunk their respective myths.

Some people will doubtless find it surprising that I should move effortlessly from this preamble to make my next point. Forget Take That - there has been another loss to the world of entertainment that I rank as greater than the precipitate departure of the funky five. Generations of television viewers will remember the wonderful world of Rainbow. Yes, that's right - cuddly Bungle, fey George and testy Zippy with, of course, well - Geoffrey, who wore jumpers that were far too tight for him with panache and an apparent lack of fear of the style police.

At the heart of Rainbow in those early days in 1980 was a singing trio called Rod, Jane & Freddy. They were so successful at bringing their own brand of upbeat and gentle music to that programme, that they were awarded their own series - understandably, if predictably called - *Rod Jane & Freddy*. They seemed to have a limitless ability to come up with catchy melodies with engaging lyrics. They sang about

anything from hanging out the washing to the virtues of root vegetables. They donned silly costumes to impersonate those great favourites - the Wobblies. They sang haunting gentle songs about Edward Bear and raucous foot-tappers called Mr Ooompahpah and Om Tiddly Om Pom. They did all this with style, charm, energy and warmth and were loved unreservedly by all the children who came to see them. Adults who had been jaundiced by previous trips with children to stage versions of Biker Ninjah Grasshoppers from Space or Milkman Jim, found to their relief that they were attending a performance that was funny, charming, tuneful and even, whisper it quietly - educational!

But last month in Tunbridge Wells, of all places, they performed their last gig. No more will theatre goers be enchanted by Rod's conspiratorial twinkles, Freddy's cheeky charm or Jane's purity of voice and youthful slender form. They have hung up their stripy T-shirts and too-short long trousers. They have winked their last wink and wobbled their last wobble and they will be missed long after Take That have been consigned to the same repository of curiosities as Dexy's Midnight Runners and Manuel and his Music of the Mountains.

Maybe some television executive will seize the opportunity to bring them back to our screens. Thank goodness Blue Peter has survived - and rightly so. But I am sure many like minded parents would welcome the return of some of the old shows so that a new generation of children can appreciate the charm of *Noggin the Nog*, *The Woodentops*, *Rainbow* or *Rod Jane & Freddy*.

15th September 1995

On my first visit to the United States, when a shop assistant exhorted me to "Have a nice day!" on the conclusion of our business, I was deeply moved and thanked her effusively and warmly for this delightful expression of her concern for a fellow human being.

The growing look of suspicious animosity that then appeared on the poor girl's face gave me the impression that, had she been a fully paid up member of the terrifying National Rifle Association, she might have dropped to one knee and fired a warning shot into my

head. It was only when I visited another shop that I realised that my reaction to this parting nicety was the equivalent of responding to,

"How are you?" with a detailed description of the effect of the passage of the years upon my knees and memory. Despite the ritual nature of the "Have a nice day" valediction, it is an indication of the American attitude to the sales assistant/customer relationship. In the States it's 'okay' to be in a service industry in the front line, so the grudging, surly waitress or shop assistant is a comparative rarity.

Even though, in Britain, the nail buffing sales girl chatting to her colleague about their respective boy friends' deficiencies, all the while studiedly refusing to meet a customer's eye, is undoubtedly a sit-com stereotype of the type superbly realised by Victoria Wood, nonetheless, like all such clichés, it is based on more than a germ of truth. We have all encountered the bored, unmotivated teenager, who is defensive because she erroneously thinks you have an attitude about her because she is working at Jeans-U-Like.

Not too long ago I decided to give fellow members of the cast of a play appropriate books as first night gifts (instead of the usual flowers or bottles of wine.) I arrived at a local cut-price book shop at about 5-10 p.m. and by 5-30 had selected about ten books which were piled up by the till. I was searching for two more when the cashier said,

"I'm closing now." When I replied that I would only be a minute as I only had two more books to get, I was told, unapologetically, that they closed at 5-30 and would I please pay for the books I had selected and leave. I explained that unless I could get the two more there was no point in my buying any. That was fine by him, he said, standing by the door with the key already in the lock. I left, empty handed, expressing my aggrieved and avowed intention never to return again. I gathered that this would not cause him any loss of sleep. Now the young man was clearly not the owner of the shop and was probably not on any kind of commission - and if the shop closed at 5-30, then he was undoubtedly entitled to close up on time. But - it surely cannot be beyond the wit of the shop's owners to set up a system whereby the doors close at a certain time leaving those inside fifteen minutes to complete their purchases and to employ their clock-watching shop-assistants on that basis?

On another occasion, I wanted to buy repeats of a particular kind of ladies' shirt that my wife had liked very much. I had retained the receipt for the original purchase, planning to get more of the same as a birthday surprise. I went to the shop in Marlow where it had been bought, armed with all the information from the garment's label only to be told flatly that they didn't sell them and never had. My continuing insistence that I knew otherwise was not met with any hint that they might have heard of the old maxim that 'The customer is always right' - in fact, the customer in this case was plainly a blessed nuisance coming in there trying to buy things, for heaven's sake! However, misguided I might have been, in their eyes, in my persistence, I am still surprised that common sense did not lead them to humour me in the hope that I might be impressed enough by their kindness to such a dullard to allow them to relieve me of some of my money.

It was only as I left, loudly recommending that the couple coming into the shop should go elsewhere if they wanted to avoid similar treatment, that the manageress followed me into the street, with her Hermes scarf billowing behind her, to ask if she could show me something else? Courtesy perhaps?

8th September 1995

Bill Potts devoted his column in this paper last week to the subject of Anthea Turner, 'a fat cat presenter ... and toothy, dizzy mophead ... who would not appeal to any audience demanding more than a Barbie Doll intellect".

He suggested her earnings were disproportionate to her talent, and went so far as to state that "she can't sing, can't dance, can't act, can't tell a joke and I would guess, can't even juggle." The fact that Bill only guesses that she can't juggle implies an absolute knowledge of her other areas of ineptitude. Are we to understand that he has researched poor Anthea with such zeal that he has personally witnessed her failures in these other areas of activity? And how relevant are these imagined deficiencies to the job she is actually being paid to do - that of a presenter?

I would hazard the guess that Jon Snow's *King Lear* might be somewhat lacklustre and that Peter Sissons wouldn't survive 15 minutes doing 'stand-up' at the Comedy Store. So what? That's not

their job. Miss Turner, whom I do not know personally, has committed that most heinous of crimes. She has made a difficult job look easy. Bill Potts has fallen into the same trap as my daughter, who believes she can run as fast as Linford Christie, and all those people who have competed on *The Generation Game* and having watched potters potting, paper folders folding and cake icers icing have signally failed to duplicate their achievements.

Skilful practitioners make their craft look deceptively easy. How do I know this in Miss Turner's case? Because I've tried! I co-presented *Children in Need* for the West Midlands area last year. We were surrounded by apparent and actual chaos. People bellowed incomprehensible instructions down our ear-pieces while we were trying to talk to the camera and look relaxed. At the same time members of the public are doing their innocent best to have fun and make your job impossible. My colleague on the occasion was a Children's TV presenter, who looked as if he wouldn't be served in a pub, but who sailed through the evening with an admirable and effortless mastery.

Last year a television producer thought, in his wisdom, that I might be a suitable presenter of a quiz show. It was based on current affairs and involved six contestants and buzzers. I recorded a pilot of the programme, at the end of which I felt that I had swum the Channel 32 times. Throughout, you have to be aware of the rules of the game, desperately try to remember the contestants names, which camera is on whom, whose buzzer has just sounded, what the scores are and how long you can spend on each section in order for the programme to come to an unhurried and effective conclusion after precisely 23 minutes and thirty seconds. Simultaneously the ear-piece is giving you streams of information, some of which you need desperately and a lot of which is just so much distraction and floor managers are performing gyrations in your eye line to speed you up, slow you down or tell you that your flies are undone. And all the time you have to appear confident and relaxed and encourage the reluctant contestant whilst controlling the over-enthusiastic! Any hint of tension or uncertainty and that camera will pick it up and magnify it a thousand times. Add to that the knowledge that, in addition to the studio audience, millions will be watching.

As far as Miss Turner's pay packet is concerned, unlike Directors of public companies who can vote themselves and each other provocative and excessive pay rises, her salary is freely negotiable. If the Broadcasters feel that her talents are essential to their programme and that they have to compete with other Companies who may wish to employ her, then she is perfectly entitled to make the best deal she can. And good luck to her! Very few presenters can expect a career in front of the camera for anything approaching a full working life. If, as a result of our pithy and controversial columns in this paper, Bill Potts and I were asked to contribute our undoubted talents to high circulation, national glossy magazines and could name our prices - I know how I would react (provided, of course, that I could continue to contribute to the Bucks Free Press!).

13th June 1997

I used to castigate my mother for failing to force me to persevere with piano lessons when I was a child. I would have loved to be able to sit down at a piano at the drop of a hint and casually knock off a swift Chopin Nocturne or songs from the shows, while accepting drinks from a grateful and respectful audience. But I have reluctantly concluded that even had my mother been the 1950's version of the pushy Mum, the likelihood is that I would still sound like Les Dawson's brilliant pastiche of the pianist with the errant fingering. The truth is that our talents are not limitless. Despite all attempts to make the silk purse, sometimes all you end up with is a very well polished, embroidered and out-of-place sows ear, which, unless you're an upwardly mobile sow, is of little use or decoration.

The trophy wife, the neo-Georgian house, the expensive German car, the membership of the right golf club and the holiday in Mustique have evolved over the last generation as a signal to the rest of the world that the owner (pace women's lib) has arrived.

It's all comparable to the gorilla beating his chest and the baboon showing his highly colourful nether regions to others of his species less gloriously endowed in fundamental baboon terms and more easily impressed.

We used to hear about DINKIES (Double Income No Kids). The child as trophy is the latest bolt on accessory to the successful SICKIES. (Single Income Clever Kids). There is a corresponding

version where both parents work. Traditionally, the wealthy middle class male has sired his required number of children and packed them off for someone else to bring up and educate as soon as possible, very often despite their own less than joyous experiences and their spouse's very natural reluctance. Those who actually choose, for whatever reason, to live with their children on a permanent basis and opt for State Education now seem driven to feel that those children have to be seen to achieve as much as possible as soon as possible. My mother was a teacher, but having entrusted me to the care of others of her profession, whilst being supportive and helpful at home, never made me feel that I was being hurtled along towards the competitive and cut throat world of adulthood at the expense of my childhood. Certainly, until I started secondary education at the age of 11, I had no homework. I played, read when I wanted to and took part in family life. I was lucky to have a mostly carefree existence for the first six years of my schooling.

Today I see parents who seem to view their children's education not as a means of bringing out all the many and diverse abilities of that child, (which is after all the meaning of the Latin roots of the word), but as an opportunity to cram in as much as possible whether or not the child is ready, willing or indeed able.

The chimera of the league tables is a case in point. The Thatcherite legacy has led a generation of parents to believe that the comparative attainment levels of children at certain ages are dependant only on the quality of the teaching they receive. Whilst that is one of many factors, it is by no means all. Mercifully children are not homogeneous. In order to have an average ability, by definition and inevitably, there must be an equal number of children whose attainment potential is above and below that average.

This ability, of whatever level, is pre-programmed in the genes and is no respecter of class or money. It cannot be bought. To tutor and cram children in order that they may be selected to attend a school only to struggle for the rest of their school lives is not a kindness. Good teachers recognise that and have the unenviable task of communicating it to parents who sometimes confuse their own ambition with the natural desire to give their child every chance in life. After love, time is the most precious commodity a parent can give a child. I urge parents to question, and I do not exclude myself ,

their real motives in wanting their child to learn the piano, dance a gavotte, play sport for the county, learn a foreign language, be civilised high achievers and love us at the same time. If we all eased off just a bit, we might just re-invent childhood.

27th October 1995

When I realised that I was writing my thirteenth contribution to this column, I found myself drawn to pondering the whole question of superstition. Should I think of this as 'Number 12A', just as some hotels pretend that they don't have a thirteenth floor, in the hope that guests won't register the fact that the staircase leads directly from the twelfth to the fourteenth. Are there really enough triskaidekaphobes to justify this absurdity? I suspect there are just as many people who, like me, walk under ladders deliberately, but carefully, to demonstrate that they are not superstitious.

Most superstitions, however, are firmly grounded in common sense. Ladders are liable to have people up them, who may be wielding heavy objects, which just might tumble onto a passing cranium. No great surprise then that this particular superstition came into being.

The Theatre has more than its fair share of superstitions and there are very few actors who are foolhardy enough to flout them deliberately. Our profession inhabits a world of fantasy and imagination. It is hardly surprising therefore that we are arguably unusually susceptible to what some might consider fanciful fears. People working in theatres are liable to go into a terminal decline if someone quotes from or uses the word 'Macbeth'.

Before you admire my recklessness, this selective prohibition only applies inside a theatre. In the undramatic safety of my home, it's perfectly acceptable. The usual explanation derives from the presence in the play of the weird sisters, whose chanting, it is widely supposed, are real, full blooded, witch's turn-you-into-toads-with warts-on curses. It is certainly true that Macbeth seems to have had more than its fair share of accidents in sword fights, compared with, say, Hamlet or Richard III. Regular readers of this column - (May you prosper and your numbers increase) - will recall my recent example of an inglorious effect of the Macbeth curse! But I believe that it is more the result of the nature of the particular kind of fight required by the

play in terms of the emotional point the combatants have reached, than it has to do with any intrinsic malignity.

It is now accepted that the superstition derives from the fact that in the 19th Century Macbeth was considered the final-gasp box office attraction to fall back on if the rest of the season hadn't gone too well. So, if you heard people muttering lines from the play or mentioning it in whispers, it could presage the end of the engagement, as the management's finances were rocky. A prosaic enough explanation with which an actor of any century would readily empathise.

The other great crime in the theatre is to whistle - again for very practical reasons. Today the stage manager presses a button which illuminates a light which tells a technician to raise or lower a piece of scenery. Before the luxury of electricity offered this instant and silent cueing, it was effected by soft whistles, audible to the crew but not the audience. It requires no great leap of intuition to deduce that unsolicited and arbitrary trilling could produced undesirable results - in terms of wanton scenery hurtling up or down in a manner respectively embarrassing or life-threatening. No wonder actors came to view the practice with alarm.

You will be relieved to hear that actors are, however, a practical bunch. The show has to go on whatever solecisms have been committed - so there is an antidote available for the effects of both the above crimes. The offending quoter/whistler is compelled to quit the room, turn round three times, spit, swear and knock to request re-admission. How that improves things, I am, however, unable to explain. Another superstition proscribes the uttering of the last line of a play until the first night. I have worked with many senior actors who have refused to finish the play in rehearsal for fear of bad luck. That most delightful and eccentric of actors the late Sir Ralph Richardson appeared once in Shaw's *You Never Can Tell*, the very last lines of which are:

"You never can tell, sir, you never can tell." - giving the reason for the title of the play. True to tradition, he did not deliver the lines in rehearsal and on the first night, when the cue came, there was the slightest of pauses and those unmistakable, tones confided

"You never know, do you?"

22nd September 1995

It has long been my ambition to be there in the Albert Hall for that great British institution - the Last Night of the Proms. I'd love to savour the atmosphere, albeit jingoistic and chauvinistic, to wave the flags and pop the party poppers and be unashamedly and sentimentally British, for just one evening, before returning to the less heady reality of late 20th Century Britain. I do not share the puritanical view of those who condemn all things overtly patriotic on the basis that they somehow distract us from the struggle for lasting world peace.

Of course, it is undeniably true that blind nationalistic fervour and racial prejudice are, and have been for centuries, the cause of pointless wars dealing 'devastation's dire dark doom' to millions. But I really do not believe that anyone can persuasively argue that the promenaders, music lovers, socialites, chattering classes, or even those responsible for bombarding the about-to-be-greatly-missed Richard Baker (no relation) with festoons of coloured paper - attend the Last Night because they are celebrating their membership of a master race and harbour frustrated imperialistic ambitions.

It's more that, for that brief time, once a year, we luxuriate in the wonderful, stirring and uplifting music of Elgar, Arne and Sir Henry Wood, which tradition and familiarity have elevated to an even more potent position in our collective consciousness; and anything that binds us together constructively in these days of fragmented communities and lost national self esteem must be worth retaining. Old-fashioned does not necessarily mean expendable or worthless. This year, as in previous years, I found myself watching on television and wishing I was there- that was - until the beginning of the second half. The use of words like 'interesting', 'challenging' and 'different' as an introduction to Harrison Birtwhistle's *Panic* should have set the discordant clappers clattering at the cracked warning bells. I suppose the best I can say about the piece was that it was aptly named.

I experienced a growing sense of panic that the cacophony would never end and that I would be unable to find the remote control unit and turn it down.

For a while the 'Emperor's new clothes' syndrome operated and I tried to convince myself that the repetitive dissonances were something that I could, and should, learn to appreciate. After all, the

engagingly boyish and charming Andrew Davis gave every appearance of believing that he was privileged to be conducting the premiere of this exciting new work by a modern, and undeniably respected, British composer. He even summoned the revered Harrison onto the stage to accept the lengthy applause of an audience comprised of the handful who understood it (I can't bring myself to write 'enjoyed'), those who wanted to give the impression that they belonged to that first category and those who, like me, were just grateful that it was over (and remember - there were no remote controls in the Albert Hall!).

I reminded myself that some of my favourite people, paintings, pieces of music, wine and books are ones that I did not warm to on first acquaintance. Tastes, after all, do change, develop and frequently benefit from greater knowledge and understanding. But then I told myself that, in the case of people for instance, those eventual favourites did start off as members of the human race, with the usual complement of physical attributes - like faces and limbs! As a rule of thumb, and at the acknowledged risk of accusations of Philistinism, I have always believed that the certain knowledge that I could have created a particular musical work or picture was a fair indication of its lack of merit.

It hardly needs to be said that I could never have composed the Elgar Cello Concerto or painted the ceiling of the Sistine Chapel. But I have seen pictures in Exhibitions of Modern Art, which I know I could have daubed and on Saturday night I heard a piece (well the first eternal five minutes of it, anyway) that sounded exactly like what I imagined would be produced if I were to randomly strew notes across a stave for some hapless musician to reproduce.

The undoubtedly gifted saxophonist I exonerate from all blame, he has a living to earn and I have had to breathe some form of life to some pretty lacklustre and self-indulgent scripts in my time. Never were Pomp and Circumstance and Jerusalem so welcome in this green and pleasant land!

18th July 1997

I spent last Sunday afternoon watching a village cricket match in near idyllic circumstances. I have been an irregular follower of cricket since the days when my brother and I used to play as children. I was

the entire English cricket team and he was the Australian team. Given the fact that he was six years older than me and could have been whichever team he darn well liked , I am, in retrospect, grateful that he allowed me to be Hutton, Washbrook, May, Graveney, Wardle, Evans, Locke et al while he had to impersonate the foe in the form of Lindwall, Benaud, Miller, Hassett and Grout. I also used to watch Lancashire play under the captaincy of the great Cyril Washbrook. Occasionally, I got to a test match but whilst I enjoyed the cricket, I was never fond of the crowds. I now watch the tests on telly with the sound turned down and the radio commentary on. Even without John Arlott and Brian Johnstone, the feeling of being a privileged eavesdropper remains - although the conversation is just a shade less likely to ascend to the infectious levels of overgrown schoolboy mirth provoked by the wonderful Johnners.

His inability to speak to Jonathan Agnew, after the inadvertent double entendre when Botham straddled his own wicket, was so infectious that it remains able to make me laugh out loud on every hearing.

And who says cricket is boring? How can a sport be boring which boasts amongst its greats the languid David Gower, the inspiringly competitive and laddish Ian Botham, fiery Fred Trueman the archetypal dour Yorkshireman and David Sheppard, Bishop of Liverpool? Cricket is in my opinion the popular team sport which is least attributable to a specific class; it is capable of being played on many different levels and by participants of a far greater age than most other sports.

This is particularly true of village cricket where senior citizens mingle on the pitch with schoolboys and, provided the distribution of both is more or less even on each team, a good game can be had. No other sport is quite so in tune with our national characteristics; and for spectator and player alike it appeals to all the senses simultaneously. The sound of willow on leather is of course a cliché, but like all good clichés is founded in accurate observation.

There is, too, something calming about the distance of the sound, the inaudibility of the voices of the players and clack of the scorer's tin numbers mingling with the occasional noise of the outside world punctuated by the sound of the cups and saucers being set out in the ramshackle pavilion. The smell of new-mown grass, lemon cake,

linseed oil and beer. The sight of the whites and less than whites against the green of the grounds and the blue of the sky (if you are lucky as we were on Sunday). The fact that gentle periods of longeur are punctuated by flurries of activity and bursts of applause as the President executes a rather nifty late cut. It is as if H G Wells or you know Who had taken us all back a generation or two to a calmer world where we all had the time to play without feeling guilty and when leisure was regarded as an important ingredient in a wholesome life. I hope that cricket survives for future generations, which it will if our schools are encouraged and enabled to continue to provide facilities for it in our erratic summers.

There was something profoundly relaxing about sitting with the foaming tankard in hand whilst children played pseudo-cricket in the nets keeping a casual eye on the cricket and chatting idly with similarly unpressurised spectators. I commend it to you.

28th March 1997

A friend recently told me that my chances of winning the lottery were roughly comparable with my being able to walk up to a stranger in the street in Wycombe town centre and correctly guess their phone number. We all know this, of course, but choose to continue to give a little to a good cause in the hope of a possible awful lot for ourselves. And anyway most weeks at least one person harnesses the powers of chance. Events occur in all our lives which one could have had pretty good odds against happening if we had been able to have a little bet beforehand.

I have never in my life committed any minor transgression without fate stepping in, aided and abetted by coincidence, to prevent me from enjoying the fruits of my peccadillo. At my primary school, when a group of us disobeyed the interdict against going near the brook at the edge of the playing field, I was the one who slipped and fell in. No chance of dissembling there. Ruined clothes and instant retribution in the form of the dreaded strap in front of the whole school - (remember those days?). The only up-side to the sorry saga was that my failure to snitch on my fellow transgressors elevated me from being a bit of a wimp into a temporary heroic status amongst my contemporaries.

Later in life, I went one afternoon to see a dubious film in the West End with a group of similarly indolent and lubricious fellow law students, when we were supposed to be at a lecture. On exiting, we were confronted by jostling reporters and blinded by flash bulbs. Guilt led me to the instant conclusion that I was their prey. I could see screaming headlines proclaiming "Law student ducks lectures to see girlie film." I was relieved therefore to realise that I was not the focus of this media interest. Next door to the cinema was a bank, from which security guards were at that precise moment, carrying the infamous Lucky Gordon tapes which were to prove such crucial evidence in the trial of the unfortunate osteopath, Stephen Ward, in the wake of the Keeler/Profumo scandal. The following morning, every paper on every breakfast table in the land bore a front page picture which included at its periphery this columnist as a startled teenager, slinking out of a Soho flea pit and blinking at the barrage of flashlights immediately in front of a large picture of Brigitte Bardot at her poutiest. My parents were chagrined, to say the least, that I had opted for 'And God Created Woman' instead of the less alluring complexities of Constitutional Law.

The fickle finger having discovered me has refused to move on. In 1978 I was doing a play at The Grand Opera House in Cork in Eire. I was at one of those many phases in my life when I was trying to lose weight. In fact, if I added up all the pounds I have lost over decades of dieting, I have probably lost far more than my current body weight. Now there's a bizarre notion.

Anyway, I had let everyone know that I was on a diet, deliberately, in order to bolster my frequently unreliable will power. On my Sunday off, I drove some 50 or so miles over Macgillicuddy's Reeks to the beautiful Ring of Kerry. I walked several miles along the shores of Dingle Bay with my Irish Setter, Cleo, the wonderful haughty beauty whose portrait still hangs in my study. Invigorated but peckish after this robust activity, I succumbed to temptation and entered a tiny village shop where I bought a Mars Bar, which I ate on the drive back to Cork. The following day, when I returned to the Theatre,   I was greeted by the Stage Doorwoman.

"Hello Mr. Baker, did you enjoy your Mars Bar in Kerry yesterday? And there we were thinking you were on a diet, to be sure - you're a wicked man!" - or words to that effect. It transpired that the Kerry

shopkeeper was her cousin Eileen, who naturally felt that the sucrose intake of an actor passing through her village was a piece of information that had to be passed on to her relative at the theatre at which he was appearing. Now if I were to buy a lottery ticket from a Spice Girl in a sauna...?

13. Milestones

And now back to where it all started – the first finger to keyboard as a professional (yes, I do get paid – amazingly) columnist, I used to think I could call myself a 'journalist' as a result of my writing for a newspaper, but I was soon disabused of that brief delusion by proper journalists, who do a lot more than sit around airing their views without let or hindrance.

It is interestingly a topic that never goes away – the question of how we allow our children to develop and grow whilst protecting them from the outside world that each generation considers to be less friendly than was true in their childhood. The pendulum swings backwards and forwards and we all worry as parents that we are being too protective or too permissive. I suppose it will always be the case. All we can do is our best.

Tim, Tim the editor man has come up with a selection of milestones here – a visit to the Baker Hundreds which as I live in the Chilterns has a certain relevance. I was interested to note that the subjects were childhood, fame, the press itself in its worst manifestations, George W. Bush (remember him?), my column (talk about navel gazing!), political correctness (of course), recycling, and Christmas cards. Now there's eclectic for you.

2nd January 1995 – the first column

The recent horrifying examples in the press of what deranged and/or evil human beings can do to the most defenceless amongst us - our children- has once again sparked off speculation about the allegedly idyllic post war childhoods of my generation.

In common with many others, I am sure, I would love someone to do the research that would tell us, once and for all, whether we really were that much safer in the forties and fifties. Are our memories of wandering far and wide through woods and moors, without the slightest perceived danger from strangers, accurate? Has the incidence of child abuse and murder by opportunistic perverts increased as dramatically as all too regular reports in the press would lead us to conclude?

I suppose what we really need to know, if such records exist, is specifically how these appalling incidents relate to population sizes then and now. Are the reporting patterns different? Or, have we produced such a corrupt society that there are, per capita, more

depraved creatures, whose imagination, humanity and pity are so distorted as to allow them to perpetrate such vile deeds upon those whom every decent human instinct urges that we protect?

When I was 8, I went to school, on my own, by public transport. This involved a short bus ride into the centre of Rochdale to connect with another bus, which took me the three or four miles out of the town to my Primary School. Even in the early 1960's, my wife, at the age of 7, went, unaccompanied, by bus into the centre of Portsmouth for her regular Irish Dancing lessons. I very much doubt if any parent would allow that now.

Unrestrained as it was by the understandable concerns of parents today, my childhood seems in retrospect utterly carefree. I think the worst thing that ever happened to me took place in a summer not unlike the one we are currently experiencing. I had persuaded my older brother to allow me (aged 8) to tag along with him (aged 14) on a cycle ride. I think my mother had succumbed to that temptation we all recognise as parents - to buy a few minutes blessed peace by bribing (usually) an older brother or sister to humour the blind adoration of a younger sibling for just a few hours.

We had both ventured a little further than we had before into the countryside around Rochdale, when we found ourselves looking down from a hill-side onto a most unusual terrain - acres and acres of what looked like a sort of mud-coloured crazy paving. It may be that my big brother knew where we were and what we were gazing down upon. It may be also, for reasons that I can only guess at, that he decided not to share with me that we were on the perimeter of a sewage treatment plant.

Nowadays, of course, there would be vandal proof perimeter fencing, and warning notices. I can recall very little that impeded my headlong rush down the hill to run onto that inviting expanse of "crazy paving" What else could it be there for, for Heaven's sake? Have you ever seen one of those cartoons where Bugs Bunny tricks Yosemite Sam into hurtling off the edge of a cliff? And Sam manages a few paces onto thin air before stopping, looking down for a brief second and then plummeting?

So, dear reader, did the younger (and definitely lighter), Colin take several steps onto the sun-baked surface before gravity had its way with me. I started to sink into that which I have found myself

(figuratively speaking anyway) many times over the intervening years. I don't recall it being a terrifying experience as much as a massively unpleasant one. I suppose the slow approach of an elderly gentleman with a long hooked pole was reassuring. Either he didn't feel that my imminent immersion should make him break into a sweat, or long experience had taught him that the great oblong pits of human by-products were shallow enough to cope with the troublesome boy that was sinking into them.

He grumbled, fished me out and delivered a pithy homily about the relationship between the size of my brain and the activity I had just undertaken. He had an unassailable point. My brother followed me at a very respectful distance as I pushed my bike the few miles home. His flow of comments was, predictably, limited to his ability to locate me with one of his senses with considerably more ease than the other four. My mother did not take me into her arms and console me when we got home. She despatched me to the far end of our garden, where I was hosed with freezing cold water for what seemed several hours, until the last evidence of my trespass was removed. I was then marched indoors for the first of many baths and scrubbings.

As you can imagine, my brother, having been chastised for allowing me to do such a stupid thing, was not too disposed to remain silent about it.

"Phew, what's that terrible pong. Oh yuck!" followed me around for many weeks. It did prepare me for the day many years when, as *Doctor Who*, I had to rub dirt into my face to disguise myself as a miner. I bent down, took a handful and applied it to the Baker mug to discover that the carefully placed, clean, BBC prop dirt had proved a magnet to the dogs of the neighbourhood since it had been placed there. The crew were as sympathetic as my brother had been all those years ago - and seemed to share his sense of humour. They say things go in threes. I avoid zoos!

27th June 1997 – the 100th column

I suppose that some might envy the trappings of fame. I am not one of them. My boring British lower middle class roots would stop me from ever really enjoying the fruits of the kind of fame that enables you to jump queues and get the best tables in restaurants. I couldn't bear all that hate and would have to do lots of sheepish

shrugging, as if it really wasn't my idea, for heaven's sake! Nor do I envy the goldfish bowl atmosphere in which the real stars live. (The word star is much abused today. It seems to be applied to anyone who has been in a TV soap for five episodes - so it's hard to find a word to describe The Seans, Clints and Arnolds, without resorting to hyperbole of the super-duper-megastar kind).

But I wouldn't want to have to wear a disguise in order to live a normal life. It may sound a bit bizarre, but I would hate not to be able to pop into Asda for the dog food whenever I wanted to. It might seem attractive to be able to pay someone to do that for you for a while, but I suspect the novelty might wear off. However even the modest level of television notoriety that I have achieved as a result of being Doctor Who ten years ago has significant disadvantages.

But before I list them I wish to make it quite clear that I am not complaining, I chose the acting profession, for some reason, three decades ago, so must take all the consequences. Indeed, I have little patience with actors who object and become all precious or simply rude when people ask for their autographs and stop them in the street to express appreciation or even simple recognition.

One disadvantage is that you can never allow yourself the luxury of being in a bad mood in public. The one time you complain or mutter an imprecation when you get bad service, is the time that will be remembered by the recipient of your wrath for the rest of their lives. Whenever you appear on the screen, they will inform their friends that you are horrible, unpleasant and arrogant; the friends will seize on this with rapacious glee and pass it on. By the time a few weeks have passed there will be universal amazement that you have not been put on trial for crimes against humanity. For some reason, I am still surprised when people treat me in an odd way when I meet them. Perhaps that is naive of me. I know that I would probably not behave normally (whatever that means) if I were to meet a sporting hero.

But when you are you, if you see what I mean, you really do forget that other people see you as HIM. Accordingly people can be impressed and over effusive or ostentatiously unimpressed or downright rude. Sometimes the rudeness stems from simple embarrassment admittedly.

My wife was amazed recently when at a public charity event a total stranger embarrassed her young son who had stopped to get Doctor Who's autograph by saying,

"My goodness, you've put on a lot of weight since you were Doctor Who. You weren't as fat back then were you?" I am used to this reaction and inclined to be philosophical about it. I can't deny the truth of it certainly. But I would never dream myself of making such an observation to a friend, let alone a complete stranger.

But if I replied in kind, as I did once to a lady in Sweden who detailed all my physical drawbacks, in that forthright Scandinavian style, at length for some minutes, then I would be regarded as appallingly rude. What did I say? Well it was twenty years ago and even though I felt good at the time I wouldn't do it again. I said,

"How kind of you. Do you know you have a very fat bottom?"

28th May 1999 – the 200th column

This being my 200th consecutive column in Freetime, I had intended to celebrate my long service with a lighter piece this week. But the news bulletins about the Dallaglio farrago deflected me. There is a vast difference between the content of a national newspaper and that of local papers. I may have had the odd tussle with members of the species *subeditorialis irritatus* over my prose, (usually about the length of my sentences – have they never read Bronte or Austen?).

But I have never felt obliged to spice up the subject matter. There is in the case of those certain Sundays however, a very clear agenda to not only dig dirt but to facilitate the creation of dirt in order to bring in the JCB's. Tip-toeing carefully through a legal minefield, on the face of the statements of our ex Rugby Captain about the methods used to lure him into the folly of drunken ee-aye-addio Dallaglio bragadoccio about alleged drug related activities, which may or may not be true (phew) – I am left with an impression of tactics which if, say, employed by the police would be ruled as entrapment and consequently inadmissible as evidence.

We have seen several very high profile examples of this in recent years. I was reminded of a less damaging incident that happened to me a quarter of a century ago. I was attracting some publicity as a result of playing the J.R Ewing prototype, Paul Merroney, in a BBC

series called *The Brothers*. I was approached by one of those Sundays for an interview. I declined. I was assured by the persistent reporter that her paper was trying to shake off its past lurid image and become more serious, with a bias towards the Arts. She would ask no personal questions – merely discuss matters professional and talk about my career.

Yes, alright I was naive. And I fell for it. She took me for lunch. She was in her fifties and appeared to be safe and respectable. We talked theatre, art and the meaning of life for an hour and a half. No probing questions, no danger signals. She put her note book away and we chatted as I walked her to her car. She told me she was worried about her daughter who was only 19 and had just told her that she was moving in with her boyfriend, whom she had only known a couple of weeks, and with whom she was having a relationship. Wasn't that appalling? I tried to help. I explained to the clearly distressed mother the facts of life for my generation in the brave new world of 1973. She was not convinced.

"You wouldn't sleep with someone you'd only know for a couple of weeks, would you?" Failing to spot the bait, I tried to help her understand her probably mythical daughter's profligacy. I said that I could imagine circumstances where that might happen. It was not unusual. The conversation continued from there. You're ahead of me, aren't you? My flatmates had great delight in chorusing the headline the following Sunday. It was along the lines of:

"I bed girls I've only known a few seconds" bragged actor Colin Baker to our reporter Lotte Slander, etc., etc., etc... I read the article and envied this fictional me his racy life. It did me no harm professionally or indeed socially at the time. Taxi drivers gave me knowing winks of approval. But I had an awful lot of explaining to do to my Mum. But was it really in the public interest?

27th April 2001 – the 300th column

A survey was commissioned by the Northern Irish Government earlier this month to discover American attitudes to our Foot and Mouth outbreak. Apparently it made grim reading. The tourism minister reported to his assembly that we are perceived as a diseased country, with no food for the tourists to eat, (or at least none that would be safe for the delicate transatlantic palate). Incredibly, some

Americans were under the impression that their hands and feet would fall off, if they were to be infected themselves - by a disease that has arguably only affected a couple of human beings this century and which, however unpleasant, is rarely even fatal for animals.

The same nation that has this fastidious attitude to Foot and Mouth, (which they call Hoof and Mouth, even though the hoof is unaffected) is the world's premier polluter; and it has a president who has declined to allow his country to join the rest of the industrialised nations in setting modest greenhouse gas emission reduction targets with the intention of preventing all our grandchildren inheriting a poisoned, overheated planet.

This then is 'Dubya', a man whose function seems to be to make other nation's leaders look articulate and statesmanlike. He is on record as having said,

"It isn't pollution that's harming the environment. It's the impurities in our air and water that are doing it." Ah, how silly of us! But then what is to be expected from the man who also momentously pronounced,

"It is time for the human race to enter the solar system." And for wee Georgie boy to return to whichever bizarre planet he came from, presumably. The laughter provoked by these "thoughts of Chairman Bush" rings somewhat hollow in the context of his awesome power. As he himself prophetically uttered,

"People that are very weird can get into sensitive positions and have a tremendous impact on history." You can say that again, Dubya. Human nature being what it is, none of us are going to give up our greedy planet consuming ways unilaterally. But we fondly hope that those who seek high office do so on our behalf, at least in part, because they want to be seen to make a difference.

Some nations at Kyoto, and subsequently in The Hague, have been brave enough to risk short-term inconvenience and financial loss to their own countries' citizens in order to slow down global warming and reduce pollution. It is significant that the Earth's richest country is the one declining to ratify the Kyoto protocol.

To the credit of the European Union, its ministers are urging member countries to continue to meet the emission reduction targets even if the United States refuses to join in. It's a rather telling indictment of the American national mentality that telling a lie about

a sexual liaison, (properly only really the business of the parties involved), is seen as a greater crime than poisoning the world at arms length, by adopting a chauvinistic protectionist attitude. It is, of course, only to be expected from a Texan president, who previously governed that state and has received over two and a half million dollars in campaign funds from pollution control exempt Texan petrochemical industries. Small wonder he would rather dance to their fossil fuel tune than worry about the environmental cost to future generations of foreigners and democrats!

"The future will be better tomorrow." – guess who!

28th March 2003 – the 400th column

This is my 400th consecutive contribution to the Bucks Free Press since this organ's august and revered editor, Steve Cohen, (praise him all you readers for his wisdom and inspirational leadership!) invited me to write a weekly column. I derive some small satisfaction from having thus far contrived to share the thoughts of this strolling player and occasional scribe without feeling the need to head for the hills pleading writer's block.

This is partly due to the advent of computer technology which has enabled me thus far to despatch my inconsequential ramblings from places as diverse and far afield as Cyprus, Cornwall, Los Angeles, Turkey and this week – a hotel room in Norwich. When I have completed this week's offering, the kind staff of the Theatre Royal will e-mail these words to the throbbing hub of the Bucks Free Press empire in High Wycombe, while I entertain the matinee audience who, despite the balmy spring weather, are kind enough to find the prospect of seeing Peter Duncan and me trying to kill each other irresistible.

This will, I hope, be the last time that I have to rely on the internet capability and generosity of others to get my copy to the editor. After months of fiddling and prevarication, I have resolved to admit defeat.

Tomorrow I am taking my laptop and my blue tooth, infra-red all singing and dancing mobile phone to someone who might have better luck than me in negotiating their way through the impenetrable messages and options offered to frustrated would-be computer buffs like me, when they try to negotiate with these frustrating devices.

Just as the nice man at the auto-entertainment specialists here took no more than three minutes to get my car radio working again after I allowed my battery to go flat and confuse it, so I expect that someone who (unlike me) is not afraid of the words "you have committed an illegal operation." will dance through the arcane mysteries of the codes and technobabble that still stop this baby boomer in his tracks. Then will I be happy, I wonder?

I suppose it all started when, as a boy, I used to set myself arbitrary targets unrelated to anything of real importance. I would think that for some unspecified reason I had to see three red cars before I turned the next corner. I recall the steadily mounting anxiety as my pace slowed more and more to enable that last post office van to pass.

Other self imposed targets might have included counting lampposts, holding your breath until you heard a bird sing (that would be a tricky one these days!) and the good old not walking on the cracks in the pavement.

As an adult, there are too many real hourly, daily, monthly imperatives for us to have to invent them. Mortgages, bills, household tasks give us a delightful vista of unending targets. But there are still milestones to be marked. One such is this four hundredth article making it into print.

Another will be my hoped for connection to the internet while on the move via my mobile phone. And yet another will be achieved when my teenage daughters pick up their clothes and put them in the washing basket, or bring their empty cups and glasses back downstairs – even if my wife or I still have to wash them up. But (heavy sigh) one thing at a time!

25th February 2005 – the 500th column

The groundswell of universal public distaste for political correctness in all its ridiculous manifestations ought by now to have stemmed the tide of official nonsense that is blighting public life. But our dislike clearly hasn't percolated through to the grey men in grey suits with even greyer minds to convince them that we've had enough.

Even though I have never met anyone who is prepared to defend the worst excesses, there are still clearly a hard core of deranged

bureaucrats with the spare time to find new ways of increasing the blood pressure of the rest of the population.

Some of them work for the Lottery Grants Commission and decide how to dispense the money to good causes by applying politically correct catch-all criteria that bear no relation to the nature of the application or indeed the spirit in which we all believed that the lottery money should be distributed.

So, for instance, the Caister lifeboat in Norfolk, which is the only independent lifeboat station outside the RNLI, has been refused much needed Lottery funds to replace its old boat on the basis that it does not provide a service for disadvantaged people! Clearly, the two thousand and more people who have been plucked from the sea by the brave volunteers manning the Caister lifeboat over a century and half were all diving (in the football sense as well as literally) when their plight occasioned the launch of the lifeboat. Harry Barker, chairman of the Caister Volunteer Lifeboat Service, said that they had also been told that the majority of the calls they dealt with were also ineligible as they were industry related.

"If we rescued someone from a ferry, that would come under the shipping industry, and if we rescued a holidaymaker adrift on a dinghy, they were part of the holiday industry."

The Sheffield branch of the Samaritans failed in their lottery bid to provide premises for their one hundred and twenty volunteers because they did not target groups such as asylum seekers, ethnic minorities, the young or the elderly. So presumably only middle-aged ethnic majorities get sufficiently depressed to call the Samaritans. Perhaps they're all driven to despair by the Lottery Commission's bizarre approach to dispensing our money.

And it gets more nonsensical yet. The Lake District Park authority has been told to discontinue its free guided walks in the fells on the sole basis that the service is used mainly by white middle class middle aged people (that awful unworthy lot again!). The money saved was to be used to meet Government targets for attracting visitors from minority groups.

What makes the whole nonsense even worse is that these pen pushers are creating divisions where none existed before. When the Passport Office rejected a seven-month-old child's passport photograph because its bare shoulders were visible, on the grounds

that it might offend Muslims, the Muslim Council of Great Britain protested,

"They are imposing ridiculous morality on us, without consulting us." But it is interesting that this week Ken Livingstone, whose administration has been guilty of marching to the politically correct drum on more than one occasion, should be called to account for characterising an in-your-face journalist as a concentration camp guard when the hack used "just doing my job" excuse to justify his intrusive behaviour.

Ken's refusal to apologise for succumbing to the urge to offend the offender is hopefully a good sign for the reduction of political correctness emanating from the People's Mayor.

26th January 2007 – the 600th column

We are all being encouraged, quite rightly, to recycle. The residents of Baker Towers are getting better at it all the time. The contents of our wheelie bin are dwindling weekly. Paper, cardboard, glass, metal, plastic bottles are all deposited at one of Wycombe's many recycling points – and never a special trip – always when we are going to or past that place anyway. It is tricky sometimes to get full information. This week, for instance, we learned that the tetrapaks that contain fruit juice are not required on voyage in the cardboard recycling skip because they are waxed and therefore not recyclable. Oops! Sorry. But the more we do our bit, it seems the less effort the retail outlets and manufacturers make.

The packaging in which goods are sold gets steadily more comprehensive, to the point now of ludicrous excess. Why do computer programmes on a CD have to be packaged in a box that would comfortably contain another hundred of them?

Why does glass have to be smashed and reconstituted before it can be used again? Why can't we re-use them – a practice to be seen frequently in Europe? And what about bananas sold in a plastic tray covered in clingfilm and then placed in a larger plastic bag?

The debris left after Christmas, when goods are given yet another layer of wrapping, was phenomenal and completely dwarfed the pile of goodies carried off by my children.

All right, I am honestly not being Scrooge here, but if the goods themselves weren't already triple wrapped, then the festive tradition

of wrapping gifts in colourful fancy paper wouldn't jar quite as much. I bought a replacement ink cartridge for my printer recently. I opened a cardboard outer box, a foil bag, two outer plastic trays surrounding the replacement cartridge – and then, like a goodie in a lonely game of Pass the Parcel, I discovered the cartridge itself. The manufacturers will only change their current practices if they feel we really mean it when we say,

"Enough." I still mourn the departure of the old hardware shops when the blister pack was not in evidence and you could buy as many loose washers, screws, brackets and nails as you needed and pop them in one brown paper bag. And the friendly man selling them knew about his products and you could handle them before buying.

"Wake up Mr Baker – you're dreaming again."

26th December 2008 – the 700th column

Yet another year when I failed to get my act together in time to organise my Christmas card list properly, by which I think I mean courageously.

Most of us share an ecological anxiety about happy glades toppling just to fuel next week's recycling bonanza, in order not to be thought of as having completely forgotten people whom we last thought about, if we are honest, in the second week of December last year. Amongst the cards I sent out were many to people of whom I was very fond, when I lived near them or worked with them decades ago, but whom the pressures of busy life have prevented me from seeing, in some cases, for years. And, if any, those are the ones to send cards to, rather than people we see regularly, work with or who live just around the corner.

The money spent on these festive disposables could probably fund several open air swimming pools and free parking for the disabled throughout the county. And then there is the Christmas letter - I have lacked the courage myself to send out a pamphlet detailing the doings and comings and goings at Baker Towers.

I know what my reaction is to some of my correspondents' desire to proclaim that their offspring have sailed the Atlantic single handed while studying for a degree in microbiology in between typhoons or have discovered the tangled photon.

On the other hand I am diverted by one of our friends' annual letters which paints a picture of a very real family, warts and all, where their offspring are clearly just like ours – like the little girl with the curl in the middle of her forehead? We are all proud of our children's achievements but trumpeting them abroad should be restricted to grand-parents and elderly spinster aunts. No one else really wants to know, any more than I needed to know one Christmas when I was about eight that my clever cousin had learned the Jabberwocky by heart. I then spent hours doggedly learning it myself and it is now the only poem I could recite hanging upside down playing table tennis, (should I be asked to do so) such was my humiliation when my mother told me about wonderful cousin John. Next Christmas I will be brave and only send out cards to those for whom it would mean a lot more than just something else to stick on the mantelpiece.

14. A Red Top to a Bull

Mark Twain once wrote "There are laws to protect the freedom of the press' speech, but none that are worth anything to protect the people from the press." It is unlikely that in the one hundred and thirty odd years since he wrote those words that much has changed to alter his opinion.

It might on first glance seem odd, if not dangerous, for me to dare to criticise the press and media whilst myself contributing to a newspaper. Talk of feeding hands and biting springs to mind. However there is and always has been a marked difference between the readership and therefore the agenda of local newspapers and national newspapers. And within the latter category there is a huge difference between the ethos and content of different mastheads. I suspect I don't need to elaborate.

But the local paper, whilst not exactly addressing its readers in the menacing tones of the residents of Royston Vasey and demanding confirmation that they are 'local', knows that its readership is almost entirely and exclusively local. And in a smaller community, interestingly, the worst excesses of some of the nationals would simply not be tolerated.

It seems that I have railed against these scrabblings and scribblings in the mire on several occasions, as you will see from the selection that follows. I have no doubt that I will have occasion to do so again, until that far off day when we stop being drawn by the salacious headline to find out more.

And we all do on occasion, don't we?

6th August 2004

Shock, horror! The unmarried manager of a national football team may have (to put it in words that readers of Private Eye would remember), 'discussed Uganda' with an unmarried secretary. If, every time something of that nature took place between an executive and a female employee, the newspapers devoted the same amount of space to it as they have to Sven's alleged horizontal activities, the renewable forestry industry would be hard pressed to meet the resultant demand for newsprint without driving the world's population into the sea. Some idiot provokes some other idiot to deny any impropriety and the dung beetles of the press seize the excuse to swarm over the resultant mess with all the unctuous

censoriousness of a Uriah Heep. And I just don't care; and I suspect that you don't care either.

Nor should you. There are things happening in the world that should be in headlines ten feet high. On the same day that the FA was 'tottering' and 'in disarray' when they should be saying.

"Oh, please! Get a journalistic life!"

I heard a speech from a sixty-year-old woman who was virtually single-handedly rescuing from the streets of India children who were by their culture labelled 'untouchable'. Their families numbed by generations of abject poverty and disease either sell their children into prostitution or cast them out at the age of three or four to fend for themselves. Sadly, that information wouldn't shift a lot of red tops in the newsagents. But could anyone deny that it is much more worthy of headlines? I have over the years had many dealings with the dung beetle end of the press.

Last weekend I was in Somerset attending a *Doctor Who* related event organised by a young relative. I was to give an interview with a popular tabloid about the fact that Daleks will not be appearing in the upcoming new series. The BBC were apparently unable to agree terms with the estate of Terry Nation who first wrote the word 'Dalek' in a script in 1963 and who therefore shared creative rights in the resultant phenomenon's popularity. I did not wish to get involved in that particular debate anyway, particularly in a newspaper that past experience had taught me would not quote me accurately and would, indeed, if I said so much as a word to them, then print whatever it was they had already decided to print anyway. However, later in the day, as I was walking along a pathway by the River Axe, a clicking camera was thrust into my face by one man, as another's plangent and insistent tones, accurately stereotypical of tabloid toe-in-the-door journalists, demanded,

"What do you think of the BBC not having Daleks in the new series, Mr Baker? Don't you think it's a disgrace?" I put my hand up in front of the camera lens to have the cameraman, clicking away like a cricket on speed, snarl at me.

"Don't touch my camera!" while the reporter repeatedly droned on at me about Daleks. I said nothing. It remains to be seen whether that is how it appears in their alleged "newspaper". Having got near enough to take a photograph, they may now claim I said whatever

they like and it is my word against theirs. Remember that next time you read that a pop star has thumped a photographer! I wanted to! And I know what I would put in Room 101, if asked.

3rd June 2000

There is a terrible weary, desperation about the way that the tabloids insist on mistaking us for people who give a damn about the lives Messrs Hurley and Grant etc. Apparently they believe that the activities of these seemingly shallow folk sell papers. If so, then come friendly bombs and rain on Fleet Street! I know this has the unwanted effect of bringing their names to the fore once again, but it's hard to protest without being explicit.

There is a myth perpetuated by the media that all performers crave the drug publicity in order to lurch gloriously from one visible income stream to the next. For a very small number it is perhaps true that their continued existence in the gossip pages serves to affirm their stranglehold on that glittering bauble – fame. But most actors do not crave publicity. Whenever an employer is contractually obliged to pass some of his precious cash over to me in exchange for my daily attendance at a theatre, he is understandably anxious to ensure that bottoms, with wallets in close attendance, are scattered liberally on the seats in that venue.

One way to achieve this is to ensure that everyone within the catchment area of that theatre knows that I am there and is moved to want to attend in order, say, to see my trousers fall to the ground (in my case at The Theatre Royal, Windsor the fortnight commencing 12th June – I have no shame but a solid sense of irony!) The producers therefore pressurise the actors to be interviewed or attend functions where the press will be present. Perversely, it is only the very big "I vant to be alone but in a BIGGER Winnebago" stars who can get away with that magnificent, brooding reticence that guarantees increased media interest.

Any British actor who behaved as some American stars do in that respect would very soon find themselves discovering the joys of the Job Seekers allowance. But they inhabit a different world. Donald Sutherland recently even insisted, successfully, that a sloping stage floor be levelled before he would strut his Canadian stuff on it. We both trained at the same Drama School in the 60's. I can do raked

stages (as they're known in the business) – presumably he missed that class and the one about inspiring the affection of stage crew. But where publicity is concerned, I am never eager to surrender myself to the variable prose and judgement of others by doing an interview. This column is, I protest, different. It is local (therefore good) – I do hope you are all local! It is also within my control. It says what I want to say. My experience with national papers has rarely been beneficial, even though it may arguably have persuaded someone to watch whatever programme, or attend whatever play that I am currently gracing with my presence.

But do you know anyone who really wants to read endless dreary prose and not very creative fiction about Liam and Patsy, Posh and Becks, Holden and Morrissey, Liz and Hugh? Were the minutiae of their relationships really the most important things that happened in the eyes of the red top editors that day? The public and the poor young people involved would all benefit if we let them do whatever it is they're doomed to do privately. Though I am optimistic about the Beckams. He has a prodigious talent and they are clearly fond of each other and their baby. Oops – I showed an interest! Let the rest be silence.

20th April 2007

They say that we get the media we deserve. If that is the case, then we must be a pretty undeserving nation. The stories that the print and visual media have led with over the last couple of weeks are a sorry indication of the health of the third estate. The Queen's eldest grandson has broken up with his girl friend. Okay. Leaving aside the inescapable conclusion that the girl has had a lucky escape, as the failure rate for marriages in that particular family is probably higher than the national average, is the fact really worthy of more than a mention at the bottom of page five? Are we really going to have to endure endless pictures of the lucky escapee for the rest of the summer? And are we to look forward to insider stories and endless speculation during the course of the next dozen or so relationships that a young man might reasonably be expected to have over the next decade with, in his case, yet more pin-ups from Tatler and Country Life? The other headline grabber, despite the implicit irony, is the castigation of everyone involved, right up to the Army Minister and

probably that nice Mr Blair, in allowing a couple of the sailors captured by the Iranians to talk about their ordeal to the – erm – media, for money. Shock, horror! Although, dear reader, you may be staggered to learn this, I have myself in the past on occasion been briefly besieged by the national media in search of a story. I discovered then that the best way to defuse the situation was to sell the story that they were all after to one paper (with copy approval), thereby removing the insistent pressure, which can simply be overwhelming for those unused to it (like girlfriends of princes).

It may not have been a wise decision in the case of those advising the servicemen, but I don't begrudge them their bonus and I hope we're not going to be discussing it for the next month or giving more airtime to opposition politicians demanding endless judicial reviews. Maybe the tide will turn – or am I being naively optimistic?

I had the distinct impression that some of the television news presenters in particular were looking somewhat unenthusiastic about some of the recent prince watching items. But then I listen to radio phone-ins and realise that sadly the media do reflect the public they serve.

28th April 2006

Over 3,200 people were killed on our roads last year. 800,000 people suffered injuries playing sport. In 2003, 6,580 deaths were recorded which were directly related to alcohol abuse. The national media report these facts and offer occasional thought provoking pieces or programmes on the subjects. But they don't approach them with the same degree of frenzied disinformation and panic that has greeted the possibility of bird flu having any impact in the UK.

Yet, as a result solely of the bizarre media brouhaha, it is being reported that parrot and small bird owners are releasing their feathered charges out into the wild, in case they should bring plague and pestilence into their owners' homes. Duh?

Were the same approach to be employed in the other cases I have cited, where very real deaths in large numbers can be attributed to cars, to sport, to alcohol, we would see citizens releasing their cars to the tender mercies of breakers' yards, closing down sports fields or demanding the closure of pubs and off-licences. So why this frenzy of terror for a flu virus that claimed 41 lives worldwide last year and

37 so far this year? 1050 people died in plane crashes last year. Yet our desire to fly grows exponentially.

To put it even more into perspective the total number of fatalities from the H5N1 strain of bird flu is a fraction of deaths caused each year by seasonal flu, which usually claims between 250,000 and 500,000 lives annually worldwide, according to the World Health Organisation. Furthermore, in almost all human H5N1 cases, infection was caused by very close contact with sick or dead birds, such as children playing with them, or adults butchering them or removing the feathers. One swan dies in Scotland and the media goes into meltdown. Jose Mourinho, that great tactician and thinker, says when questioned about the threat to Chelsea posed by Manchester United, "For me, pressure is bird flu; I am feeling a lot of pressure with the swan in Scotland."

He claimed he was being serious, too. Why do you have to have a common sense bypass in order to work in the national media?

10th September 2004

I'm glad that the British media were not in their present destructive form when we were fighting the Second World War. Can you imagine the reaction after Dunkirk if the national newspapers were in the hands of the current lot? They would have been baying for Churchill's blood and demanding the replacement of the entire military staff. Never mind the size of the German army, or the fact that we were playing away from home for the whole contest.

We are 'Great' Britain, after all. Our citizens expect victory; we had known nothing else in any significant conflict since 1066. Lord John Gort was the winner of the Military Cross, the Distinguished Service Order with two bars and the Victoria Cross for outstanding bravery in World War 1 and was the commander of the British expeditionary force. Forget his past record, however. He failed to secure a victory in his first away match of a long campaign, so clearly the media would have demanded his immediate replacement.

Fortunately, in the mid-twentieth century the national character was forged from sterner and more generous stuff. The battle was not confused with the war and the need to support and encourage was recognised, not just by the population at large but by those who had the power to shape and change opinions in the newspapers. I will

leave aside the arrogance of the assumption that Austria and Poland (two countries that may have reason to be grateful that our self-destruct button was less accessible sixty years ago) are insignificant opponents who might not have their own thoughts about who should win a match on their own turf.

There are no pushovers in sport any more – with the possible exception of Formula One Racing – and that makes most competition all the more interesting and challenging. But there does seem to be a proliferation of pundititis about, exacerbated by a discernible envy of the salaries paid to footballers.

"We pay their astronomical wages and this is how they repay us! A draw away from home!" A goalkeeper makes a mistake. Of course it is regrettable but does it really justify the red top rage that was visited upon him, or indeed the viciously gleeful reporting of his replacement for the next match. No celebration of that victory, but scorn poured on the replaced goalkeeper. Maybe we should re-think the word 'supporter'. It has become somewhat of a misnomer for the fair-weather fans who attend football matches. And the ability to turn on former favourites is not restricted to former golden boys.

"How dare Paula Radcliffe give up in the Olympic Marathon? We had the champagne on ice to toast her victory! Selfish woman. She wilfully deceived us by being really successful for a long time and then what happens? She let us down. Twice!"

And, "The sprinters only won the 4 x 100 in the Olympics because the Americans messed up their baton change!" - overlooking the fact that the baton change is as much a part of the race as the running bit. Martyn Lewis the BBC newsreader once lamented the fact that good news gets insufficient airtime.

It's certainly true in the tabloid press, which has the undoubted potential to encourage and motivate readers but prefers to spread gloom and despondency in between sententious muckraking.

I don't blame the England team for declining to talk to the people who had done their utmost to demoralise them.

15. 21st Century News

The first decade of the third millennium has produced its fair share of dramatic stories, dominated perhaps by the corrosive phenomenon of terrorism, which dominated the media after the 2001 destruction of the twin towers in New York. Even though I write for a local newspaper it would have been unthinkable to ignore such a calamitous act of destruction and mass murder.

It was also the decade of Jean Charles de Menezes, whose death on a tube train shocked the nation, of Iraq and its never found weapons of mass destruction and of the abduction of Madeline McCann whose little face is imprinted on all of our minds forever, as the years slide inexorably by since her disappearance.

Not exactly at the other end of the scale, but certainly of less international significance there were shenanigans in Big Brother, and just that element of schadenfreude around when we learn that our representatives in the mother of parliaments, (who like Caesar's wife, ought to be above suspicion) – have been a trifle free in their interpretation of what was reasonable when claiming expenses.

Every tax payer in the country watched to see whether the same degree of assiduity would be employed in scrutinising their receipts and expenditure as the rest of us endure on an annual basis.

15th September 2001

The events in America this week have impacted on our lives to such an extent that it would seem unthinkable to write about anything else. War excluded, I can think of no single event in my lifetime that has had a greater potential to change our lives irrevocably. Indeed, many regard this attack as an act of war. So much that our generation has taken for granted is possibly gone forever and much of what has gone can be summed up in one word – freedom.

In the face of fanatical mass murderers with as little regard for their own lives as anyone else's, we will have to surrender rights that, in less troubled times, we would fight to retain. No-one wants a police state. No-one wants to be challenged repeatedly to demonstrate innocence of intent. No-one wants to endure extra hours of identity checks, searches and loss of privacy.

However, despite the criticisms in the media of the intelligence services for their failure to pick up any advance warning of the terrorist attack, it is not impossible that a handful of human beings,

whose mental states the rest of us can only struggle to begin to understand, armed with penknives, with little contact with anyone else and no requirement for rogue state funding, simply hijacked four planes full of aviation fuel. A low tech crime with cataclysmic and devastating results.

It is impossible to eradicate completely the possibility of fanatical terrorists committing similar atrocities. But even to even reduce the risk, which clearly we must now do, will involve the necessary erosion of what many would regard as civil liberties. But I will tolerate searches, x-rays, document checks, luggage examination and earlier check-in times. Any minor irritation will vanish instantly in the face of my memory of images that I fear are permanently and indelibly printed on my mind.

The people who planned and committed the heinous acts were motivated by a hatred of you and me, as well as the anonymous thousands who died in America. We are all, apparently, legitimate targets in the promotion of their political or religious beliefs. They may delude themselves that our beliefs, our democratic institutions, our capitalist society are evil but it is a huge step from that belief to the wholesale destruction we have witnessed. I pray that the reaction of what we believe to be the "civilised world" does nothing to provoke further hatred of our society where there may be none at the moment. I hope we do not create more martyrs to deluded causes. Fanatics throughout the tortured history of humanity have evolved from or attached themselves to religions.

The incidents of intimidation and terrorising of children on their way to school in the Ardoyne area of North Belfast, on the sole spurious basis of their adherence to religions that worship their same God in a slightly different way, are manifestations of the same cancer in human society that leads to suicide bombings in the name of a different religious belief. Just as the leaders of the Roman Catholic and Protestant Churches in Northern Ireland do (and must continue to) condemn all the atrocities committed in their names, I fervently hope that the leaders of all religions, worldwide and locally, will feel able to categorically and unequivocally reject terror and wholesale massacre as a legitimate tool of their followers. People of all faiths and political beliefs now have a common cause.

24th October 2003

It was announced this week that the National Institute for Clinical Excellence have recommended that all pregnant women should be routinely tested for Down's syndrome. The acronym for this organisation is, somewhat disarmingly, NICE, which is arguably less than appropriate in this instance. It must be implicit, in the offering of such a test, that the mother might then wish to take some remedial action in the event of the test proving positive. Otherwise, why test? We are, however, warned that the tests will miss four out of ten babies who have Down's and furthermore that one in twenty will be incorrectly identified as carrying the extra chromosome, when in fact they do not. Not only is it clearly distressing to think of a healthy baby being terminated because of an incorrect diagnosis of Down's, but we should also, as a society, think very carefully before we let ourselves mark for possible extinction a group of people who are merely different to the rest of us, not (by any reasonable diagnosis) ill. The quality of life of those with Down's is as variable as it is amongst the rest of the population. If worth were to be measured by the capacity to show affection, then people with Down's would in fact rank much more highly than the rest of us.

When I attend conventions and events celebrating *Doctor Who*, there are sometimes fans there who have Down's. They are invariably more open, effusive and simply affectionate than their peers. Who is to say that someone who runs up to me, enfolds me in a vice-like hug and says,

"I love you, Doctor Who!" is less worthy of existing, than someone who thinks of themselves as 'normal' but whose reticence leads them to be less demonstrative? It is only initially an awkward moment because I, the recipient of the seemingly disproportionate affection, am less uninhibited. The only real disadvantage that those with Down's have is our prejudice; and prejudice is always a by-product of ignorance.

My wife and I lost a baby when he was just short of two months old. This has perhaps resulted in my heightened sensitivity to the fragility of new life. I can understand a desire to terminate a pregnancy when there is convincing medical evidence that the baby, when born, will be suffer from some illness so painful or handicapping as to make its life intolerable. I would argue that

Down's does not fulfil either of those criteria. One newspaper this week included an article on this subject, giving the example of Anya Souza, an articulate girl born with the syndrome who works successfully as a stained-glass artist and lives in North London with her boyfriend. She is offered as compelling evidence as to why we should not automatically think of a diagnosis of Down's babies as being an indicator for termination. The validity of that point is undeniable, but it somehow begs the question about all those other Down's children who may not discover such talents and be able to care for themselves, but who have every bit as much right to live.

Not that I would advocate it, of course, but if those nice people at NICE could come up with a test that would predict those who will become violent thugs, drug dealers and racist yobs – then that would be a different matter. I've never yet heard of a person with Down's syndrome indulging in any of those activities.

13th September 2002

This week I heard an American journalist giving a most perceptive analysis of his nation's inability to comprehend that there is any real alternative to the American way. He drew a very neat parallel our own country's international strategy in the 18th and 19th centuries. Our leaders then spoke of 'bringing civilisation' to lands that, we can now see, might have benefited more if we had left them alone. And, however naively well intentioned the mass exportation of our values, customs, religions and laws might have been, history has repeatedly demonstrated that gratuitous interference in the social and belief structures of other nations inevitably results in payback time generations later. One needs look no further than Ireland or the Middle East for proof of that.

When you are demonstrably the most powerful nation in the world, it must be very tempting to believe that your values are universal, particularly when you see yourself as democratic and the majority of your voting population enjoy a standard of living significantly higher than that of most other countries.

Even more so, when those countries show every sign of welcoming the arrival of your fast food, your footwear and your entertainment. Self interest tempts one generation of political leaders to arm and equip the unelected leaders of smaller (and often less democratic)

countries who are then able to counteract a potential economic, or even military, threat from one of that aided country's neighbours. A few changes of administration down the line and the self interested generosity of yesteryear becomes the nightmare rogue state scenario of today. Those of us who are powerless and can only watch and wonder at the developing situation concerning Iraq cannot help but doubt the wisdom of drastic action unless it is absolutely necessary. There are scores of other less than salubrious regimes worldwide who have mad scientists beavering away to produce any manner of nasty biological, chemical and mass destruction weapons.

Why arbitrarily pick on Iraq, whom even America has not accused of being responsible for the events in New York a year ago, if not for reasons connected with oil? And it strikes me that perhaps the one thing that one shouldn't do to someone who has ferreted away something nasty and destructive is to start shouting and yelling at them and provoke them into doing something silly with whatever it is that they might have. The benefits of telling a madman with a large nasty hidden weapon that you and your mates are going to come and sort him out, at some unspecified time in the future, elude me.

And just because we have been pally with our former transatlantic colonies for a couple of hundred of years is no reason why we should be so anxious to hold George Dubya's coat while he goes and lights a fuse in the Middle East which may not go out until an awful lot of innocent people in an awful lot of countries have very good reason to hate us even more than they are already predisposed to do.

One doesn't automatically associate the USA with the concept of irony. But there seems to be not the slightest acknowledgement by the nation that possesses enough destructive firepower to obliterate the planet several times over, that there is anything even slightly hypocritical in insisting that an inconvenient regime should be prevented from acquiring a tiny fraction of that potential.

17th September 2004

There have been the usual flimsy arguments this week from the hunting apologists. For starters - **We provide a useful fox control service for the farmer** and **we don't kill many foxes anyway**. Well, those two cancel each other out in my book. Gathering dozens of people horses, hounds and people together to pursue one terrified

mammal and then to failing to do so justifies neither the former statement nor the claim that it is the most effective means of fox control.

They are 'vermin' – a convenient, meaningless label to justify an unjustifiable activity.

It'll be fishing and shooting next. Why? Fishing and shooting provide food. Most of us acknowledge the need to kill humanely for food. Fish, pheasant, partridge etc are edible; foxes are not.

It is an erosion of our civil rights - like the banning of bear baiting, child labour and speeding infringed the civil rights of those who had previously enjoyed indulging in those activities.

The 'Town v Country argument' is just a fabrication. There are Londoners who hunt and farmers who dislike fox hunting … a rather unworthy attempt to persuade country dwellers who might otherwise be antipathetic to hunting to support the hunting lobby.

People will lose their livelihoods - yes, like workers in the coal and steel industries had to retrain when their employment became no longer viable for whatever reason.

Foxes are ruthless, sly and savage killers. Leaving aside the naïve anthropomorphic nature of this argument, foxes kill more than one chicken at a time because of the way we keep them for our own benefit. They can't fly off and perch to get away from the fox. A fox is just being a fox. He has evolved to survive by pouncing on things that flutter and squawk. We have created an environment where the fluttering and squawking goes on and on, as the chickens can't escape. I have chickens and they live in a reverse engineered, very comfortable Stalag Luft HP14.

This ban turns decent law abiding folk into criminals. Erm – you mean like every other law that has ever been passed that contains punitive sanctions. I used to drive at 100mph down the M1. Since the arrival of the National Speed Limit (which infringed my civil liberties) if I do so now, I get punished. Lots of us don't like it, but we have to accept it. It is typical of the arrogance of the hunters that they announce their intention to select the laws they obey.

There are more important things to do than ban hunting. There are always more important things to do than anything except 'the most important thing' – whatever that may be. A whole raft of

laws is passed every year varying from the really terribly important to the arguably less important. No one complains then.

Foxhunting is a centuries old British tradition. In fact it really only became truly popular when stag hunting declined in the middle of the 19th Century; as a result foxes became so rare that they were actually imported from Europe by the Hunts. Most of the red foxes we see today are descended from those Swedish imports.

It is a political move by 10 Downing Street to keep backbenchers happy by honouring a manifesto promise ... and to keep happy an electorate who voted them in and rarely have the experience of seeing manifesto promises actually honoured by any party.

29th July 2005

I left England for Australia a day after the first terrorist attack on London and am here for a further two weeks. I have therefore been watching events unfurl in the UK through the eyes of a population on the other side of the world. It is indicative of the fact that terrorism is now a whole-world problem that the monstrous acts perpetrated by these deluded young men have occupied the same position in the Australian media as at home.

There is the same distress for the bereaved and injured; there is the same incomprehension that any belief system can produce a mindset that sees random killing as acceptable; there is also the same determination to refuse to allow the perverted, the murderous and the depraved to dictate how we live our lives.

There is the same overwhelming sadness that a Brazilian electrician has perished at their hands too. And, however much we regret that further tragic, unnecessary death, it is clear beyond doubt that it is the direct responsibility of the perpetrators of the first and second attacks and not the unfortunate police officer or officers who obeyed their difficult instructions in a situation where a decision had to be made in a heartbeat and there were scores of other hearts that might stop beating if the wrong decision was made.

The policemen that killed that young man are further victims of the mad distorted ideology that spawns murderous mayhem. And that memory will be with them for the rest of their lives. But it has been helpful and comforting as a Briton half a world away from home, to

know that the Australian nation, which somewhat unpredictably and illogically recently voted to retain as its nominal head our Queen, still shares our sorrows as if they were their own.

The single exception to that lies on the cricket field. Their triumphalist glee and use of words like 'thrash', 'whitewash' and 'obliterate the Poms' are, however, put in context by their sympathy and compassion in the 'real world' of terrorist activity. It has been interesting, too, to see the reaction of the media down under to the astonishing detection benefits of the use of CCTV cameras. There is a nationwide demand from politicians and commentators alike for serious investment in CCTV in order to give Australia the same ability to at least detect and identify (if not deter) terrorists. Our own CCTV cameras have in this case been demonstrated to enhance rather than restrict civil liberties.

2nd February 2007

It can be quite tough standing up for what is right and the extent to which an individual in the public eye is prepared to put his or her head over the parapet is a pretty good measure of that individual's worth. Despite all my efforts, it was impossible not to be aware of the recent events in Celebrity Big Brother.

Like many people, I had little interest in the events unfolding on Channel 4 until the racism controversy surfaced and the viewing millions increased dramatically to watch the tawdry behaviour of that sad creature Jade and her weak minded acolytes. And I use the word 'creature' advisedly. Jade was created and turned upon by the media just as Mary Shelley's Dr. Frankenstein created his monster and then turned upon it. We are all pretty much agreed now that the despicable behaviour was quite simply common or garden bullying.

Had Shilpa Shetty had ginger hair, worn glasses or had any of those other characteristics fastened onto by bullies then the focus for the jealousies and inadequacies of her tormentors would have been on that difference rather than her race. That kind of bullying exists everywhere and will always exist to some extent in schools, workplaces and other closed environments despite the best endeavours of those running them to eliminate it.

What really saddened me was the fact none of the other inmates (for such they were) really confronted the issue while it occurred.

They expressed their discomfiture to the camera, but not in any positive or effective way to the bullies; and that was perhaps even less palatable than the bullying itself. The intelligence and education of the perpetrators went a little way to explaining if not excusing their behaviour. The passive witnesses had less of an excuse. Had I been present to hear such nastiness, I cannot believe that I would not have strenuously confronted it whether there were cameras there or not; and I am sure many of you would too. I think a good yardstick by which to judge the decency of a society is whether its citizens are prepared to stand up for what is right.

When uncomfortable matters of principle arise it can be tempting to avoid involvement, to hide behind the illusion that neutrality is an honourable position and allow others to fight for what they believe to be right while they protect their own interests.

18th May 2007

The ongoing case of poor abducted Madeleine McCann is impossibly hard to bear even for those of us who do not know her and her family. For her parents and immediate family, we can only pray that they can somehow endure the seconds and minutes and hours of unimaginable, visceral dread and uncertainty that lie ahead, clinging, as they must, to the hope that the little girl herself is not suffering and may be restored to them.

For all of us impotently observing events unfold, there is the awful awareness that we belong to the same species that has perpetrated this hideous cruelty to a four-year-old child and her family. That any human being could even contemplate doing what has been done, let alone execute it, simply defies belief for the rest of us and calls into question just how thick is the veneer of civilisation we might otherwise fondly believe that we display.

However rare these cases might be, we are also faced with the dilemma of how we prepare our children to live in a world where child abduction and abuse exist, without at the same time paralysing their ability to develop healthily. Educational and other professionals today are much better at delivering appropriate and balanced information to our children. My wife remembers being told when she was five years old "not to take sweets from strangers." Full stop. It is

hard to believe today but, like me, she used to travel to her primary school on a public bus, on her own. A different world, indeed.

She recalls very clearly once being offered a sweetie by an old lady who was sitting next to her and who travelled on the same bus every day too. But she was by, definition, a stranger. Five-year-old logic battled between displaying the rudeness implicit in refusing the lady's offer and obeying the 'stranger' rule. She resolved the problem for herself eventually by accepting the sweet but not eating it. For her the sweet was the danger, not the stranger. She had avoided the 'poisoned' sweet and proudly handed it to her mother when she returned home, to demonstrate her obedience.

Clearly, we are today (and need to be) more careful in how we prepare young children for the awful truth that wandering among us, like a pernicious cancer, are very, very few individuals who belie their human appearance.

31st October 2008

Ever since the first caveman got a cheap laugh, comedians have pushed the boundaries of taste into areas previously regarded as offensive or unacceptable. Humour has been used very effectively to challenge powerful individuals and oppressive regimes throughout history by brave writers and performers.

However, there are occasions when comedians misunderstand or misuse the licence that audiences willingly give to entertainers. One such is Russell Brand. I must acknowledge that he is not aiming his act at me, or indeed anyone I know over the age of twenty-five. However, his particular brand of humour and his proclaimed lifestyle is only tolerable (if unappetising) until he delivers his random obscenities on the radio at identifiable individuals who cannot respond. It is reported that he telephoned the elderly actor Andrew Sachs and left prurient macho ramblings about Andrew's grand-daughter on his answer machine.

Even Bernard Manning, whose humour was consistently racist, sexist and offensive, confined himself to performing to audiences who knew what was on offer and opted to go and listen to it. Brand and Jonathan Ross were broadcasting on Radio Two, hardly a niche channel for bar room humour. The programme was recorded, but still broadcast with all the offending schoolboy smut and cruel jibes

intact. And for that, the BBC must take some blame. It may sadly be that Brand and Ross are paid so much money, (the indecency of the amount of which is matched only by the content of their respective programmes), that the, by comparison, lowly paid producers of their shows have little power to rein in their preening stars' excesses. After seeing Russell Brand a couple of times, I realised that he was not for me.

I have tolerated Ross despite his occasional forays into the humour of the lavatory wall, because he can also display an amiable quick witted charm. But this sorry episode has ended my tolerance. I want to be able to watch television and listen to the radio with my family secure in the knowledge that the broadcasters value all of their audience. Aside from the appalling discourtesy to the lady concerned and her grandfather and family, this whole sordid incident is also a clear case of bullying, something that as a nation we are trying to eliminate from both schools and workplaces. These two smug foul mouthed idiots have not helped that cause.

15th May 2009

So, the little piggies of Westminster have been immersing their greedy snouts in the trough we have to fill through our taxes. What astounds me is that there isn't a bigger furore and more strident demands for wholesale resignations.

We live in a world where benefit cheats are imprisoned and we accept that as a sanction on the poorest amongst us, when they make fraudulent claims. We live in a world where if you break the speeding laws you may lose your licence for a period of six months or more (a personal gripe – I freely acknowledge). Our legislators have decreed that those are the penalties and we have to accept them, as did the chief executive of the firm that makes and supplies speed cameras this week when he fell foul of his own products. I admit it, a tad of schadenfreude there.

We are all bound by the laws that politicians enact for the greater good, we fervently hope. We have therefore an absolute right to expect that they should be, like Caesar's wife, above suspicion themselves. It can only be arrogance that leads them to believe that they can behave quite so immorally with impunity. When I work away from home in my profession I get a 'touring' allowance that covers

only a fraction of the real cost of living away from home and I have to lump it. That's the real world. If I handed a producer a receipt for the theatrical equivalent of cleaning out my moat, or mowing my helipad or even buying a new toothbrush, he would either have me committed or burst into laughter. Perhaps I was naïve to think our elected representatives wouldn't cheat or play the system in such a cynical way, like the worst benefit cheat or tax avoider. But now Pandora's Box is open and they haven't closed it in time for any Hope to remain. A plague on all their houses, say I. Yes, some of them are now, shamefacedly, shovelling back their ill-gotten gains. But none of the cheats, the 'flippers', the greedy opportunists – for that is what they are – should ever be allowed to stand for public office again. The rest of us can't write our own rules.

We have to obey the quite restrictive rules they write for us. It is beneath contempt to provide themselves with such generous loopholes and then quite so shamelessly exploit them.

24th July 2009

Living, as we do, in a world where the majority appear to see fame as the holy grail, it is interesting that most of those who might truly claim to be 'famous' regard fame as an unwelcome consequence of whatever it was that propelled them into the public eye.

The classic example is Neil Armstrong, the first human being to set foot on 'luna firma' – to stand somewhere else in the universe and look at the planet Earth. He has resolutely refused to allow himself to become part of the spaceman circus that could easily have grown up around him, had he felt inclined to court that kind of attention. However for him, as for most very successful people, fame or money are mere by-products of what really interests them – the striving, the work, the achievement of personal goals.

The fortieth anniversary of his and Buzz Aldrin's and Michael Collins' achievement was rightly celebrated this week. Like most people who were old enough to remember the event, I know exactly where I was when that "small step for (a) man" was taken by Armstrong. I was standing in the middle of Stonehenge listening to his words on my transistor radio. In those days Stonehenge stood majestically in the middle of an unfenced field. I was driving back from Cornwall that evening and found myself sometime after three in

the morning driving past Stonehenge. Given the supposed connection between the moon and Stonehenge, I decided to park and walked into the centre of the stones to listen to the distant drama unfold. I can't remember now whether the moon was actually visible or whether it was clouded over.

But I do remember listening to Neil Armstrong stepping off the bottom rung of that nine rung ladder and telling me and many millions worldwide that humans could escape their planet and walk on the moon. A moment that I will never forget and which is infinitely more uplifting than those other events etched on our memories – the shooting of John F. Kennedy and the destruction of the twin towers.

Knowing the worthlessness of fame, Armstrong has studiously shunned it. There are many who would love to just 'do what they do' without the accompanying ballyhoo, but are under contracts to studios, to clubs, to production companies that demand their participation in the publicity circus.

Way to go Neil!

16. A Sporting Life

I have always enjoyed watching sport more than I have partaking in it, unfortunately. Because I was undersized in my earliest years as a child, which may be hard to believe now, I was always, to all intents and purposes, sidelined when my contemporaries picked teams or when I took part in school sport. As a result, I thought I couldn't 'do sport' and therefore had little interest in it beyond supporting Manchester United and going to matches when I had the chance, in a family where sport wasn't even <u>on</u> the family agenda, let alone low down.

It was therefore in later life – well after school – that I started to play tennis and squash and discovered that sport can be fun, as long as you find someone of comparable ability with whom to play.

Then a decade or so ago I accompanied a friend to see Wycombe Wanderers play Reading in a local derby. I hadn't been to a live football match for years and started going regularly to support 'the Chairboys' - as Wanderers are known because of the chair making history of Wycombe, my nearest town.

My wife and I are now season ticket holders and agonise with and for them on a weekly basis as they struggle for promotion and then struggle to avoid relegation. We have a wonderful community of stalwart supporters in the area of the stands where we sit, all of us longing for the opportunity to leap to our feet in exultation, if only to get warm, which happens far less often than we would like.

After the match, we walk through fields and up a steep, wooded hill to get home, which takes its toll on my lungs and limbs, leaving me every bit as exhausted as the players probably are at the same time, with much more reason. Lower league soccer has a lot going for it. So at least sport is providing me with some exercise, even at this late stage of my life!

The more sport there is on television - the happier I am, particularly if it is football, cricket, tennis or athletics. I'll even watch golf on the big occasions.
This does not always make me popular in a house where there are four daughters whose viewing habits are slightly different. Mercifully my wife shares my interest in most sports.

Over the years I have tried to do my bit in my column to support our local team, as you will see. In one such article I mentioned having met the former Arsenal captain, Tony Adams, in the street in London, while he was manager at Wycombe. Our very brief exchange was matched only by his brief tenure at the club, which he left abruptly when he discovered that players in the bottom division

of the league don't have the same skills as footballers in the premiership, (otherwise they would be in the premiership – doh!).

I think he had already made his decision to leave when I spoke to him as he showed no signs of relishing the opportunity to chat with a fan. I made a mental note at the time about how to deal with fans myself. Even when I'm busy or rushed, I try to at least explain that and have a quick chat. Fans remember the snubs, real or imagined, longer than they do the pleasant encounters, unfortunately.

30th July 1999

My earliest memories of participating in sport were not promising. Thankfully even the casual sadism of the sports' teacher who blighted my early secondary years was insufficient to permanently deter me from later participation in some sport and the considerable enjoyment of watching others compete in almost every sport.

It would give me enormous pleasure, I am ashamed to say, to blazon his name across this paper for the damage he did to me and the other boys at my school who were not at the front of the queue when six packs, co-ordination and testosterone were being dished out. However slim the possibility, my persecutor may have relatives with rosier memories, which I prefer not to tarnish. He has at least, no descendants. He was a catholic priest, a short, chunky, super-fit Scot. One of his favourite tricks was to demonstrate a jump over a pommel horse and then make pretence of selecting one of the class at random to be the first to attempt to emulate him. More often than chance alone could possibly explain, it was myself, Colquhoun or McGrath whom he would select, secure in the knowledge that he would then be able to increase his status in front of his fans, the physically co-ordinated, first team boys whose bodies were not, like ours, utterly unsuited for demonstrations of physical prowess.

His sporty boys would suppress sniggers as the tubby McGrath, lanky Colquhoun or the smallest boy in the class, weedy, bespectacled Baker would make an utter pigs' breakfast of it and land in an undignified and painful heap on the mat. There would be a briefest of pauses before the inevitable, "Right, that's how not to do it." He would then select a known athlete to have a go. The smug youth would then nonchalantly execute the manoeuvre that I had just inelegantly attempted and failed. Immaculately, of course.

On sports' days, we would repair to the playing fields where my tormentor would nominate two of the sturdier first team players to pick sides. No free tickets to Wycombe Sports Centre for guessing who were the last three unchosen, shivering wretches.

"Alright, I'll have Baker if I can pick ends, have the better changing room, the clean kit and the phone number of your sister's friend at Loreto Convent down the road."

"Done!"

I was spared a sizeable chunk of my routine humiliation because my school operated a bizarre punishment policy for boys who forget to bring in their PE or sports kit. Clearly, some genius had concluded, boys love sport and hate reading. So forgetting one's kit resulted in – turn your face to the wall my dears if you wish to avoid the horror of it – an afternoon in the library, engaged in silent reading.

"Oh – er – right, gosh, sorry sir. That'll teach me!" (Shades of Brer Rabbit and the briar bush). The sad thing was that it was years before I realised that playing cricket, football and tennis could be fun, if you got to play those games, or any game, with people who were either of a similar standard or who saw no point in deterring others from participation in a sport that they clearly enjoyed themselves. I still however regret those missed opportunities to rush around and compete and fail without the certainty of the scorn of the one person whose job it was to enthuse me. Teachers have great power. Mercifully today's generation of teachers do seem at least to realise that.

13th June 2003

By the time you are reading this, the whole David Beckham transfer saga will have occupied a few more thousand column-miles of fevered speculation and journalistic fiction. The whole business resembles a rather unseemly meat market, inviting comparison with an age before human emancipation, when people were commodities to be bought and sold. Alright, I acknowledge that there is a fairly dramatic difference between someone earning millions of pounds in one place being compelled to go and earn millions of euros somewhere else; but in terms of the basic underlying principle of personal freedom behind the process, there is very little difference. Those of us who rather admire the talent and/or the persona of

David Beckham are inclined to believe the view that he would rather continue to demonstrate his prowess at Old Trafford, with the colleagues and friends that came with him through United's excellent youth training scheme. Although a Londoner by origin, he is in that sense a Mancunian by adoption and apprenticeship. I am just glad that TV and theatre companies can't adopt the same cavalier attitude to personal liberty with actors and that my present employers - (by the way, I am currently appearing in *Corpse!* – "an excellent comedy thriller" - at the Swan in High Wycombe, seats available at all prices until Saturday!) – can't sell me to another producer who is putting on *Ooh – Er, Where's your Trousers?* Or some other similarly uplifting piece of allegedly comic drama And just imagine the possibilities - Corrie's Ken Barlow on a free transfer to Eastenders. Jeremy Paxman on loan to Blue Peter. I can think of no other area of paid human activity, outside football, where an employee can be flogged off quite so shamelessly. But it is a sign of the extent to which all of sport has become the biggest of big businesses. Where there is such a massive popular appetite for sport in the media and at the turnstile, it is small wonder that business practices – and all that they entail – move into areas that, in the halcyon days of the amateur, would have been unheard of and, indeed, probably viewed with distaste.

Today, Wimbledon Football Club can go to Milton Keynes and yet try to maintain the conceit that it is still Wimbledon Football Club. It clearly isn't. It is now Milton Keynes Football Club, which just happens to employ some of the same people. They should have had the courage to change their name and move on, allowing the people of Wimbledon to have their own club and go forward. They've done it before and who's to doubt that they might do it again. Similarly, and I know that I'll be stirring up a hornet's nest here, Marlow Regatta can only be justifiably so referred to, if it takes place in Marlow. Even if the participants and the race structure are exactly the same, if the Regatta takes place in Eton, then it can only properly be called the Eton Regatta. By insisting on retaining the cachet that a century and more of competitive rowing in Marlow achieved, the town has been deprived of the opportunity of putting on its own regatta again. Although I suppose, given the precedent, they call theirs the Eton Regatta! There may well be very good reasons for the

organisers to wish to move to another venue but they should have the courage of their convictions and change the name too.

31st March 2006

Cheating is in the news. Apparently the internet offers the opportunity to university students to borrow the work of others to incorporate in their essays and dissertations with a little, or in some cases no, tweaking. It has triggered a debate about honesty in all areas of society. Things have moved on since, (and I confess it here after all these years), I cheated in my History 'O' Level all those years ago. I wrote the dates of the two Jacobite rebellions on my wrist. I was clearly incapable of remembering them at the time, although I have never forgotten them since - 1715 and 1745. I think writing them down like that immediately rendered the act unnecessary. Cheating by sportsmen has also triggered the current debate and it is very difficult to persuade young people to be scrupulously honest in their dealings when the common perception is that everyone is at it, so you're at a disadvantage if you don't.

Some sports are plagued by the general suspicion that performance-enhancing drugs are the principal reason why records tumble so frequently, which must be infuriating for the athletes who improve and progress without such artificial aids.

Of particular concern is the appalling upsurge in diving in football. The footballer who rides a tackle and tries to stay on his feet, come what may, is as rare in the Premiership as the footballer who tries to persuade a referee that he was actually not fouled by an opponent that the referee has just unjustly penalised. If that were a frequent scenario, we would not all remember so clearly Robbie Fowler's honest admission that he had simply fallen over and not been fouled, when he was awarded a penalty in that match at Arsenal an amazing nine years ago. And in that case, the referee was so traumatised by the admission, that he obviously thought Fowler deranged and declined to rescind the penalty.

And when that former sporting bastion, cricket, now produces more batsman who remain defiantly rooted to the crease, when they know full well that they are out, in the apparent hope that they will get away with it, then you know that the country is in big trouble. If our young people truly do see footballers as role models, as we are

repeatedly told, then what they are learning at the moment is that if you don't cheat like everyone else, you'll be left out in the cold.

8th July 2005

Winning is in such short supply if you are British in the 21st Century, that the announcement from Singapore that London is to host the 2012 Olympics was doubly delicious. All the more so because, being who we are, we all feared deep down that it wasn't going to happen, however much we talked it up publicly. At Baker Towers the air got a severe punching and Arthur, our dozing Jack Russell, was rudely awakened from his dreams of muddy puddles by the whoops of celebration. I hadn't realised how much I cared.

The boost that it will give to UK sport is tremendous, and the next seven years will hopefully move schools further away from the notion that competition is a bad thing and damages the psyches of young children. Those sports days without races or healthy competition struck despair into those of us who love sport and know how beneficial it can be not just to the individual but to society in general. The boost that the creation of the infrastructure and the upgrading of transport links will give to London in particular and the country at large is incalculable. Even those who are indifferent to sport will now be hard pressed to deny that the legacy of the next seven years of building, preparing and creating the 'best ever games' can only benefit the next generation of citizens and sportsmen and women alike.

We can only hope that the money will also be available to provide facilities for the young people who need them today to reach the standard that will enable them to compete for their country with distinction in 2012. Sports funding for training programmes and facilities must not be allowed to suffer to accommodate the vast investment in stadia, buildings and roads.

And then there is the shameful feelings of satisfaction in beating the French, who thought they had it *dans le sac* and said so a little too loudly. Given that the votes were 54 to 50, one can only fantasise about where the Finnish votes went after those inopportune (opportune?) remarks by Jacques Chirac about British food being exceeded in awfulness only by the Finns', thereby perhaps writing a very definite "FIN" at the end of the French bid. Someone reading

this article will have a child who will be competing at the London Olympics in 2012. I can think of a couple myself. Fantastic!

25th January 2002

I was still terrorising the citizens of Canterbury in my role as Abanazar last weekend, so my wife accompanied my daughters to Adams Park to watch the Wanderers play Cardiff. She hadn't been to a football match since the late 60's, when she regularly went with her grandfather to watch West Ham or Portsmouth. He was apparently a proper football supporter of his era. He watched televised England matches wearing the full kit and brandishing a rattle. Remember rattles? So, it was interesting to hear her impressions of the difference between the footballers of Bobby Moore's era and those of today. The first thing she noticed was the amazing difference in the speed of the game and the distance covered by the players. The level of fitness of today's players was abundantly superior to their baggy-shorted predecessors. She remembered stockier 'blokes' who had time to dwell on the ball and jiggle a little from side to side while team mates jogged steadily into positions where they could receive an eventual pass. The pace of today's game, as viewed from Row C at Adams Park was, by comparison, frenetic, she felt. There was a significant police presence at the match, apparently. Whether it was any more than the usual complement I do not know, but suspect that the influx of Cardiff fans, after the recent events of the Leeds match, may have guaranteed a somewhat tighter scrutiny of the crowds.

However, my family were impressed by the level of commitment of the Cardiff supporters, who despite occupying less than a quarter of the available seating, apparently provided noise and vocal support that belied their inferior numbers. It has long been acknowledged that the Wanderers' supporters are not as vocal as those of other clubs. Indeed, there have been occasions when I have felt somewhat self-conscious when shouting out words of encouragement in the company of my girls, to find those around me looking somewhat surprised. My wife also was amazed by the mass exodus of alleged fans, whilst there were still several minutes of the match left.

The reasons for this are clear. The former practice of allowing the road from the ground to become temporarily a one way only exit has been terminated on the instructions of the police, so it can take up to

an hour to get away after the game. Some are not prepared to pay that price to watch the team they purport to support until the end. Therefore, Chris Vinnicombe has to take a throw-in in the last minutes of the match while the less well mannered amongst our numbers trudge past him with hardly a backward glance; and certainly without any apparent embarrassment. I know it is a sight that is commonplace at every club in the country, but at a small and intimate ground like Adams Park, besides the discourtesy to the players, it becomes even more irritating to anyone in the first few rows who has to peer round their shuffling bodies to see what just might be that last minute equaliser.

So a public plea to all fellow supporters – more vocal support for the lads please and do try to stay to the bitter end and put up with the delay in getting back to *Pop Idol* and Cilla. And couldn't we have our two lane exit back? But my wife's visit does mean that we now have Wanderers pillows cases. Sweet dreams.

2nd July 1999

By the time this edition has hit the bottom of the recycling bin or been used to make papier mache brontosauruses, whether or not Tim Henman managed to fulfil the nation's hopes and expectations will be but a fading memory. We will then be able to get ourselves into a state of excitement or terminal apathy, depending upon our preference, by the doings of our all-batting, all bowling, re-vamped highly motivated national cricket team. Hmmm.

But back to Tim Henman. His customary impassive, controlled demeanour made it somewhat surprising that our clean cut Middle English hero risked alienating half of his natural supporters by characterising women tennis players as greedy because they were seeking parity of prize money at Wimbledon. Irrespective of the merits of the case, anyone who dismisses the quest for equal rights as mere greed is clearly several volleys short of a rally.

The argument that the men play five sets and the women only three doesn't really hack it. They train the same amount; they travel the same amount. The ticket prices at Wimbledon to see their matches are the same. Indeed, I would not be alone in believing that the game played by the women tennis players is very often more entertaining than some of the rally free power tennis played by the men. In most

other spheres of activity it is now accepted that women doing the same job as men should receive equal payment for that job. At the US Open, at that delightfully named venue – Flushing Meadow – the best lady tennis player receives the same prize money as the best gentleman. And although the men only play three set matches in the States, the women say that they would happily play the five at Wimbledon, if that's what it takes to get fair treatment. Good luck to them say I; Tim should perhaps keep his head down for a while and let his racket do the talking. It's taken Richard Krajicek three years to live down his even less thoughtful public utterance that all lady tennis players were fat pigs. Nice one Richard. Doubtless all the Martinas and their colleagues were very sympathetic when you failed to make the second week this year.

I used to fancy myself as a tennis player thirty years ago. My high self-esteem was probably the result of years playing the same person who was the same abysmal standard as me. It evaporated one day in Regents Park. I had been asked by my flatmate if I would play a couple of sets with a 68 year old American who was over visiting a mutual friend and who liked, I quote, to potter around the court for exercise. Somewhat reluctantly I turned up to play with this poor old dodderer, who barely did more than potter for two hours while I slid and crashed around ineffectually in a pool of my own perspiration. My demon serve, of which I was inordinately proud, was patted politely back into the furthest corner of the court relentlessly.

He seemed to know exactly where I was going to put the ball and strolled over to meet it with a flick of the wrist. At one time I began to fear that he might set out a deckchair by the court so that he could relax between strokes. He trounced me 6-0, 6-0. I stammered excuses. He was magnanimous in victory. He sympathised, explaining that he'd only managed to take a couple of games off his good friend Rod Laver the week before. Two sets to love. And one set up!

2nd November 2001
I spent my childhood in Manchester and was a fan of Manchester United, an attachment half a century long, which today, somewhat annoyingly, always has me on the back foot.

"No really, I may live in High Wycombe now but….."

I took my daughters up to Old Trafford a little while ago. Some sixty six thousand people were cheering on the mighty Reds and we were lucky enough to sit a mere dozen rows away from Messrs. Beckham, Giggs and Kean, whose name invites comparison with the great actor. And if only theatre could capture a small part of the excitement, immediacy and involvement of a major football match. At one time perhaps it did. But there is no doubt that the real stars of live performance today are the modern gladiators who strut and compete for us without a script on a stage made of grass. And now, you may well think I am losing my grip but I derive as much, if not in some ways more, pleasure from going down to Adams Park with my daughters on a Saturday afternoon to watch the Chairboys compete with less financial backing, less fanfare and a smaller following in the 2nd Division. We sat by the touch line in the family stand on Saturday and abused the referee roundly when he failed to acknowledge a blatant Swindon handball, penalising our brave lads a moment later for a clearly accidental similar infringement.

We cheered the great goal from Richard Walker and groaned in unison at (an admittedly impressive) equaliser from Swindon, whose fans were small in numbers but great in voice. It is undeniable that the Wanderers' six thousand or so regular supporters are behind their team, but other teams' followers are much more vocal. And after a few times of hearing one's own voice echoing alone across the pitch, you gradually join the silent but intense majority who watch and wait for the opportunity to explode with delight when striker Andy Rammell powers one into the net, or when the best English goalkeeper in this or any division, Martin Taylor, keeps Wycombe in the game yet again.

This week my enjoyment was marred by two armchair know-alls sitting behind me. Only my daughters' certain embarrassment stopped me from wheeling around in wrath to suggest that they could have discussed their tedious theories about football loudly at home without the apparent inconvenience of having to do so surrounded by people who wanted to watch a rather good game of football. When the droning bores left three minutes before the end I wished I had. Clearly the players have better concentration than I do, when streams of grossly discourteous, impatient alleged fans trickle distractingly across everyone's vision in the last few minutes of every

game. The real fans watch till the end and show their appreciation. We are lucky to have a great football team in Wycombe, led by a committed and ambitious team of manager and trainer; they could so easily go on to even greater things than the fairly impressive record they have had over the last decade. But when our frankly far from demonstrative or rowdy fans are unwelcome in our town centre pubs, then I would question whether we deserve the great team we have.

I propose to only frequent pubs that will welcome me in Wycombe shirt. I say,

"Support our team or we won't support you".

15th October 2004

David Beckham's recent activities throw up some interesting moral dilemmas. It is a measure of the former icon's fall from grace in the eyes of our fickle opinion-forming media, that it is not his spectacular goal against Wales that is making the headlines, but his admission of a deliberate foul committed in order to wipe the yellow card slate clean while he is recuperating from the rib injury he sustained earlier. Interestingly, he is now being vilified more for telling the truth than he would have been had he simply done what every other professional fouler has done from time immemorial and performed the verbal equivalent of spreading his arms out wide and assuming a look of pained innocence; just as managers miraculously tend to be unsighted when their own players commit transgressions readily visible to everyone else. Commentators must have been rubbing their hands together like a shoal of piranhas when an overweight buffalo decides that it's time for a wallow (alright, I know piranhas don't have hands – but you know what I mean).

In trying to demonstrate his tactical smarts, the ludicrously tattooed one managed, of course, only to confirm his naivety, but he did nonetheless tell the truth. He owned up – and as a child it was impressed upon me that whatever you did, the repercussions would be considerably less painful if you told the truth. In a game where the professional foul is depressingly common and tacitly tolerated and when players seem to be trying to exchange shirts throughout the game, such is the ferocity of the constant shirt-pulling, for someone to actually own up to a foul is perhaps refreshing. And, of course, this particular foul was not committed to gain advantage in the game or to

stop another player from scoring, it was committed to ensure that the team could benefit from his presence at a future date which, while arguably not in the spirit of the game, is somewhat less unsporting than actually trying to win a game by cheating.

But this is David Beckham of whom we speak, so people who have never done anything in their lives to offer an example to youth, thunder on about his responsibility to set an example, his untold wealth and his lifestyle. I am, I acknowledge, adding to the column miles by commenting on it, but I am weary of the pious moralising of pundits whose columns and airtime would be empty without such a high profile victim to regularly berate.

The whole business of fouls in football needs to be addressed. Why should the team fouled against not benefit from the punishment of a transgressor, rather than the next team faced by the banned player's team. The sin bin works well in other sports and if the foul were to be committed near the end of the match then the player could be banned from playing in the next match played against the same opposition. And while we are talking about sportsmen setting an example... in a sport where the family stand is usually immediately adjacent to the pitch and we are trying to attract a new generation of supporters, why can't the players be encouraged to express their feelings to each other in language more appropriate to a family environment? Ten minutes in the sin bin for each expletive could encourage footballers to convey their meaning more quickly and effectively, by simply eliminating the unnecessary expletives.

3rd September 2004

I spent Tuesday in London contributing to a television programme about sci-fi. Part of the conversation was about fans and their reaction when they get to meet Doctor Who. As I left the studio and started to walk along the Kings Road, I saw a familiar figure coming towards me and experienced first hand the feeling those fans have when encountering me. Most actors are fanatical about some sport or other. Many very successful actors will freely profess that they would much rather have played cricket for England or Ryder Cup golf than achieved any success as an actor. Football is my passion and I have been lucky enough to meet many successful players. A recent highpoint was chatting to David Seaman when we were both guests

on The Generation Game. I recall his amusement when I was so engrossed in our conversation that I failed to notice that Melinda Messenger was standing right behind me and accidentally made contact with the part of her that was nearest to me. But I had never met an England captain – and certainly not one who was manager of Wycombe Wanderers. For it was Tony Adams who was heading towards me, accompanied by (presumably) his young daughter. Coincidentally,   I was on my way to meet my daughters who had been trawling the Kings Road while I was working. Then fan boy took over. I have to say something. I can't miss the opportunity. What do I say? I heard myself saying,

"2-0 yesterday. Well done!" He smiled graciously and said, "Yes, we're doing alright!" and we continued on our separate ways. It was very salutary indeed to have the fan boot on the other foot (and talking of boots, I do hope that they listen to Tony and stop that awful hoofing that we saw in the match against Rochdale).

I had another football experience last week. I went to see Manchester United's home leg against Dynamo Bucharest. On entering the stadium of dreams, I bought a fizzy drink and waited resignedly to have the cap removed from the bottle, as happens at the Causeway Stadium. It wasn't. I explained to the chap I bought it from that at Wycombe Wanders we weren't allowed to have something as dangerous as a bottle top, in case we threw it at the players. He was genuinely perplexed (as I have been for some time, in common with 6,000 or so other Chairboys' supporters, whose profile is demonstrably less pugnacious than that of Fergie's barmy army).

"But a plastic bottle top wouldn't even reach the pitch, let alone do any harm if it did." I could only agree. And I was actually nearer the pitch at Old Trafford than I am in my seat at Wanderers!

The other Causeway ban is on the use of cameras. At Manchester United, the cameras were flashing away all night. If the reason for our ban is to do with sales of photographs, then I would respectfully suggest that the likes of Giggs, Scholes and Rooney are more likely to attract the attentions of the keen photographer than Rhino and Roger Johnson, although I am second to none in my admiration of both of them. And if photo sales aren't the reason, I'm at a loss to understand what is. It can't be the flashes; they didn't seem to bother Alan Smith as he popped a couple into the net.

17. Childhood Memories

I am not sure whether this is common to all people when they reach my time of life – grumpy old git now and doddering old duffer-hood imminent – but I am finding that I think of my childhood more often today than I ever did over the last few decades.

The memories take the form mainly of quite arbitrary snapshots, when something otherwise prosaic lodges in the synapses and stay there forever. Standing in the street in Rochdale; holding my mother's hand as she chatted to friends; collecting dandelions in a yellow tin; playing cricket with my brother; playing 'I-Spy' in the car – a Hillman Minx Reg No LND 39; cleaning the ashes out from the fire; being entrusted with a shopping list and the money and going for the groceries; the horse and cart that delivered our milk and bread daily – and Mr Fairclough the dairyman; the flaking whitewash on the walls of the outside loo – most of the memories are of sounds and feelings but the strongest of all the senses for memories of childhood is smell. The smell of a leather football and dubbin for the boots, of bicycle oil, of my mother's fur stole with the poor fox's head and paws dangling reproachfully at either end (can you imagine that now?), the milkman's horse's breath, mothballs, lily of the valley – the list is endless.

The next few selections are drawn from some of those memories.

26th April 1996

I suppose acting became a part of my life when I was about four years old and my family moved from London up to Rochdale in Lancashire. The move was for the usual reason. My father's company had offered him promotion which entailed what is now known as 're-location' (only then there were no re-location grants! If you wanted the job, you moved.) So I started my formal education in an infant school in a town where cotton mills, clogs, shawls and cobbled terraced streets of back to backs were the norm. To say that it was robust would be a euphemism. It was a land where the natives called a spade a bloody shovel and 'spoke as they found', where a polite,

"I beg your pardon?" if you wanted someone to repeat what they had just said, was countered with the baffling rejoinder,

"I don't boil my cabbages twice."

I had spent my previous four years in Balham, where my mother had been a teacher in an infant school. I spoke with a London accent,

not a cockney one and certainly not the 'posh' accent, which I was instantly accused of having by my peers at Oakenrod Primary. And that really was the name of the school! I was as conspicuously different in that school as a budgerigar would be in a rookery. And with much the same results.

Like all creatures that survive the evolutionary minefield, I had to adapt or perish. After a period of intermittent and painful perishing, I adapted. Bitter experience is a hard but effective teacher. Not having those physical or mental qualities of toughness that might deter my persecutors, I opted for an alternative method. I eased into their accent and way of life and attempted to be invisible. If that was impossible - then I would entertain. But like a chameleon on a tartan, it wasn't always easy. I then learnt that what was acceptable at school was far from acceptable at home. My new 'Ecky-thump, I'll go to the foot of our stair' persona might fool some of the Lancashire Inquisition at School but attracted parental wrath.

So I underwent a change of personality on the short walk home, which had to be accomplished in virtual silence, lest one or other of the factions saw through my disguise and the whole fragile house of cards came tumbling down. Of course having friends round to tea was out of the question. Fortunately that was not as common in those far distant days of baggy shorts and tank tops.

My other problem was that I went to School able to read quite well. My mother was a Montessori trained teacher, so it was to be expected that my young mind had been well and truly stimulated. I learnt from her a love of books which gave me an entree and escape into other wonderful worlds of knowledge and adventure which have never left me. Bizarrely, at a school I went to when I was older, the punishment for failure to bring one's sports kit into School was that you had to spend the afternoon in the library. Yes, the library!

The idea was that we should reel back in horror at the thought of missing the ineffable joy of being twelfth man for the fourth eleven on a muddy field in South Manchester. The threat of being forced into a large quiet room full of books would focus our minds even further. Much like Brer Rabbit crying "No please, do anything, kill me but don't throw me in the briar bush!" I was despatched regularly to the library by the sadistic Neanderthal who taught PE and got regular laughs from his youthful pre-pumping iron fitness fans in my

year by getting me to demonstrate how to use some monstrously high vaulting horse in the certain knowledge that I would come to spectacular grief. But I digress. That need to minimise those qualities which made me a target for violent xenophobes turned me into an actor. When I later worked in a Solicitors' office I became very 'Oh yah' and 'County'. I still find myself attempting to blend into the background. Within hours of being in the States I am talking about sidewalks, faucets and trunks and asking buddies how they're doin'. My success at it should be judged by the fact that I am frequently asked what part of Australia I am from.

4th February 2000

When I was six years old, I was in love with Miss Taverner. She was my primary school teacher and embodied all that a six year old expects in a teacher. She was kind; she was, by whatever standards I then applied to such things, beautiful; and I wanted her to believe that I shared her love of times tables, spelling and punctuation. After I realised that any female other than my mother could be significant in my life, she was, I suppose, my first love affair.

We wind forward a few decades and I am attending one of those events where several hundred are gathered together to celebrate the BBC's most celebrated time traveller in Manchester. A young man tells me that his neighbour, a retired lady named Miss Taverner, believes that she may have taught me in Rochdale many years ago when Everest was unclimbed and His Majesty reigned. My heart and memory surge in recognition at the name of that first and too long forgotten, love of my life.

In truth, I cannot recall her face, which surprises me. But I do recall my feelings. Insofar as a six year old can romanticise about skipping off together hand in hand into the setting sun, Miss Taverner was the designated back-lit skippee. I was also astounded that, all those years later, given the hundreds of runny noses attached to small boys that she must have surveyed, she should associate the middle aged actor, (with let us face it a fairly unremarkable name), with the earnest, bespectacled boy whose short-trousers were held up by a belt with a catch in the shape of a snake. I asked my informant to pass on my recollected devotion and it was only after his departure that I regretted not asking for a contact address. It would have been good

to have the chance to tell someone, who may just have forgotten, that her choice of vocation had been more than validated by at least one grateful pupil. A couple of years later, I met my former teacher's neighbour again and took the opportunity to rectify my earlier omission, only to learn that Miss Taverner had since died. I was gratified to learn that she had been pleased to receive word of my fond memories and childhood devotion. It was partly because of this missed opportunity that I decided to try to make contact with the English teacher whose love of his subject inspired me when I was in my teens. I wrote, care of my old school, and was delighted to receive a reply from "Spike" (a nickname whose provenance is apparently as obscure to him as it is to me). He seemed genuinely pleased, and even bemused, to learn how significant he was in inspiring my love of our language and a continuing wonder at what our great writers can conjure up with it for us. We have now exchanged a couple of letters. I must confess I am finding it hard to use his Christian name in our correspondence, as he requests but I am delighted to report that his flair with words is as undiminished as the sense of humour which singled him out from his more routine and, it has be said, less inspiring colleagues. A good teacher resonates on down through the lives of the children they teach and I was delighted to be able to thank my inspiration for his input that enriched my life. If you were lucky enough to have a similar experience – do the same – I recommend it.

11th March 2005
My late mother used to tell stories of her exotic grandmother who lived in "a big house in Belgravia with footmen and flunkies". As a little girl, living in Stockwell in London, she was occasionally paraded on a Sunday afternoon in her best bib and tucker for her maternal grandmother. She would sit quietly in the corner while the grande dame held forth and demanded to know, as every older generation has from time immemorial, how she was getting on at school. At a school charity auction of promises last year I bid for and won the services of a splendid lady who offered to undertake genealogical research for the successful bidder. I had always casually hankered to know a little about my ancestors, so surrendered what information I had into the hands of this generous archivist and

waited. She achieved a lot in a short time and unlocked the mysteries of a couple of generations on all sides of my and my wife's family.

This stimulated my own curiosity to investigate further, particularly when I discovered that I could get back to the 1830's without leaving home, via the ever-increasing resources of the internet, made available by hundreds of industrious folk who have transcribed the old censuses and records of births, marriages and deaths. I found myself scurrying from record to record in the small hours, following the census entries for ancestors from three generations back, as they moved from place to place; as their children left home and married; and occasionally as the mother and then widow of the family ended up living alone or, on one occasion, as a 'pauper' in the poor house.

I finally found 'great grandmama' after pursuing many red herrings and having to start again from scratch on a couple of occasions. Delightfully, I discovered that the family hailed from Tregony in Cornwall, a village near which my family have holidayed for the last few years and in an area for which we have all developed a great fondness. Could it be in the genes? I was then able to investigate further and unlocked a mystery that my mother was clearly not privy to as a child. Grandmama was in service. Her parents and all her siblings were servants in the homes of gentry.

When my mother sat in awe in the Belgravia mansion, she was sitting in a grand drawing room possibly while the master and mistress were out, perhaps even without their knowledge. We will never know. My mother-in-law, on the other hand, was told as a child of her descent from a family that lived in a castle in Ireland. After my recent discovery, might it be that they were in the dungeons? At least next time I go on tour, I will have a mission – it's the parish registers next!

8th April 2000

I spent last week working in Stoke on Trent – a resort that I cannot honestly recommend for a spring break, unless you have an interest in pottery that cannot be satisfied by opening your kitchen cupboard or visiting your local branch of Crockery-R-Us. Its most significant feature is the fact that the city centre of Stoke-on-Trent is not actually in Stoke-on-Trent, where you might reasonably expect it to be, but in Hanley, another of the cluster of towns crying out for urban renewal

which make up the Potteries. And the theatre is in an area of Hanley flagged, with a commendable community bravado, by those little brown directional signs as – 'The Cultural Quarter.' Ye-es? My stay there was uneventful, until I received a note telling me that one of my former teachers was coming to see the play with his wife.

Being fascinated by that distant and unknown land - the past – I am always willing and eager to re-forge links with my childhood. My feelings, however, were mixed - curiosity mingled with a strong memory of 'Ron' (I shall call him) - the tall, slim, energetic martinet who walked into the Lower 4th Classical and seemed to fix each one of us simultaneously with his gimlet eye. Whether in words or by some mystical process of educational osmosis I know not, but he managed to make it abundantly clear that not only would he not brook bad behaviour by thought, word or deed, but he also expected us all to study Greek until blood poured from our brains.

Consistent failure to reach the expected standard in Ron's weekly tests resulted in trips to the School Prefect (an amiable and somewhat apologetic priest who had to administer corporal punishment in the form of a leather strap). Being not fond of ritually administered pain, I took extraordinary pains, of a less formally applied kind, to ensure that Greek and I were on pretty familiar terms.

Whether my love of language stemmed from his hard sell methods or was lying dormant anyway, I know not. But I became rather good at Greek. It was my best subject probably. But in the decades since, my thoughts of Ron, when they came into my head, were - it must be admitted - not warm. I recognised him instantly. The years had not diminished his stature or radically changed his appearance, but the first thing I noticed was that the eyes were twinkling with pleasure. He seized my hand warmly, introduced me to his charming wife and we went for a cup of tea.

Three hours later I had a new friend. A man who, as a new teacher faced by 35 adolescent boys, had adopted an alien persona that he softened apparently over the years. We were his first batch straight after Cambridge and two years national service. He had received dire warnings about the results of letting the boys walk all over him from other teachers who bore the scars. Ron was a fund of anecdotes.

He shared memories of his own life, of playing football for Oldham Athletic, of his family and of me and my peers. In doing this and

patently being a thoroughly good, dedicated, witty and kind man, he gave me a new perspective on our shared past - previously seen through the distorting mirror of the teenager that was me – for which I am very grateful. We have arranged to revisit my old school together in a few weeks time. Funny old world, isn't it?

12th November 2004

I am, to my wife's resigned irritation, a hoarder, partly on the basis that 'it might come in useful one day' but probably more for deeper psychological reasons. Perhaps I should join Hoarders Anonymous, the acronym of which would be a very appropriate HA! Occasionally the clutter even surpasses my tolerance levels. I recently had a rather liberating clear out of all those useless things that men traditionally get given for birthdays because the donor is desperately trying to avoid the sock\hanky\tie option. We boys are apparently very difficult to buy for. So they go to those shops that only sell things that absolutely nobody ever buys for themself, but which, oddly, they will happily buy for someone else. Seaside towns are full of these emporiums of landfill fodder. A statue of an inebriated golfer with some jovial inscription at the bottom; a plinth bearing a model car with a bonnet that opens to display a rudimentary plastic engine: a pint tankard bearing a 'humorous' non-PC legend; little plastic feet which hold your socks in pairs in the washing machine, so that you don't have that drawer full of single socks whose partners have gone walkies (or is that hoppies?).

Part of my hoarding instinct derives from having a mother who gave away all my childhood toys while I was away discovering myself as a student. This profligate generosity to some charity included my teddy bear every contour of whose loved-to-baldness furry frame I am convinced I would recognise by touch to this day. I am ashamed to admit that (Christopher Robin like), I had temporarily forgotten our halcyon childhood together when I was released into a world offering less passive objects of affection. However, when that novelty wore thin (like Teddy's fur), I returned to claim my old friend and was staggered to be dismissed by a matter-of-fact,

"Oh, I gave him away with all your other toys months ago!"
It is sad that I remember this summary ejection of my most treasured possession more vividly than the undoubtedly countless nurturing

and maternal moments of my childhood. My 'other toys' included my Bayko set – a post war house construction kit using metal rods and plastic bricks, windows etc that I had built up over successive excited birthdays and Christmases. It vied with Meccano to occupy my childhood winter evenings and indeed the latter company eventually bought out Bayko from its original manufacturers. It is because of this ancient loss, therefore, that I succumbed to temptation through that great junk dispersal website eBay recently and have now amassed a quantity of Bayko that probably exceeds the amount I had as a child. My subsequent efforts to impress my 21st Century daughters with the quality and educational value of the less sophisticated toys of yesteryear have so far failed to convince. I guess it's a boy thing.

At the end of January, after my current tour of The Haunted House (Windsor Theatre Royal for the next fortnight) and panto (Nottingham Theatre Royal December and January) I shall discover whether Bayko can revive my childhood enthusiasm. I am not sure whether it is an omen, but I am told that the UK Bayko 'fan club' meets four times a year at Lane End Village Hall, here in Wycombe. Now all I need to do is find that teddy bear. It's only four decades ago – the trail may not be stone cold yet!

18. Treading the Boards

Do you know, I still haven't had time to sit down and build something with all that Bayko that has been sitting in my bedroom cupboard for five years now. But one day I will savour the joy of popping the red roof on top of all those rods with bricks slotted in between and stretchers holding the whole edifice together. I really will.

Until then I am still earning my living by pretending to be someone else most of the time. In the 70's and 80's most of my pretending was done on television. Since then I have returned to the theatre. A common question is "Which do I prefer? Stage or screen?" The usual answer from actors is either "Both" (safe) or "The theatre". The lure of the greasepaint and smell of the crowd and all that stuff. For me, after a prolonged spell of performing in one medium, it is nice to return to the other.

But if I am really honest, I must admit to a very 'unactor-ish' slight preference for working in front of a camera. I love what the Irish call ' the crack' – the feeling of a group of people focussed intently on one moment and co-operating to get it right and then moving on. The theatre has the buzz of a live audience, of course, with all the immediate gratification and feedback that that entails. But there is a different buzz to be had in the knowledge of the mutual support of a whole group of professionals from different disciplines.

I may, of course, give a completely different answer another time, after a particularly uplifting job in the theatre, a medium that has been very kind to me for many years and which has not only allowed me to support my family as they have grown up, but has also given me the additional satisfaction of knowing that countless audiences have derived pleasure and entertainment from what I have done.

6th August 1999

I cannot honestly say that I enjoy watching modern horror films. I have seen *Psycho* a couple of times but there are two scenes that I have yet to see in their entirety – the one where poor old Martin Balsam climbs the stairs in the Bates House and the one in the cellar at the end when Mrs Bates makes her first appearance in the flesh as one might say, although, I gather, not entirely accurately. I was once a guest in the home of some Californian friends who rented a movie for the entertainment of their buddy from Britain, back when the

notion of renting a film to bring into your home to watch was a truly beguiling novelty. Sadly, the film they chose for my delectation was *Nightmare on Elm Street*. I had to ask my hosts' forgiveness and slope off to bed after a very short time. I suspected that if I were to see the whole thing, my slumbers would be troubled by phantasms conjured up by my own uncontrollable imagination and the very cynical manipulation of that susceptibility by the filmmaker. I was cajoled and bullied into watching the rest the following morning and was very glad that I had the rest of the day to forget the bits I actually saw between judicious moments of eye resting.

Alright I am a wimp, I admit it. The *Hammer Horrors* of the sixties and early seventies were a very different kettle of fish. (Why do we say that, by the way? Why not 'tin of newts' or 'box of weasels'? Answers on a postcard to...) Those films had wonderful casts. Vincent Price, Ingrid Pitt, Christopher Lee and Peter Cushing were skilled technicians and absolute masters of their craft. But they chilled, thrilled and spilled blood without leaving a nasty aftertaste and without straying too far down the path of gratuitous graphic detail. Those films were scary, but not so much so as to boost the sales of caffeine for days as the shell-shocked audience attempted to avoid sleep. It has been a great source of regret to me that I had never had the opportunity to appear in a classic horror film, but all that has changed.

This week I have been filming in one of the many Victorian mental hospitals which were vacated when that masterly misnomer 'Care in the Community' discharged its victims blinking and confused into a community which in fact cared very little but wanted their taxes reduced by good old Maggie. The film, called *The Asylum*, is set, (conveniently), - in a disused mental hospital. Various people learn to regret their very good reasons for popping in and visiting its gloomy, doom-laden interior. But good news for those of my delicate sensibilities. Not only is the imperious Ingrid Pitt in the film, but her daughter Steffanie Pitt is carrying the torch of terror for the new generation with her mother's panache and her own star quality. And, it is a horror film made in the old style, where your imagination supplies just the amount of grisly gore that you can tolerate, without relying on an ever more detailed virtual reality wallow in anatomical detail. Fortunately, as my character moves inexorably towards his

particular fate in this truly spooky building (which is soon to be turned into luxury apartments – can you wait?), I am surrounded by an affable crew of seasoned filmmakers.

Were I truly on my own there, it might be a different can of worms (bottle of frogs?).

20th March 1998

Two weeks ago, I opened in Colchester in the play *Kind Hearts and Coronets*, based on the 1949 film of the same name starring Alec Guiness and Dennis Price. It tours the country until mid-July, stopping for the week after Easter at the Swan in Wycombe. You have been warned. Having returned to the theatre after a couple of years' absence from 'shouting in the evening', as my *Doctor Who* predecessor, the late and much missed Patrick Troughton, used to call it, I find myself marvelling yet again at that rare entity called an audience. At the moment that the curtain goes up, a thousand disparate and individual human beings coalesce into a single and quite particular unit, which is palpably different each night. Actors tend to pass each other information about audiences in the wings.

"They're a bit sticky tonight" or "Great house" and even "They hate me, I can feel it!" And occasionally, I regret to say, "There's a real cracker in the middle of the second row!" And however much one tells oneself, "There's no such thing as a bad audience - they've paid their money and if they want to sit in surly and disapproving silence as we give our all to entertain them, then that is their prerogative", nonetheless, you cannot help wondering why something that moved an audience to paroxysms of mirth yesterday will land in their laps like a plate of cold tapioca pudding at a funeral today. One can attempt to analyse the chemistry of the moment. Simple things like someone coughing at the wrong time, the central heating not working or, even worse, working too well, can seriously jeopardise the will or ability of the audience to send those waves of love and approbation that make the performer feel that they are doing their job properly.

It can be very salutary to peep through a chink in the set and observe the audience. It is rare that more than two thirds are giving the play their undivided attention. The rest are hunting in their handbags for that tube of polo mints, scratching, telling their

companion what the actor just said, explaining a joke, sleeping or checking the programme to see if the actor playing the murderer really is the one who was in that awful comedy series about estate agents in Ruislip. When you are playing Shakespeare there are also the people who are following the text with the aid of penlights, in the same obsessive way that some classical music lovers have the score with them at concerts. They are inclined to make exasperated tutting noises when they encounter cuts in the sacred text, which have been made by the director in order to avoid the wrath of paying customers who miss their last bus, if *Hamlet* lasts four hours.

I write these words having just returned from a performance attended by a lady who was suffering, if not from consumption, then certainly from the worst and noisiest cough ever endured by a human being. Clearly the best place to go to forget about her condition was the theatre. Naturally she sat in the front row. Not only is it distracting and frustrating for we humble entertainers, but it is also increasingly infuriating for the rest of the audience, as the paroxysms inevitably reach their pertussive, percussive crescendo at exactly the moment which prevents them from hearing the punch line of a joke or that... "The murderer was ...." COUGH! COUGH!

It happened tonight. My deeply moving death by poison as the 9th Earl of Chalfont was neatly counterpointed by her first sneeze. Not an embarrassed, stifled, furtive atishoo but the full blooded, toupee removing, explosive variety. We briefly toyed with the idea of asking her to join us for the curtain call.

11th February 2000

Someone once said that critics are as much a part of the actor's life as fleas are a part of a dog's. It is certainly true that whenever we take on any role we are exposing ourselves to the possibility that someone will, for reasons varying from outright malice to fair comment, take it upon themselves to pour scorn on our efforts. Many actors adopt strategies to deal with the possible pain of receiving a bad review. Some ask friends to show them only the good or constructive ones. Some refuse to read any interviews at all. Others only read them when the play is long over. Their logic in the latter case is, I must admit, persuasive. Robert Powell, with whom I toured two years ago in *Kind Hearts and Coronets*, felt that his performance was developed in

rehearsal with the director and other actors and, however others might subsequently regard it, it was the deliberate result of painstaking work. He didn't therefore want to be distracted from doing what he thought was right by the subjective opinion of third parties. But I am not made of such stern stuff. I cannot resist nipping to the newsagent the morning after the first night to see what the critic from the Burton on Trent Bugle or the Totnes Trumpet thought of the results of my weeks of rehearsal, sweat, toil and occasional agony. And like any normal human being if the review is good I get a spring in my step and if it's not, my shoulders slump and I begin to question whether or not they might just be right. Ultimately however they all get forgotten, as is evidenced by the fact that to quote a single review I would have climb up into the attic to drag out the box of those old clippings that I have always intend to paste into cuttings books one day.

The only time I ever get cross is if the review is inaccurate, ill informed or unnecessarily personally offensive, like pointlessly referring to the fact that I am not the lean young thing I was twenty years ago. So what? Some reviewers use the opportunity to parade their wit at the expense of the poor performer. And we are easy targets. There is no actor so talented that he cannot on occasion turn in a real stinker. And often you may not be aware of it at the time. But heaven help you, if there is a James Agate or Ken Tynan out there. Fortunately their barbs were directed mainly at performers whose status could survive their vitriol.

But it must have hurt Peter O'Toole, when his infamous and to put it mildly – brave - Macbeth received reviews like "O'Toole staggers round the stage sounding as if he were spitting out words he had inadvertently swallowed." And, "He delivers every line with a monotonous tenor bark as if addressing an audience of Eskimos who have never heard of Shakespeare." At least O'Toole hit back.

"What's all the fuss about? It's only a bloody play. They just didn't get the jokes!" And the ill fated musical "Wham!" received the one word review "Ouch!" My particular favourite appeared in the Denver Post whose critic, one Eugene Field, wrote of Creston Clark's King Lear, "Mr. Clark played the King all evening as if under constant fear that someone else was about to play the Ace!" Small wonder that the playwright Christopher Hampton once ventured that asking an actor

what he thought about critics was not unlike asking a dog what he thought about lamp-posts.

13th June 2008

Sir Jonathan Miller has complained that West End theatres put celebrity ahead of quality. He bemoans the fact that producers won't back ventures that don't have star names. This is in the wake of his recent production of *Hamlet*, which attracted critical praise but not West End producers. There are however currently two other planned productions of *Hamlet*, starring respectively Jude Law and David Tennant. Whilst I sympathise with the frustrations felt by the directors and the excellent but unknown casts of productions praised by critics when they don't get a commercial afterlife, nonetheless that is, (sadly one might argue), the way the theatrical cookie is currently crumbling. However much we who work in it might wish it were otherwise, theatre has to fight its corner in a competitive world and more brave producers have lost money than have ever made millions from putting on plays. Such is the power of television and film that the lure of a star will tempt more theatregoers to leave the comfort and security of their homes. That star may be an actor, even a composer (e.g. Andrew Lloyd Webber) or indeed simply a high profile musical, a genre that currently dominates the West End. Where Jonathan Miller weakens his argument is in his dismissal of both the two star names he has chosen to illustrate his point - as being unworthy of that status - and also of the audience for wanting to see them. He is reported to have decried the fact that the Royal Shakespeare Co. has cast

"...that man from *Doctor Who*" - which if true is rude and dismissive. David Tennant worked with distinction at the Royal Shakespeare Co. long before he achieved his recent television notoriety – and is demonstrably a fine actor. Jude Law, despite being impossibly handsome and a film star has also earned his acting spurs in the theatre. That Miller should so peremptorily dismiss actors who are successful already in favour of his *Hamlet*, Jamie Ballard, who thus far isn't (but may doubtless achieve that status one day if he is as good as Miller claims) surprises me. I once spent an evening in his company and found him charming, brilliant and witty. I am disappointed by his apparent belief that fame and talent cannot go

together. And I promise you it is not just *Doctor Who* solidarity that provokes my defence of David Tennant.

9th March 1996

I am currently touring the country with a musical production of Great Expectations. Being in my first full scale musical has proved interesting. One thing that has struck me forcibly is how seriously understudying is taken. I suppose this stems from the fact that throat infections are common in this country all year round and, whilst you might contrive to croak your way through *Run For Your Trousers Vicar* without damaging the deathless prose too much, it is unhelpful when you're attempting to sing top C's, backed by the Philharmonic Ensemble. Hence, whilst many plays have only nominal understudies who may or may not get the odd rehearsal, musicals tend to employ understudies who are at least every bit as talented as the star or featured players but lacking that elusive lucky break. The show must go on - apparently.

This noble tradition was probably started not by actors, but by those who employ us. But it is deeply ingrained. More than twenty years ago I left my car smouldering on the M4 in order to get to a Saturday matinee at Windsor's Theatre Royal. I had officiated as Best Man at the wedding of a friend. Having done my bit in the Church I had to miss the reception in order to get to the Theatre to give my *Laertes*. As I was driving my Mini Cooper (remember them?) past Slough, there was a loud bang, as something called a 'con rod' went through the side of the engine. The car burst into flames. A very public spirited chap leaped out of his car and rushed up with a fire extinguisher. Having doused the flames, he offered to take me to get assistance. However, true to my calling, I said,

"Forget the car, take me to Windsor. Please!" Bless him, he did. He dropped me at the stage door, with only minutes to spare before curtain up. I thanked him profusely and offered him compensation for his petrol and time etc. When he declined, I offered tickets for the play, as a partial recompense for his Good Samaritan act. He asked what the play was. I told him - *Hamlet*. There was a fractional pause and he uttered the immortal line,

"Ah! No thanks, mate, I'm in the building trade myself!" There really was no answer to that. Meanwhile my car had re-ignited itself

somehow and committed Hari-kari. I subsequently received a bill from the Fire Brigade for their efforts on my unattended vehicle.

The only time I have actually understudied, was in a gentle comedy called *The Holly and the Ivy* in Guildford in 1970. I was in a 'Theatre in Education' group touring schools and youth clubs. For an extra couple of quid a week we understudied whatever play was on at the main theatre. When I returned one Saturday morning from a performance of *Shakespeare - Cabbages and Kings* to a handful of spectacularly uninterested teenagers, I was seized by the Stage Manager and crammed into an ill fitting soldier's uniform.

The regular actor had a septic finger - (Well, really!) - and I would have to go on for the matinee at least, while he went off to the hospital. I had never seen the play. We had had no rehearsal but I had, sort of, learnt the lines. I was introduced to the other members of the cast for the first time and after a flurry of desperate instructions made my first entrance. I recall that my first line was,

"Hello Aunty!" There were two elderly ladies on stage. I took my chance and headed towards one, whose alarmed expression and inclination of the head made me veer off towards the other.

I spent two and a half hours lurching around the stage in erratic parabolic curves. Kate O'Mara, with whom I worked again many years later was in the play and remembers vividly this young actor betraying no outward signs of any concern, ambling through the play drinking other peoples' cups of tea, leaving props in the wrong places and kissing the wrong people. I got through it: I even got one or two laughs - and not just because I made mistakes.

But I was mightily relieved at the return of the regular member of the cast with his lanced and bandaged digit. I am not sure that the adrenalin would have got me through a second show!

2nd March 2007

I am delighted that Dame Helen Mirren's talent has been recognised at the recent Oscars. I have not seen *The Queen* but intend to, despite an ambivalence about films about real people such a short time after the events portrayed. This is particularly relevant in the case of the queen when, by definition almost, no one can truly know what was said or done (let alone thought) in the period the subject of the film. However, the clips that I have seen are sufficient to confirm

for me her status as the most superbly gifted and meticulous performer. Who would have thought that what would at one time have been critically dismissed as a bio-pic would be the vehicle that carried her to the red carpet which she trod with such style that stars three decades her junior could not eclipse her on the night?

Not only is she talented, but she is also one of the most strikingly attractive women in the business, irrespective of age – and she is so old that she is a contemporary of mine. I worked with her once when she was just Helen, in one of her early television appearances after successful seasons at the Royal Shakespeare Company.

It was one of those classic series that the BBC used to make regularly and which are greeted with such amazement and joy these days, *Cousin Bette*, an adaptation of a Balzac novel. I was playing a naïve Polish count and sculptor (I still have one of 'my' bronzes as a souvenir.) The script required that we be caught in bed together by my screen wife as a result of the scheming of the eponymous Bette. The wardrobe department asked me if I would like to wear flesh coloured knickers or go au naturel. I opted for the safety of the former. Miss Mirren, then in her mid twenties, was more adventurous. I have never, before or since, seen more crew on a set, all, of whom with very important things to do, it seemed. I needn't have been so modest. No one even glanced in my direction.

She was then, and seemingly remains, completely uninterested in anything except the quality of the work and being true to herself, which manifests itself in her resolute unstuffiness. I am glad to see that she still maintains that actors are and should be vagabonds. Nice one Helen!

17th December 1999

Pantomime is an extraordinary beast. Most musicals rehearse for at least six weeks and often more. The RSC and National Theatres spend at least that amount of time exploring dysfunctional families and the architecture of balconies in pre-renaissance Italy for Romeo and Juliet. Hmmm. Pantomime, which combines elements of almost all the performing arts, has less time for the minutiae of character development. They invariably open within a week or ten days of the performers' first meeting in a rehearsal room over a cup of coffee. After that the dancers disappear with the choreographer to the

biggest available space in the building and in seven days flat learn up to a dozen complicated dance routines, any one of which would take me a month to have any chance of stumbling ineptly through.

I try to avoid choreography at all cost. It's not just laziness. It is the simple realisation some bodies look graceful in motion under stage lighting and others were meant to remain pretty well static in the corner of a darkened room. The musical director spirits members of the cast off one by one to another cubby hole, where he has set up his all singing, all electric mini orchestra on a pedestal.

Trained singers will discuss phrasing, keys and tempo. I usually share my first ever review as a performer, in a school production of Gilbert and Sullivan's *Iolanthe*. It read "Colin Baker threw himself with great verve into the part of Phyllis and rarely strayed more than half an octave from the note". At the time, I must confess, I was rather proud of that review having but a hazy idea of the precise nature of an octave - half of which was clearly a fairly negligible thing. Whenever enough people available aren't tapping or trilling, what we like to refer to as 'the script' gets some rehearsal. There is not a lot of agonising over motivation. Now, at the end of those few intense chaotic days, I stand nightly in the wings of Wycombe's Swan Theatre, waiting to harangue the unwary and terrify the tiny and I still get that tingle down the spine when I hear the band strike up.

Or the buzz of excitement when I watch a slickly choreographed, upbeat version of *When the Going Gets Tough* during which teenage girls in the audience squeal at the laid back charm of ex-broom cupboard resident - Simeon Courtie. (A Wycombe Abbey contingent were particularly vociferous!) Or see Gary Wilmot, deceptively effortlessly, sing a delightful song with the children; or a slyly droll Brian Cant get the audience involved in a wonderfully slick and silly routine about his hat. Or Lynette McMorrough's fairy-next-door, unashamedly born within the sound of Bow Bells, singing an unexpected and sweetly poignant song from *Chorus Line*; or Richard Cawley's Dame, in the most stunning costumes which he has made himself, doing a Shirley Temple tap that no television chef has any right to have the ability to perform. Or feisty Johanne Murdock's gentle, bittersweet Sondheim number during which even the rowdiest "'E's be'ind yer" audience is captivated and still the best cat I've ever seen in a panto and a Sultan of Morocco who sings like John Hanson. And three

guys and six girls who dance their socks off in the most exciting dance numbers to be seen in front of a panto set for years. What more could you ask for? The drummer who used to play in the Tornados? Well we've got him too!

19th September 1997

I spent the whole of last week in Sunderland being Captain Hook in Peter Pan with a local cast of Lost Boys, Red Indians and Pirates. Like you, dear reader, I was not entirely sure what prompted the theatre to think that the week after the schools returned for the new academic year was the ideal time to present a lavish musical which might be more marketable at Christmas. I would have thought that the last thing on a parent's mind after the long summer break and its attendant drain on the financial resources would be an expensive trip to the theatre; and the schools would not have been back long enough to organise class outings with all the to-ing and fro-ing of letters home with tear off slips and requests for money. It was an unusual experience. Around a hundred local children were involved, most of whom had no previous experience of theatre at all apart from their school nativity. It was certainly a far cry from the financial constraints at Christmas time when a Captain Hook would be hard pressed to muster half a dozen pirates on the Jolly Roger, many of whom would be rather more graceful than one might expect, with rather stylish bandannas and far from muscular sword arms.

The large choruses of pantos of my youth are long gone. There was a recent production of Snow White and the Seven Dwarfs in the Midlands where Doc came on stage with Dopey and shouted off into the wings "You five wait out there".

Last week we had the reverse problem. Despite having two teams of lost boys, it took forever to get fifty of them on and off stage. In the end they were sub-divided again so that half did the first act and half the second. Only their mothers noticed. I encountered one gently sobbing six year old girl 'lost boy' in the wings one night. It must have been a bizarre sight, this six foot, allegedly fearsome, black-wigged villain with a hook attempting to console a waif in sacking. Apparently she had never yet made it onto the stage. Every other performance she had been too frightened.

"But I did all the rehearsals" she added with some pride (justifiable pride too - those dance teachers can be far more frightening than a whole shipload of pirates!). But her mother was in the audience tonight and she was desperate. I eventually found out that the big bang at the end when the bomb goes off was the problem.

We decided that she could sneak off into the wings just before that bit and I told her that when I was waving my hook at the cowering children and haranguing them, I would give her a special wink so that she knew I didn't mean it. I hope no- one in the audience noticed the conspiratorial nod and huge smile she gave me in return. It is undoubtedly salutary to an old cynic like me to work with children. One cannot help but remember the enthusiasm of my own youth with affection as well as the odd cringe. The other side of the coin is of course that I was always on the receiving end of some very forthright questions and comments.

"How old were you when you used to be an actor?" asked one young pirate, chillingly. Another absolutely insisted that I was related to Tom Baker, even after I had repeatedly denied the fact, because he "had read it in the papers." I winced at, "My grandma used to watch you on telly!" And the most wounding of all was from a Red Indian who came to my dressing room for an autograph, and on spotting a picture of my wife on the table asked,

"Is that your daughter?" I really shouldn't have told my wife about that one.

15th March 2002

For many years the acting profession managed perfectly well without directors. Leading actors would undertake that function themselves, deploying the rest of the cast in suitably non-distracting positions around them, with a view to stealing the limelight for themselves, literally and metaphorically. Directors have been a very recent phenomenon in terms of the history of theatre.

It is undoubtedly beneficial to any play to have a common approach and a detached view of where the focus should be at any particular time. It is no good if Hamlet is playing it for laughs and Claudius is going for the tragedy. It is also useful to have someone out there to arbitrate and stop powerful actors from overwhelming those who are less dominant, and to orchestrate movement and

positions on the stage. However, the director has achieved an importance that perhaps wasn't envisaged when the first actors employed one to help them put a play on. Now the director chooses the actors, rather than the other way around (except in the case of very big stars who can pick and choose). A director too will also often have a very strong idea of how he sees a play, which may be at variance with the author's original intentions. In the case of someone like the great Peter Brook, this can produce wonderful ground breaking creations like his circus version of Midsummer Night's Dream, which may not have been at the forefront of Shakespeare's mind when he wrote it, but one cannot doubt that he would definitely have approved. But geniuses like Brook are as rare.

The leather clad biker Julius Caesar I once endured in Yorkshire would not have delighted our Will, any more than it did the audience. And many directors in search of a reputation have visited similar indignities on actors and audiences alike. Too many of them feel the need establish their place in theatre by being different for the sake of it, with no regard to the play, the actors or the audience. An even greater crime, in my book, is the director who fails to see that actors perform better if they are encouraged to do what they can do rather than bullied. These are the 'destroy to recreate brigade', who take no prisoners in their march to critical acclaim. The ones who major in theory and doctrine and have zero man management skills. They try to impose their will on the actors and invariably have whipping boys, usually the least confident member of any company. They exist throughout society, of course, in entertainment, business and education. Their 'vision' (that much abused modern mantra) is paramount and they see their position at the top of the pecking order as a licence to bully others into serving their vision.

But actors are no different to salesmen, factory workers or teachers. They produce their best work if an environment is created in which they feel valued as professionals, supported and encouraged. It's basic stuff, you may think, but it's amazing how often it is overlooked by those who talk a storm about vision but can't actually see what's happening in front of them. For me the skill of the director lies in directing without seeming to do so. The very best directors can often be the ones whose input during the rehearsal period is minimal but who have a particular talent for casting well.

19. The Mundungus Chapter:
Phobias, Dreams, Fags, Phones and Loo Rolls

Grouping my articles into nice, comfortable chapters was always going to be a challenge for any compiler. The titles could easily have been Rants, More Rants, Ranting Again (get the picture?) or Guess What Happened To Me This Week?

In any house some items defy easy storage as they don't quite qualify as being similar to much else and end up in what someone I knew many years ago called their 'Mundungus Room' – I have never known whether this was a creation of their own or was borrowed from somewhere in fiction and it was long before J. K. Rowling invented the character of Mundungus Fletcher in Harry Potter and the Half-Blood Prince. I have just looked up the word and find it defined as 'stinking tobacco' 'tripe' or black pudding'. All of these are, I suppose, things that some people don't know what to do with – so I have now adopted the word to describe the content of our next selection.

25th April 2008

There was a story in the media this week about a lady in Waterlooville who suffers from koumpounophobia. I am not sure who devises the names of all the new phobias recognised every year or, indeed, whether they have the approval of the Oxford Dictionary, but this is the name that we are reliably informed (well, in a national newspaper?) describes an aversion to buttons. Why we can't call the condition 'buttonophobia', I have no idea.

However, before we look askance at such a bizarre aversion, I must share with you that I have a relative who shares this phobia. She has brought up her children struggling with nausea every time she has had to deal with her children's school clothes. It has, in fact, been suggested that the phobia could be rooted in an association with school uniform for those who found school less tolerable than the rest of us. The zip and Velcro mercifully provided her with options for clothing for everyday use. In every other respect, my relative is as unremarkable and sane as you and I, insofar as those descriptions can accurately be applied to anyone. An enormous number of us have phobias and aversions that others do not share and therefore find strange. I have struggled for years to remain calm while daddy long legs, those poor aimless, inoffensive creatures, are blundering around

me. I even know when the problem started. As a fourteen year old, I accompanied my parents to the cinema to see James Stewart in 'Rear Window.' Being a Hitchcock film, it delivered fear and suspense without ever showing the murderer dismembering his victim.

As I lay, still terrified, in my bed that night, there were half a dozen daddy long legs dancing around in the yellow street light that spilled in across my bedroom ceiling. I have associated them with a feeling of dread ever since but have, thank goodness, succeeded in suppressing that feeling. Having children can help. By the time I had removed a few of the fluttering spindle-shanks from my daughter's infant bedrooms, my anxieties diminished to tolerable levels. Clearly my fears, being based in identifiable origins, were less crippling than those others have, though that does not always apply. So before we deride the ludicrous fears of others we should perhaps walk a mile in their shoes. Unless, of course, we suffer from ambulophobia or podophobia.

20th January 2000
One day the occupants of those alien space craft that have been keeping careful tabs on us for the last few short millennia will finally decide to make contact on a more formal "Take me to your leader" basis. There must come a point when they are no longer satisfied to show themselves only to people that no-one would ever believe – (which I guess is most of us) and decide to come out of the ethereal closet. When they do, I suspect it will be because they will be consumed with curiosity about certain peculiarities of our behaviour for which no casual, objective viewer could ever find a credible explanation. Indeed, some of these idiosyncrasies of our self-styled civilised world are inexplicable even by our own misbegotten standards. Were I the grey, hairless hominid with the tear drop head and big dark eyes depicted in the X-files, even after aeons of observing our ever exploding population, (and indeed our population exploding everything), one of the great imponderables would be - why do we apparently have a need for pretty patterns on our toilet paper? Why do we use our finite and dwindling natural resources to bleach and then add swirls of colour to paper tissues in order to then consign them to an unceremonious fate? Likewise kitchen roll. Do we really have to look at a pastel floral motif as we use the stuff to mop

- 239 -

up the evidence of the baby's antipathy for apples and custard or the dog's disinclination to go out on a cold night? And if our extraterrestrial visitor were interested in studying our computer software, he would acquire it in a disproportionately large, garish and enticing cardboard box containing another cardboard construction within which nestles a shrink wrap encased plastic case carrying the CD containing the programme. Explain that to a bemused alien, if you can. And it will know, as we do, that the population of our planet in the backwaters of the Milky Way has now exceeded 6 billion.

It took many thousands of years for the evolved homo sapiens to number 1 billion, in 1804. A mere 150 years later there were 3 billion of us. Every year the human race is increasing by a staggering 78 million, many of whom are users of toilet paper. Despite the fact that that in 61 of the world's 91 countries, the birth rate is mercifully dropping below the population replacement rate, barring natural or man made cataclysm, by the year 2050 the world will contain 12 billion consumers. And we continue to consume the planet's resources as if we were just passing through Planet McDonalds before moving on to somewhere more interesting.

We allow ourselves to be hoodwinked by manufacturers into accepting a culture of rampant profligacy. They want us to replace rather than repair. The future is disposable. Apparently. And how would Fox Mulder go about explaining to a superior entity the logic behind one of the greatest and most arcane mysteries of all? Why are envelopes manufactured with those little parallel slits in the flap, at right angles to the gummed edge? Go on – have a look. Could it be that the manufacturers don't want us to be able to re-use the said envelopes by carefully opening them and removing the contents?

Can there be any other possible explanation? Of course, any business will work to maximise sales. But surely it is morally indefensible to sabotage your own product in order to reduce its usefulness to the consumer and force us to buy more. Let's hope our alien visitors are not too judgmental.

31st October 1997

Ten years or so ago a very good and close friend stormed angrily out of my house when I did not give the answer he expected when, as he opened a packet of cigarettes, he asked us if it was okay to smoke.

He had recently taken it up again after having given up for many years and was the only smoker in the room. When I replied that I would prefer that he did not smoke, he was outraged, exploded from the room trailing colourful expletives behind him and left his embarrassed wife to make placatory noises on his behalf. He returned an hour or so later still somewhat aggrieved but ready to discuss the rights and wrongs of the situation. He still saw me as a less than generous host however. We are still good friends all these years later and he is now a non-smoker again. This was an isolated incident, but it raised important issues even then, when we were less aware of the now demonstrably harmful effects of passive smoking.

I have always felt that when some people ask,

"Do you mind if I smoke?" they think that the question is as ritual as the "Does anyone know of any reason why this couple should not be joined in holy matrimony?" one asked in the wedding ceremony.

It would clearly be inappropriate to leap up and say,

"Well I do actually. They are totally unsuited - he is a lazy, feckless, drunken oaf with all the personal charm of a multiple axe murderer and she is a frightful slapper well known by regulars at The Firkin and Gusset". Tempted though many have been in the past, it is certainly not what is expected. However, asking if it's okay to smoke is surely a question that might reasonably evoke a response in the negative or affirmative. Otherwise why ask the question? The mere fact that most smokers do tend to ask if it's alright as they take the fag out of the packet implies at least an acknowledgement of the suggestion that their addiction might just have an adverse effect on those around them. We have got to stop being so nice, so understanding and so British. If someone visiting your home asked permission to roll up their trousers and stick a syringe full of hard drugs into their scarred leg, most of us would feel compelled to try to persuade the other person to think again. And yet, perversely, there is no apparent chance of that incident of drug abuse immediately and directly imperilling the health of the third party. Tobacco is also a drug, but it has evolved as a part of western culture since a time long before we were able to assess the dangers of its use. It is therefore traditionally less unacceptable. But the evidence that passive smoking is injurious to health is now overwhelming. The research recently published by the Wolfson Institute for Preventive Medicine is clear. Non-smokers

who live with smokers have a 23% increased risk of heart disease and a 26% increased risk of lung cancer, whether the smoker consumes ten or sixty cigarettes a day. Children of mothers who smoke suffer 70% more respiratory illnesses. The statistics continue along those lines and are frightening and simply beyond argument. Tessa Jowell, the minister for public health has promised action to promote more smoke free public places. We all owe it to ourselves, our families and our friends to be uncompromising in our attitude to smoking in our homes, schools and workplaces. The unreconstructed smoker who lights up with a cheery "Rules are made to be broken" is not an amiable eccentric; he or she is no less antisocial than the drunk who urinates in doorways. Smokers undoubtedly deserve our sympathy as addicts, but not our tolerance at the risk of our own lives.

4th July 2003

If you would like an article this week about the proposed ban on foxhunting, please press 1. If you would like to hear my views on the inadequate funding of education in Bucks, please press 2. If falling standards of politeness and respect for others, in all areas of life, concern you, please press 3. If you wish to discover what happened to me when I took part in Top Gear this week, please press 4. Depressing facts about waiting times in hospitals? Press 5; or for details of the service that GP's would like to provide but cannot because of contract and funding issues, press 6. If Tim Henman's Wimbledon has given you palpitations and anxiety attacks, press 7. Sick of speed cameras being located where they will gather revenue, rather than reduce accidents? Press 8. And if you would cheerfully consign every multiple choice telephone answering system and its inventors to oblivion, press 9. You have pressed 9. If you would like to boil the perpetrators and their automated torture devices in oil, press 1. If you would prefer to drop them into the fires under Mount Doom, press 2. If they should be compelled to watch Kilroy for eternity or share an office with a writer of codes of practice and policies for the advancement of political correctness, press 3.

Get the picture? If you don't, you have the patience of a saint, enjoy listening to canned music and are probably certifiable. This week, my super all-singing, all-dancing new fridge broke down after just over a week. I have always coveted a fridge with the ice and

chilled water dispenser in the door. As a birthday present to myself, I cajoled my long-suffering wife into allowing this admittedly vast item into our house. 'American style' is synonymous with big! It stopped dispensing on day 10 and displayed a fault code on its mini-screen. The instruction booklet written, of course, in badly translated Korean, warned of dire consequences if I disconnected it, after 'the showing of message of error.' I obeyed. I telephoned the electrical retail store in Wycombe. Or rather - tried to. These chain stores don't have phone numbers any more. They have call centres.

Eventually, I manoeuvred my way through a comparatively short series of options to a human voice somewhere in the North of England, who took my details, issued a repair authorisation number and told me to ring their repairers. I rang the number he gave me. Once again I entered a multiple-choice labyrinth. "All our operators are busy." I waited fifteen minutes before being cut off the first time. Then twenty minutes. Finally, fifty minutes after starting my ear heating activities, I was informed that I had been given the wrong number – they didn't repair my make of fridge/freezer.

Another half hour of multiple choices and synthesised music loop resulted in an appointment for the following day. A very nice man came, disconnected my fridge, reconnected it and it worked. He didn't know what the error code meant but told me I had done the right thing and shouldn't risk turning off the power myself if it happened again, as it might void the warranty. And don't get me started on banks and their call centres. I received a letter this week about changes in bank charges. If I needed any further help I was urged to call my 'Relationship Manager'! Ice anyone?

9th January 1998

I was raised in Rochdale in Lancashire. Perched on the edge of the Pennines; it was a typical post industrial revolution town, which then still had flourishing cotton mills. I recall on dark, winter mornings, seeing the sparks struck off the cobbles by the metal plates on the tips of the mill workers' clogs and their coats speckled with the white cotton. Rochdale's main claim to fame was the fact that the Co-operative Movement started there and that it produced Cyril Smith, Lisa Stansfield and most notably Gracie Fields (whose real name, coincidentally, was also Stansfield).

It was not the obvious place to find a flourishing theatre, but as a child I was privileged to see many splendid shows at the Theatre Royal - a gilded Victorian gem in the style of its namesakes in Windsor or Brighton. Imagine my shock, therefore, when one morning on the way to school; I beheld this magical place in smouldering ruins. The fire that reduced the theatre to ashes, also destroyed Semprini's white grand piano and Tessie O'Shea's outrageous wardrobe. Contemporaries will know the magnitude of those variety stars in the early fifties. I had no desire then to become a part of that glittering world myself; indeed to be honest, it would never have occurred to me that it might even be a possibility.

At that time, the ownership of a television set or a car were sufficiently lofty ambitions. But my few excursions into that world, where after the lights had dimmed and the last chords of the overture faded, all things were possible for a few hours, left me with the abiding certainty that theatres were 'a good thing'.

Several decades later, sadly, theatres are struggling to survive in many towns and cities, but it is a tribute to the people of Wycombe that they have understood the contribution that live theatre can make at the heart of a community. The Swan is a vital part of the heart of our town, which in many ways resembles the town of my childhood, being approximately the same size and population and enjoying a similarly rich and diverse ethnic and cultural heritage. In many places, when town centre traders suffer from the effects of the combination of out of town superstores and the lack of convenient in town parking, it is often the Theatre that helps to keep the streets alive until the latest occupants of the Town Hall recognise the vital need to breathe life back into town centres.

Yes, of course, television and cinema have had an impact on theatre attendance, as has the perceived threat of unsafe streets at night, but just as the cinema has had a renaissance in the last generation, so too could the Theatre, - but only if enough of us value and support the importance of all those activities that lift the human spirit and illuminate, in creative and inspiring ways, what it is to be a human being. The things we value the most, and which define us in the eyes of the world at large, are our spiritual and creative aspirations. These are indeed what set us apart from animals that simply feed, reproduce and die. Whatever political relationship we have had with other

countries over the centuries, our lives has been vastly enriched by the work of the composers, painters and writers of, for instance, Germany, Italy, France and Russia. Arguably, our pre-eminent contribution has been in the area of drama. Shakespeare is better known world-wide than Churchill, Newton or Henry VIII. Alan Ayckbourn's name will endure when Rupert Murdoch, Ian Paisley and Neil Hamilton occupy paragraphs of varying size in the history books. Imagination and creativity are what set us apart from the beasts. Deprived of the possibility of exploring the human condition through art, civilisation would soon unravel.The Swan is not a luxury.

5th April 1997

Every life is littered with unfulfilled dreams and broken resolutions. I, for instance, have still not taken up the piano. When I was thirty, I was assured it was not too late to start lessons and that I might still reasonably expect to be able to play a passable tune one day. When I was forty, it apparently still wasn't too late. Indeed, I would probably benefit from the extra motivation and focus that middle age can bring, despite the decreasing digital mobility. I am no longer either of those ages and, as all my contemporaries will recognise, free time is at even more of a premium. And nodding off whilst watching television is considerably less hazardous to the health than doing so at the keyboard of an upright piano.

My other daydream is that one day I will become a gardener. I relish the notion of strolling out into the garden at sunset and savouring the aroma of honeysuckle as I pass through my immaculate pergola, past the topiary scenes from Shakespeare and into a neat and formal rose garden on my way to pick some mint and borage in the walled herb garden for the evening Pimms. This dream contains no flies, wasps, green fly or visits to my osteopath. It includes no perspiration or backache. It has no truck with compost, mulching or mud. It might extend to a little gentle weeding or even hoeing to the strains of Elgar's Cello Concerto which is wafting out from the house and mingling with the gentle tinkling laughter of my clean and happy children as they play grandmother's footsteps on the clover free, lush, cropped lawn. Wake up Colin, it's time for your medicine! My dream, of course, fails to address the question of how the sloping uneven expanse of flinty clay covered in mowed green stuff that passes for

grass, though certainly not lawn, is transmogrified into this bucolic idyll. One method employs the modern version of Capability Brown - perhaps we shall call him Improbability Green - and would involve the expenditure of sums of money of Lottery proportions.

So Improbability will have to wait in line behind the notional builder who is going to provide me with a study and turn what we are pleased to call our conservatory into, well, a conservatory, - rather than the imperfectly glazed lean-to which it currently is; the lawyer who will reclaim the hugely disproportionate sum of money which I foolishly paid to a builder who sadly was not notional; the plumber who will put in the high pressure, state of the art shower for which I yearn; the white goods purveyor who will supply me with one of those vast vulgar American refrigerators with (oh such luxury) a tap in the door that dispenses iced water - the list is endless.

The other route to my rural nirvana would involve the use of my all too resistible force in a lengthy struggle with the irresistible object that is the Baker acre. To do that I would have to first of all get fit or risk doing my protesting skeleton irreparable damage. Perhaps the gym... oops, nurse, he's dreaming again. Until then, every spring I see that the grass effect substance which defies me to call it a lawn is in need of attention. I take the key down to the shed that houses my decrepit 'ride-on' and waste a few moments ruing my folly in failing to get it serviced during the winter and then I attempt to start the wretched thing. Two hours later I hurl into the holly hedge the adjustable spanner that persistently belies its name. Having done all that the amateur mechanic can with WD40 and a few inadequate tools to persuade what seems to be a ludicrously rudimentary engine to fire into life, I phone the mower man, that guru of the seeker after stripy lawns. I am needless to say the hundredth love-lawn depressive to phone him since Easter. It might be a fortnight before he can get to me. "But by that time the grass will be too long to cut!"

"Well, of course, your old Lawneezie Powerglide ZX isn't really man enough for your patch. What you really need is the Stradling Hoffer side chute model with extractor fan and 40 inch scythe cut capability."

"How much are they? Ah... join the queue... have you met my friend Improbability?"

20. Old Sixie

Well you would have been surprised, delighted, appalled, relieved or disappointed had there not been a Chapter on you-know-Who, wouldn't you? (Delete as appropriate).

I suspect that had the Tardis passed me by as I hitch-hiked my way through my career, then the likelihood is that I would not have attracted the interest of the editor of the Bucks Free Press when I wrote to him all those years ago. I would like to think that the content of that letter was so ground-breakingly original and witty that he could do no other than solicit my immediate assistance in increasing the circulation of his newspaper, but the stark truth is probably that the letter was probably okay to interesting but emanating from a lapsed time lord elevated it in the interesting stakes a tad.

That's fine by me. I have always grabbed every opportunity that has been offered to me to expand my horizons as well as my means of earning a crust, together with the rest of the loaf if I can. I am a Baker after all.

I had the best of all possible times working on the show, even though it was struggling to maintain its foothold at the BBC during those years, despite the best efforts of my late and much missed friend, as he soon became, the producer John Nathan Turner. I was in fact completely unaware of the undercurrents that were going on during my time as 'Old Sixie' as I like to call my incarnation of the good Doctor.

It was only towards the end of my three year tenure of the role that I came to learn of dissension in the production office and the lack of support from on high.

I just loved for a brief time being one of very few people in the country who could chat to children in the street without worrying about that being misconstrued.

19th January 1996

It seems that the much heralded American version of *Doctor Who* is finally becoming a distinct possibility. Since 1989, when the programme was last made, there have many rumours, some based on reality and others seemingly emanating from the more fanciful excesses of bored copywriters. Various names have been announced by the press as the new Doctor, including Eric Idle, Simon Callow, Jonathan Price, Alan Rickman and John Cleese - in fact every English actor familiar to wider American audiences except Charlie Chaplin and Hugh Grant - for very different reasons!

But it was recently announced that the American giant film and television corporation Universal has commissioned a one off exploratory special in conjunction with BBC Worldwide, which is the BBC's marketing arm. A British born producer, Philip Segal, has been put in charge of the project and is reportedly keen to preserve the essence of the programme that made it so popular for thirty years whilst ensuring that the benefits of big budget expertise bring the programme up to the higher production standards possible as we approach the millennium.

Of course, those of us who remember with great affection those first black and white episodes in 1963 starring the late William Hartnell are wary and concerned. A large amount of the appeal of the programme stems from its long and cumulative hold on the imaginations of the British family audience dating back to the exciting beginnings, when it was truly ground breaking stuff. Everyone under the age of 45 remembers hiding behind a sofa when the Daleks or Cybermen appeared and the companion screamed at the end of an episode.

We watched with dismay tinged with curiosity when Patrick Troughton became the regenerated form of the Doctor. Never has there been a more brilliant device for capitalising on the essence of a programme and ensuring its longevity. Because Patrick did such a remarkable and inventive job of characterising the second incarnation of the Time Lord the long term future of the programme was secured. I strongly believe that both the audience and his successors in the role owe him a massive debt of gratitude for that. Without his genius, I probably wouldn't be writing this article.

For reasons beyond the merely personal, I have much regretted the absence of the programme from our screens. Until recently it was a pleasure to watch succeeding generations of children discover the thrill of terror, mingled with anticipation at the sound of the familiar theme tune that accompanied the opening titles. You can actually deduce someone's age, when they tell you who their favourite Doctor is - because, in the case of the average viewer, it is the one they first saw. Alas, there is now a whole generation of under 10s that do not have their own Doctor. For my children, it's just a programme that their Dad was in, in a dim sepia past before recorded time began! And watching videos does not replace the thrill of a whole week of

fevered expectation and longing. How will the Doctor escape from the jaws of death? Will that stupid girl ever stop screaming? Why do all the corridors/passages/tunnels look the same? Will the set fall over? Even though the purists may tremble at the thought, it may just be that the fallow years will result in a regeneration of the programme as well as the Doctor. Of course, we all hope that the Police Box Tardis, the eccentricity of the main character, the Daleks and the Master will all play their part, but let us wait in hope rather than despair. I have been asked by more journalists than I can count over the last week for my advice to Paul McGann who has been announced as the 8th Doctor. I would not presume to offer advice to someone who has repeatedly demonstrated himself to be a very gifted and charismatic actor. If the film were being made in this country I would only recommend a close study of the filming schedule and insistence on a costume appropriate to the likely weather conditions. My particular multi-coloured monstrosity did at least have the benefit of being warmish in the Arctic conditions in which we usually filmed in the remote clay pits that passed for alien landscapes.

My only other advice would be to enjoy every minute of being part of the living legend that is the Doctor. I did.

24th May 1996

As I was leaving my house on Monday for a heavy session with the dentist, the telephone rang. It was Radio 5 asking me for a live comment on their news programme about the death of Jon Pertwee. There is no easy way to hear about the death of a friend, but a phone call from a BBC researcher wanting a quick sound bite is not amongst the least worst. I agreed to say a few words because I wanted to publicly mark and mourn the passing of another of that rapidly passing generation of entertainment greats. I left for the dentist which suddenly seemed less daunting and found myself following a transporter with three blue portaloos on the back. They looked just like three Tardises. Jon was the third Doctor.

I turned on the car radio to hear Bernard Cribbins being interviewed about his time working on a *Doctor Who* film with Peter Cushing. It was an extraordinary and poignant combination of events. As can be imagined from the wonderful roles and voices he has created, he was a fascinating man with a seemingly unending fund of

colourful stories from his early years in variety touring the Halls. Only a couple of months ago he came to see me in *Great Expectations* in Birmingham and he, Darren Day and I went out together for a splendid Chinese meal. Darren is currently hot news because he is about to open in the stage version of Cliff Richard's Summer Holiday. But, unlike many of his contemporaries, Darren knew class when it was in front of him and sat rapt as Jon told us about his first appearance as a stand up comic in Glasgow. He had gone on early in the evening and given his all in total silence, leaving the stage to the deafening sound of his own feet. He went to the theatre manager and conceded defeat, expecting to be paid off and find himself jobless for the rest of the week. In the event the manager expressed his surprise that the young Pertwee had done so well. This unexpected reaction was thrown into sharp perspective when Jon heard the audience baying for the blood of the rather better known and more successful comic who had followed him on to the stage. The latter was obliged to dodge missiles and torn up seating as he left the stage, half way through his act and headed straight for the station and the next train home to civilisation. Different generations will have different memories of the diversity of Jon's talent. Those older than me (yes there are some!) will remember him as a comedian and man of a thousand voices on the stage and in radio comedy. My memories are of Sunday lunch times in the early 60's listening to the wireless - The Light Programme -to CPO Pertwee in *The Navy Lark*, which with *Educating Archie* and *Round The Horne* were highlights not only of the week but of broadcasting history. Another generation will remember his *Doctor Who*. Against everything one might expect of a man renowned for character voices and madcap humour, he was determined to play the Doctor as an idealist and man of action, with only the occasional flash of the wicked humour of which he was so capable. His height and marvellous physique were accentuated by the patrician head which was crowned, even at 76, by a wonderful mane of white hair. He exuded charisma, knew it and revelled in it.

Yet another generation were captivated by *Worzel Gummidge*, the scarecrow whose wonderfully selfish personality and bizarre lifestyle gave him ample opportunity to demonstrate his prodigious vocal skills. It was a constant amazement to many of us and, indeed disappointment to him, that Worzel had such a comparatively short

run on our screens. I have seen him dressed up as Worzel and enthralling children who had never seen him on the screen. It would be a fitting tribute if someone in the corridors of broadcasting power saw fit to repeat the *Worzel Gummidge* series. I know my children would love it. To coin the words for which Jon was famous amongst *Doctor Who* fans - words which he always unashamedly substituted for the complicated technobabble in the script if he had difficulty remembering them - I wish we could "Reverse the polarity of the neutron flow" and bring him back to us.

17th August 2001

I have been privileged to share my views in this column (or one much like it in Freetime), for just over six years now. I am surprised to discover, given that topics leap to the pen less easily some weeks than others, that I have never in all that time written about the television programme with which most people associate me.

I will therefore use the opportunity of the publication of a new book about cult television programmes to do just that. Last week, it was that which we all already knew deep down was confirmed in the Penguin TV Companion. The nation's favourite 'cult' television programme is *Doctor Who*. It rose above *Fawlty Towers, Star Trek, The Prisoner* and other strong candidates for Top of the Cults. In his book, Jeff Evans defines the word 'cult' as something that, 'sets fads and fashions, generates merchandise, inspires fan clubs and conventions and pervades the national consciousness to some degree'.

Now, I'll acknowledge a certain bias, but would still argue that the adventures of the good Doctor have done all those things, with the possible exception of the fashion bit. Unless you happen to be at a *Doctor Who* related event you're unlikely to see many people trailing scarves and toothy grins in midsummer or sporting question marks on their lapels. There were several of each however at Longleat last weekend. It is amazing that a programme that has been off air since 1989 can still attract literally hundreds of people to turn up at Longleat to visit the *Doctor Who* exhibition there and meet up with some of the actors. I joined two companions of the wonderful and greatly missed Patrick Troughton, the second incarnation of the Doctor - the lovely Anneke Wills and Fraser Hines, whose knobbly knees peeked shyly out beneath a kilt as Jamie McCrimmon long

before he graced our screens as Joe Sugden in Emmerdale Farm. (Remember when that show had two words in its title and muddy boots?) It was wonderful to see how many young people had discovered the Tardis and its disparate and evolving crew, when many of them were far too young to have seen the show when it was originally broadcast. More than a decade after the BBC aired its last episode there are still enough followers to justify a comprehensive BBC website and innumerable conventions and signings through out the year. And the Beeb still jealously guards its property.

Many production companies have spent long hours and months putting together applications to make the programme only to have the plans founder, when someone at Shepherds Bush adopts that good old attitude "If you want it that much, maybe we should hang on to it a bit longer." So yet another generation is denied the opportunity of having their own special Doctor and hiding behind the sofa when a sink plunger edges into view bent on extermination! Most people can name a few of the Doctors. I wonder how many of the millions who phoned in to vote will be able to name one of the *Big Brother* contestants twelve years from now.

If a half hour programme that was shown intermittently on Saturday evenings can still command a following a decade after its last episode was aired, then it must have been doing something right. I wonder if my children will ever hide behind the sofa.

29th March 2005

I watched the first episode of the new *Doctor Who* with a mixture of delight and ruefulness. Delight because it is precisely the mix of innovative creativity and connection to the past that the future of the programme needed. Christopher Eccleston is absolutely spot-on.

He looks splendid; that's the costume I would have liked – black leather jacket, black tee shirt - although, I must admit it probably looks better on him. He has just the right mix of humour, passion, quirkiness and single-mindedness to provide the dynamo that is necessary at the centre of the programme. Billie Piper too is an unexpected revelation and has made the perfect start.

And the writing, special effects, filmic style and 'look' have been pitched at precisely the right level. All of which has contributed to a whole fresh and inspiring feel to the programme. A new audience

could not fail to be gripped and I believe that a significant proportion of the old loyal diehards will find enough that is familiar to be carried along for the ride, with a smile. Ruefulness? I would have loved to have been playing the part when all that was possible.

On behalf of my children and their contemporaries, thanks are due to the executive producer and writer Russell T Davies for having the vision to prove what we all knew – that there was life in *Doctor Who* yet. In addition he had the essential tenacity to bring all the disparate creative and administrative strands together to get the programme back on the air! One small cavil – not about the programme - just stop going on in the media about your Mancunian roots and comparing them with your 'posh' predecessors, Mr. Eccleston. You're immediately following a Liverpudlian (Paul McGann), a Scot (Sylvester McCoy - hardly a 'southern upper middle class actor' – more northern than you are actually), and another Mancunian (me) – none of whom would have been invited, or allowed, to play the role as a northerner.

Television has changed in twenty years. You had to speak 'standard English' when Tom Baker (another Liverpudlian), Peter Davison, Sylvester, Paul and I started; now, quite rightly, the media embrace and show diversity in accent, appearance and race. So be grateful, Christopher, that you're allowed to be a northerner and shut up, please. You can rely on your talent. The work needs no justification. It stands alone. The accent is irrelevant. Play the part with passion, talent and commitment (and the signs are that you certainly are doing all three) and we don't care if you sound like sound like an Etonian, a Grimsby fisherman or a Northern Irish preacher. Anyway, it's nice to have something to look forward to apart from the football results on a Saturday again.

And get that sofa away from the wall! The Doctor is back with a vengeance.

13th January 2006

If you had told me a couple of years ago that the flagship programme on Christmas Day might one day be *Doctor Who*, I would have suggested that you seek specialist medical help immediately. But building on the excellent series transmitted last year, the special festive episode introducing David Tennant as Doctor No. 10 was the

undoubted success amongst what was a predominantly lacklustre batch of offerings this holiday. In fact, it was the only programme that tempted the Baker family away from the delights of enjoying each others' company. Once again that genius Russell T. Davies has produced not only a great script and a great new Doctor, but just when you thought the story was over and the world saved, there was a judiciously crafted hefty sideswipe against those most un-Christmassy characteristics greed, selfishness and political expedience, that so depressingly regularly nudge humanity and honour out into second place. A contemporary message every bit as powerful as that in Dickens' *Christmas Carol*. To offer the viewers whirling dervish Christmas Trees and homicidal Santas without losing credibility is quite an achievement. And I am glad to be able to confirm what I already knew – that David Tennant would be a worthy recipient of the Tardis baton. He's grabbed it with both hands and has already given us exciting glimpses of a Doctor that embodies the familiar Time Lord characteristics of passion for justice, loyalty and compassion, whilst promising a greater self awareness, vulnerability and humour than his immediate predecessor.

Tennant has also been blessed with not only considerable acting ability but compelling looks and an innate charm that will prove invaluable in retaining the viewers' interest when the series returns.

I continue to envy the production values and, in particular, the scripts that are remarkably contrived to flesh out the familiar 'Doctor repels alien threat to humanity' storyline in original and witty ways. And none but the bravest and best scriptwriter could get away with overt references to *Hitchhiker's Guide to the Galaxy* (Doctor aware of the connection to that programme that could be inferred by fighting alien invaders while wearing pyjamas!) or indeed allowing our hero to stop himself in mid-rant as he realises that he is quoting from *The Lion King*. I have been astounded when die-hard fans have expressed to me a preference for the old series. Fortunately they are in a minority. It is hard to imagine how the series could be bettered. I look forward to its return.

26th June 2009

It's always interesting to have someone tell you something about yourself you didn't know. This week several people contacted me to

say how delighted they were that I was to appear in a *Doctor Who* 'multi-doctor special' for *Children in Need* this autumn. The fact that this was the first I had heard about it says it all. The source was apparently the Daily Mirror, so I logged on and checked online. Well I never! Apparently all eleven Doctors Who are to be involved in a special story. Ah yes, Oh wise reader, you know too that three of them are, alas, no longer with us. That is to be resolved, (we are told by the journalist concerned, Clemmie Moodie), by incorporating old film footage of Messrs Hartnell, Troughton and Pertwee.

An unnamed 'insider' (another clue to the likely accuracy of the article) spoke to the paper of the difficulty experienced in setting the project up.

"It's been a logistical nightmare getting all the actors together and available for shooting on the same days." Well, it will continue to be a logistical nightmare if no one actually contacts the actors. The crystal ball gazing insider even speaks warmly of us all waiving our fees.

Ms. Moodie writes of a previous *Children in Need* story – *The Five Doctors* – filmed in 1983, just before I became the Doctor. It was, in fact, part of the normal series and not a *Children in Need* story – which serves further to confirm the degree of attention to detail of the author of the piece. Had this kind of thing not happened frequently over the decades, one might forgive a national newspaper for perhaps listening to a Chinese whispers rumour emanating from heaven knows where as a result of whomever's wishful thinking.

We must assume that The Mirror didn't simply make up the story. Why would they? Well, apart from the fact that they are currently giving away free Doctor Who Magazines every Saturday?

But that can't be the reason, as they wouldn't want to be responsible for dashing all the young fans' hopes, would they? Anyway whatever the provenance of the story and the reason for publishing it without checking with the actors or their agents, the simple truth is that there has been no contact of any kind about this from anyone. I just feel sorry for all the fans who may have been falsely excited by this piece of fantasy journalism.

3rd August 2007

This week I had an unexpected opportunity to revisit an old friend. My theatre tour has taken me to Cardiff, where *Doctor Who* is filmed. By chance they were night filming just round the corner from the theatre at which I am appearing and invited me to pop in and see what was going on. How could I resist? I must confess to certain trepidation. I went back to my old school a couple of years ago and discovered it to be strange and unsettling. Things seemed the same but were different. Or perhaps I had changed and the place hadn't? And there was no one there that I knew, of course.

However, returning to a night shoot on *Doctor Who* was reassuringly familiar. The personnel had changed certainly, but the atmosphere hadn't. I had worked with David Tennant before he became the Doctor and therefore knew him. He came and chatted between takes for what looks as if it is going to be yet another superb Christmas special.

I also got to meet his companion for this story – Kylie Minogue who was relishing the opportunity to demonstrate her acting prowess on television again. I loathe spoilers of any kind, so will not elaborate on the detail of the story. What was reassuring for this old Tardis key holder was that although the programme has moved into the 21st century and manages that impossible task of appealing to a completely new audience without losing the beating heart of the programme, the process and the atmosphere on set remained as special as I remembered it. I can think of no other job I have done which would see me at 3-50 in the morning still enjoying the work in the company of others similarly motivated.

What was particularly unexpected was the welcome that Russell T Davies and Phil Collinson, respectively executive producer and producer, afforded me and the very genuine affection they appeared to have for the original programme – 'Classic Who' as it is now called. I must confess to a moment of quiet envy seeing David, impeccable in a tuxedo, surrounded by bizarre aliens doing his time lord thing.

It brought back happy memories and it was uplifting to be, for a moment, part of something that meant a lot to me and now means a whole lot more to a new generation of television viewers. Long may it continue to do so.

21. Season's Greetings

At this point in the book I would like to take the opportunity to thank all those fans of the show who have been kind enough to respond with such warmth to me and my portrayal of the Doctor. Of course everyone has favourites, usually the Doctor they first saw at an impressionable age, but ultimately I think most true fans subscribe to the view voiced by the wonderful Nicholas Courtney in his role as the Brigadier. When asked which his favourite Doctor is, his practised response is "Splendid fellow – all of them!"

In the twenty five years since my Doctor first appeared on our screens, fans have been remarkably supportive and friendly towards me. I think that they know that I view the programme with as much affection as they do and that I continue to be proud of my association with the show. The feedback I have been getting from them about my renaissance, as it were, in the Big Finish series of audios has been most gratifying.

While I was chairman of the cot death charity, The Foundation for the Study of Infant Deaths, which I joined in the wake of the death of our seven week old son Jack just a couple of weeks before I was due to start filming Doctor Who *in 1983, the fans were remarkably supportive and some of them even jumped out of a perfectly good aeroplane with me, when the Red Devils helped us to raise money for valuable research into the causes of cot death. They have supported the charity in many, many ways over the years and I, and countless parents, am/are in their debt for that.*

Whenever I go to conventions or signing events anywhere in the world, it is truly heart-warming to be on the receiving end of so much affection. And there is a whole new audience now for the programme who are slowly discovering its long history and coming along to see what the 'Classic' series is all about. I like being part of something 'Classic'.

Anyway, before you launch into my final chapter – culled from Christmas and New Year articles – I would like to say to those wonderful fans, "Look Who's Grateful".

22nd December 1995

Christmas starts earlier every year. It's a well worn truism but accurate nonetheless. My first sighting this year was on an evening in mid-November. Returning from London I pulled off the M 40 at Loudwater having spotted Tesco's clock showing that I had enough

time to pop in and get the cat food and children's breakfast cereal. As I approached the store I spotted it - the banner strung across the entrance wishing us all a Happy Christmas. A little on the early side perhaps, some 40 days in fact. But then the seasons are blurring and shifting all the time. March is no longer reliably windy, nor April showery and with the notable exception of this year summer is frequently the second Wednesday in September.

But, what if the debris of Guy Fawkes and Halloween had not yet been completely cleared away, let's give Tesco the benefit of the doubt - the spirit of Christmas is after all a potent force for good. People who have trouble mustering a smile the rest of the year thaw perceptibly when surrounded by tinsel, cotton wool snow and School Nativities, complete with nose-picking shepherds.

We all want to re-capture the magic of our first visit to Santa's grotto. Children today are, of course, more sophisticated and know that the real Santa has quite a heavy work load and therefore has assistant Santas, of varying quality, to sit in his many grottoes, caves and elfin glades to receive and pass on the children's requests for presents to the great man himself. My own children discovered this once when Santa greeted me with an enquiry as to what Panto I was doing that year. He compounded his dereliction of Santitude by then launching into a diatribe against his agent who had failed to find him an opportunity to give his Ugly Sister that year. He reached under his beard and handed me a card which informed me that he was no other than Uncle Neville - a children's entertainer, specialising in balloon modelling and comedy magic (with real live rabbit). He was clearly not a method actor. Fortunately as there were three Santas within ho-ho-ho-ing range, my daughters had already correctly assumed that these were local agents of the big cheese and were therefore simply irritated that their father's notoriety had once again interfered with what should have been their moment.

My first ever involvement in Pantomime, twenty years ago, was as Dick Whittington in Cork. The dame was a local comic whose accent was so strong that I couldn't understand a single word he uttered. I felt much as Clint must have done when performing in those spaghetti westerns, with the rest of the cast speaking Italian to be overdubbed in English later. That particular year, as the only English folk in it, Alice Fitzwarren, the Fairy and I had our Christmas dinner

together at an hotel. We were joined by the Fairy's boy friend, a yachtsman. Alice F. was nineteen and it was her first Christmas away from home. She wept bitter tears into her roast parsnips and kept rushing off to phone her Mum. The Fairy discovered a hitherto unfelt deep and eternal revulsion for her boy-friend and told him over the plum duff. He took it like a man and decided that I was the sort of chap who would like a detailed enumeration of the virtues of his sloop. He was wrong. I drank far too much Champagne, made my excuses and took my red setter for a long, elliptical walk along the beach. At the beginning of this article we were in Tesco's car park. My pondering of the earliness of their Christmas greeting was driven from my mind when I failed to gain access to the store.

A security guard opened the door when I performed an exaggerated mime conveying my dissatisfaction given that the time was only five to eight. He told me that it was 8 o'clock and the store was closed. I pointed to the clock tower above us.

"Everyone knows that clock is slow", he remonstrated, unmoved by my description of my daughter's impending day without Lucky Charms and the fact that I had only pulled off the motorway because of their ruddy clock. As I passed beneath the jolly festive banner I muttered a seasonal, "Bah Humbug!"

26th December 1997

So what's the best thing about Christmas? For some it might be the moment when the all the shopping, preparation and cooking is done and the children are still on a present induced high, but just before they start arguing about which of the indecently vast array of toys and games they all want to play with, - when you can sit down for the first time in two weeks and nod off while watching a sentimental movie on TV. For others perhaps it is in watching the children and dredging up, from the mists of time, bittersweet memories of that barely containable excitement on Christmas Eve, really wanting, yet at the same time not wanting, to go to bed. For yet others, it is possibly eating too much turkey, but still having room in the evening for the cold cuts washed down with a glass of something just a little bit more interesting than the usual supermarket Vin Ordinaire.

The more honestly venal amongst you may even admit to deriving the most pleasure from the receipt of copious and lavish gifts; for

others it may be the giving, which can often be a less complicated pleasure than that of receiving. All these things have their undoubted charms, but Christmas is summed up for me by those nativity plays, produced in nurseries and primary schools all over the country.

I am usually away from home, inhabiting the more secular world of panto, at the very moment when my daughters are wearing tea towels or gossamer wings in High Wycombe, otherwise wild reindeer, with or without red noses, would not prevent me from being there to witness those unforgettable moments; when the innkeeper forgets his lines and tells the pilgrims from Nazareth that he has plenty of room; or when Joseph picks up the infant Jesus by his head to allow Mary to prepare the straw in the infant crib, or when angels, kings and shepherds scan the expectant audience with screwed up eyes until they spot their adoring mums and dads and then give very un-biblical cheery waves before spending the rest of the performance riveted to the audience and paying no attention to the drama unfolding in the stable; when angels and citizens of Bethlehem engage in earnest conversation about what each thinks the other ought to be doing at that particular moment; and, inevitably, when the desire to visit the loo compels a diminutive sufferer to seize and hang on to his equipment in discomfort .

On one occasion I saw a five year old Mary get quite irritated when a helpful angel tried to replace on her lap the Baby Jesus, when he had tumbled unnoticed to the floor. But there is something about the charming innocence of all this that adds to, rather than detracts from, the message of the Nativity play. It is not always possible to imagine, scanning those infant faces, that from their number will come the adults of the future whose more pressurised lives will take them further away each year from the message of Christmas - which if it is about anything, must be about hope for the future.

Despite the pressure of providing cards, food, presents and time for everyone at Christmas, most people manage to summon more tolerance of the failings and idiosyncrasies of their relations and fellow man at this time of year.

There is a Roy Wood song that goes "I wish it could be Christmas every day" and, though I must shame-facedly own that I heave a very small, private sigh of relief when the decorations are packed away again, wouldn't it be nice if the mutual tolerance and the general

bonhomie could last longer? It's no coincidence that New Year's Resolutions follow so swiftly on the heels of both the generosity and indulgence of Christmas.

20th December 2003

If you have sent me one of those Christmas round-robin letters, then, of course, what you are about to read does not apply to you. Yours did not produce a desire to throttle the writer and all their descendants, because yours was not smug and boastful, nor did it contain pages of unmitigated bragging about the prowess of your children. Yours are delightful and their modest but commendable achievements do not eclipse anything my family will ever achieve. First of all I should concede that I have received two wonderful and interesting letters. One is from an old friend whose epistles I eagerly anticipate every Christmas. He is a witty, acerbic individual who entertainingly catalogues the disasters that pepper his retirement. This year he also recounts the pleasure he has taken from several books that he has read during the year, at least one of which I shall make a point of seeking out myself. That is useful and diverting.

The other acceptable letter came from a contemporary who shares the hideousness of his teenage children. He strays only briefly into the murky waters of their talent and achievements but redeems himself by disingenuously detailing their contempt for him, his values and all that he worked so hard to achieve in order to give them the freedom to despise him. These two correspondents made me laugh and are therefore acceptable.

However ... I have received a fair few examples of how it is possible to take self-satisfaction to new and dizzying heights of awfulness. These are the letters that should only be written either to very close relatives who have given a clear indication that they actually give a damn, or to people who do not have children, so no invidious comparisons can be made.

I have decided to write the anti round-robin letter. Maybe I will call it the square-grouse letter. It will go something like this.

"Well, it's Christmas again. This year was much the same as last year. The children ate more and did even less round the house. They're doing okay at school. We decided not to buy a villa in Tuscany or to go sailing around the Aegean with a lovely couple and

their delightful children that we met in Barbados last year. Mainly because we didn't go to Barbados and certainly didn't meet anyone with whom we would want to sail round the Aegean. We went to Cornwall and had a great time without any of us winning a yacht race, qualifying as a parascending instructor or meeting these really wonderful locals who taught us how to do topiary. I didn't get nominated for any acting awards (or literary or journalistic ones). Neither my wife nor I took up Tai-Ken-Pu-Chow (a wonderful physical discipline from foothills of Indo-China that combines the calm acceptance of flatulence as a manifestation of natural energy with the very gentle massage of the elbow and ankle to release the spiritually disruptive effects of the pressures of 21st Century angst.) Nor do we do this every morning in our Tudor Knot Garden (that I have not been creating for the last seven years in between sessions in my workshop where I don't make lutes using traditional methods). Our children do a bit of homework sometimes and go out with their mates. I do a bit of work and watch the telly. I'm not sure what my wife does. I must ask her sometime."

22nd December 2004

Christmas has been surrounding and overwhelming us for several months already and this is probably why I failed, yet again, to get the Christmas cards written and posted within the time advised by what I like to think of as the Royal Mail. The fact that festive goodies appear in the stores in October lulls one into a false sense of security.

There seems to be, indeed there is, plenty of time in which to get ready for Christmas, so one inevitably procrastinates. In the good old days, when the advent calendar meant something, when there was nary a hint of a mince pie or tinsel before December, we knew when we had to start to prepare. Now I am not even sure that it is actually this Christmas that we are celebrating and not next Christmas, as the marketing juggernauts appears to get rolling earlier and earlier.

For the last ten years, it seems, I have laid plans involving computers, data bases and labels that have been designed to produce, at the press of a button, neatly addressed envelopes into which I will slip the cards that have been pre-signed by each member of the Baker tribe. And each year I have produced reams of labels bearing gibberish or addresses that spread across the edges of several labels

and are completely useless. As usual, I give up and at the last minute, whilst doing twice daily performances of pantomime, end up frantically looking through old address books and attempting to remember which of the several addresses available for old friends are the ones that they actually live at now. Why on earth can't people just stay put or indeed stay married to each other?

So, I have probably sent merry Yuletide greetings to people at addresses they have long vacated and, worse naming partners they have long divorced. But it's the thought that counts, isn't it? We all really ought to have the courage to halt this mammoth exchange of pieces of paper – certainly between people who see each other regularly during the year. If the truth be told, we glance at cards for a second to check whether we have sent one to the sender, then heave a sigh of relief or rush to the address book, before consigning the card to a vacant place on the wall, dresser or mantelpiece until January 6th. Then, if you are organised you make a list of those who sent you a card so that you can reciprocate next Christmas, which when it arrives, you will, of course, be unable to find. And if you do find it, it can lead to alternating year card syndrome. You sent them one, but they didn't send you one. So next year you don't send them one. They, however, got yours this year so they send you one next year. There are actually people to whom I send cards that I probably wouldn't recognise if I met them; it is so long since I saw them.

But it does continue a thread of friendly connection and keeps alive memories of the past that can be lived again for a few seconds whilst writing the card. And how many times have we all written that we must get in touch next year? And how many times have we done it? Maybe this annual failure could lead neatly to next week's reluctant consideration of that other ritual dance – the New Year's Resolution?

8th December 2006

Christmas. Christmas. Christmas. Christmas. Christmas. That's better. I deplore the steady absorption of November and October into the whole Christmas preamble. But I deplore even more the corrosive notion amongst a minority of pallid bureaucratic functionaries that Christmas can be, by the mere fact of its existence, offensive to anyone whose IQ is larger than their shoe size.

And that's UK sizes! I would not patronise or want to risk offending any of my friends and acquaintances of other faiths by sending them cards that self-consciously exclude reference to Christmas for reason of a 'fear of offending'. I have yet to even hear of a Muslim, Jew, Sikh or Hindu who has staggered back in outraged horror on receipt of a Christmas card. Indeed, the leaders of those and other religions are now commendably going to considerable lengths to distance themselves from the ludicrously divisive attempts of some public bodies to avoid blame for anything, thereby guaranteeing precisely the opposite effect and creating a sterile world where an absence of belief, passion and difference is deemed desirable. I would feel quite chuffed if I was wished a happy Eid, Hannukah or Diwali by a member of those religions, or if I was in a country where those faiths are practised (even nominally) by the majority of the population and could witness or join in their festive celebrations.

It all started, in 1998, when Birmingham City Council renamed Christmas 'Winterval'. If ever there was a word devised by a committee, it's Winterval! In the words of the song - That's Santa-tainment! Three years later, Luton named it's Christmas Lights ceremony Luminos, exchanging the Christian tradition for – yes that much more aspirational and uplifting festival in a work of fiction - Harry Potter. But the tide is turning and much needed common sense is coming from the heart of the community that is allegedly being 'protected' from offence. Councillor Khizar Iqbal, of Kirklees Council in Yorkshire has said that his group plans to adorn all town halls with banners wishing people a Merry Christmas. In common with other adherents of non-Christian religions, he was more offended by the suggestion that he might be offended by the celebration of Christmas. Send that man a mince pie. But make sure it has a health and safety warning with it. Like many local councils – it may contain nuts.

14th December 2007

I am currently rehearsing for pantomime in Norwich where, in their wisdom, they have asked me to play King Rat, rather than the dame which I have played for the last few years. Perhaps they have been reading my articles in this paper and have deduced, quite rightly

(some readers would doubtless suggest), that the adjective 'grumpy' better describes your columnist than does 'mumsy'. Suffice it to say that my family were only mildly surprised when I donned a merry yuletide hat that bore the legend "Bah Humbug" last year. "All in the interests of humour!" I protested, to little avail. Playing the villain in panto does however have a pretty useful cathartic effect. After hours trudging round crowded streets full of hundreds of other people similarly seeking inspiration because they have no idea what to buy for assorted relatives, workmates and neighbours who already have everything they want, the opportunity to harangue a thousand people (and get paid for it) is undeniably attractive. Theatres are able to subsidise the rest of their seasons from the revenue generated by pantomime and therefore cram as many shows into that four or five week period during which parents want to re-live their own memories of Christmas and rediscover the magical world of panto through the eyes of their children. That opportunity to fill the theatres means that I shall be plotting the downfall of Dick Whittington and his cat twice daily, including Sundays, and three times on Saturdays. The most popular shows are those on Boxing Day and it is quite hard to tiptoe away at the crack of dawn with my turkey sandwiches clasped in my hand, while the rest of the house are sleeping off the excesses of the day before. It also means that drinking stops when Christmas lunch is over. To ensure I am driving off sober! But the expectant buzz and excitement of the children audience soon lifts everyone for the matinee. And at least we don't suffer quite as much as those other entertainers - footballers. Playing matches on Boxing Day to entertain us (well, those of us who aren't in or attending panto!) means that they often have to either train on Christmas Day or travel to another ground miles away if they're not playing at home. Now, that really is a sacrifice too far. Everyone should be able to spend at least Christmas Day with their families. Well everyone who wants to anyway.

29th December 2006

Did you all have a good Christmas? I hope so. I hope you didn't receive too many Christmas cards on Christmas Eve from people to whom you had failed to send one. Why do all the cards that arrive in

the build up to Christmas come from people you have remembered, whereas the last minute ones come laden with recrimination? "Have you remembered me? No? I thought not." They do it on purpose. And it's too late by then to put an advert in the paper announcing your green credentials and that you have donated the twenty-five quid you would have spent to a renewable timber project in Lapland. I hope you didn't wrestle with the tree that didn't fit into the patented tree holder-upper that you were flogged last year, which had rusted solid.

And when you succeeded in finding the one you used the year before and got the tree in it, into the house and the furniture back in place,   I hope you didn't then find the label that smugly suggested that you saw an inch off the bottom.

There's no point in entertaining any hope about the lights. They either needed bulbs that are no longer made or none of the spares you stocked up on last year actually fitted any of your lights. I hope that you didn't fail yet again to wrap anything until midnight on Christmas Eve and then realise you had forgotten that that it always takes at least two hours and you end up surrounded by bits of sticky tape that seem designed to curl up immediately on removal from the roll and determined to buy a pair of scissors that actually cut things before next December. I hope you didn't buy your children DVDs that they already had; that you didn't get irritable with them when all they were guilty of was enjoying themselves loudly and vigorously.

I hope that you didn't have to then apologise because you were a grumpy old git. I hope you didn't put the postman's Christmas box out in the drizzle after he had actually been, then not discover the soggy contents until the evening.

But I hope that like me you thought that it was all worthwhile when you realised how lucky we all are to have families that still want to be with us at Christmas. Long may it continue.

28th December 2008

Are you going to go through the annual ritual rigmarole of making New Year's Resolutions? Or, like me, are you struggling to identify a personal deficiency that you have the slightest chance of remedying?

Deficiencies I have aplenty, but ones that I have a hope of doing anything about are few. And for once I would like to have at least a fighting chance of achieving the objective of my resolution.

In fact, giving up smoking 24 years ago has been my only true success, as far as I can recall. I can however offer you some ideas for resolutions should you or your friends be experiencing similar difficulties. For instance, there may just be drivers reading this who think that turning on your rear (and indeed front) fog lights make you safer in all road conditions. Wrong! The High-way Code stipulates that they should only be used when visibility is less than 100 metres. To do so at any other time merely blinds and irritates those behind you. Or, how about cyclists (who must at other times be pedestrians themselves) resolving to only undertake their commendable transport of delight on the highway and not the pavements?

And maybe those who run our postal services could resolve to make their indispensable services actually available to all of their customers? For a town the size of Marlow to be bereft of a post office would have been utterly unthinkable hitherto. As I write this I am in Norwich, a sizeable city, the centre of which now only has one post office - on the second floor of a busy shopping mall, where I queued for 40 minutes one lunchtime last week, because I had no option given that the weight and size regulations for letters are now too complicated for us, the customers, to accurately predict the cost of our mail. Perhaps too, our fellow citizens might take the time to thank us when, in accordance with our resolutions to be more courteous, we hold a door open for someone, or stop to let them cross the road. We will continue to do it, of course, but a word of thanks is always appreciated. And yes that will be my resolution this year. I believe I am usually courteous but I will endeavour to make that always - even to the driver who chucks his fag packet out of the car window.

Well, I'll try anyway!

21st December 2007

I was invited last week by the good citizens of that lovely old coastal town, Cromer, to turn on their festive lights with my old friend Terry Molloy, who played Davros, the evil genius creator of the Daleks when I was Doctor Who. We are both appearing in panto

down the road in Norwich. The Cromer lights are entirely the work of a dedicated team of volunteers who fundraise throughout the year and supply and install the impressive festoons of light over a series of Sundays throughout the winter. This unpaid dedication to their local community was, I thought, worthy of 'bigging up', so I deemed it appropriate in my short speech to indicate that I had a few weeks earlier seen the lights in Blackpool and the Cromer illuminations were - I paused for effect - infinitely superior!

Everyone was happy with my unashamed hyperbole and we adjourned for a sandwich and mince pie in a local hostelry. When I say everyone was happy, I am sadly excluding the press in Blackpool, who somehow heard about this distant but monstrous insult to their sea front attraction and pursued me relentlessly for three days via telephone and email.

As I was in the throes of dress rehearsals for Dick Whittington, I declined to respond to their plaintive requests for a justification of my hideous and offensive slur to their town. A Blackpool councillor even suggested that I would benefit from a word with my successor David Tennant, who turned the lights in Blackpool on this year and had declared them to be superb.

Oh dear! I am now worried that a remark I made to a friend that her house was more desirable than Buckingham Palace might provoke questions in the House and a letter from the Lord Chamberlain; or that Brad Pitt might come and sort me out because I think my wife is more attractive that Angelina Jolie! Clearly the local press in Blackpool are for some reason a little more sensitive about their town than, say, we in Wycombe who know we live in a town that is regenerating and improving year by year. And if anyone who had a working fountain in their town were to try to belittle us because we don't, I like to think we would rise above it. Anyway a happy Christmas to all you sane, well adjusted and non-politically correct readers, near and far.

Afterword

I was astonished to learn from Tim Hirst, after he had made his selection of the pieces you have been kind enough to read (unless of course you have hit upon this page in flicking to the end to see how much more there is!) – that the content of this book is just a fraction of my fifteen year output.

Whether this is good news or bad news depends upon you, discerning reader. If you have been diverted and entertained to some extent during your trawl through my musings, then it may well be that another volume may be on offer in the future.

My canny publisher has already told me that he has kept back some of what he was kind enough to refer to as 'nuggets'. To those who feel sated and are holding your heads groaning, "No more, please, no more!" I offer my thanks for essaying my essays, perusing my prose and meandering through my mundungus.

On the following page you will see a list of names of people without whom this book could never have existed. Whilst I was flattered and delighted when Tim came up with the idea, I was initially unsure that there were enough people out there who might be interested enough in my chunterings to spend their hard earned money buying it. I didn't want him to lose his shirt financing my book. It is a rather nice shirt - with pictures of Daleks all over it. So he came up with the wizard wheeze of taking pre-orders to test the market, refundable naturally if it somehow failed to get to the press.

The list you will read is of wonderful people who were generous or warm-hearted or silly enough - or all of those things - to want to support my book. Some of them are friends, some are familiar names, others were until now, strangers to me - but not any longer.

I thank them wholeheartedly for their interest and faith in us and for enabling me to become a 'published author'.

For anyone sufficiently interested in my doings to want to find out more my very good friend Robert Cope has constructed and maintains on my behalf an excellent website at **www.colinbakeronline.com** *where details of upcoming theatrical and television work can be found alongside other information about me.*

Thomas Adams
Janet Adkins
Dave Agnew
Darren Allen
Kade Allen
Mark Ambler
Tony Amis
Shaun Ashton
Prakash Bakrania
Barnaby Eaton-Jones
Jane Barrance
Robin Bell-Taylor
Nick Blake
Jackie Branton
Philip Brenna
Richard Broder
Steve Bull
Lesley Byrne
Rory Byrne
Stephen Candy
Paul Castle
Lee Catigen-Cooper
Darren Chandler
Andrew Chaplin
Dino Charalambous
Alan Christison
Sheldon Collins
Martin Cook
Mike Cook
Joel Cornah
Andrew Croker
Andrew Dack
Manu Das
Paul Devine
Robert Dick
Charles Dunne
Vivienne Dunstan
Larry Dyde
Carolyn Edwards
Ken Ellington
Paul Engelberg
Mark English

Stephen Eramo
Robert Fairclough
Christopher Fewell
Richard Firth
Brian Flynn
Cynthia Garland
Richard Garner
Angela Giblin
Michael Gilroy
Aaron Gregson
Chris Griffin
Stephen Griffiths
James Grizzell-Jones
James Guthrie
David Hamblin
Michael Harvey
Peter Hastings
Jo Healy
Simon
   & Sasha Hewitt
Elsie Hirst
James Hobbs
Martin Hughes
Sinead Hughes
Daniel Humes
Michael Hussey
Steve Caldwell
   & Jacky Thornton
Maria James
Martin James
Amy Johnson
David Johnson
Thomas Joliffe
Garry Jones
Iain Keiller
Chris Kerr
Geoff King
Mike Kirby
Andy Kitching
Chad Knueppe

Christopher Leather
Alison Lee
Rob Lee
Courtland Lewis
Andy Longley
Adrian Maj
Richard Marsh
Sean Marsh
Alan Maskell
Kenneth Mason
Steve Matthewman
Kenny McCann
Roddy McDougall
James McFetridge
Sean McGauley
Michael McManus
David Meades
Andrew Meadows
Gary Merchant
Greg Miller
Jeffrey Miller
Chris Moores
Barbara Morgan
Chris Moss
Jennifer Newland-Park
Paul Norman
John O'Hare
Anna-Maria Oléhn
Richard Parker
Matthew Partis
Adrian Pauley
Ali Pearce
Josie, Romy &
Edward Pearce
Alister Pearson
David Perkins
Hollie Perry
Robin Prichard
Mike Purser

Billy Rees
Thomas Anderson
   Reid
Jason Rhodes
Justin Ridley
Dominic Romano
Charlie Ross
Robert Ross
Gary Russell
Peter Sandercock
Michael Sauers
Michael Shakesby
Stephen Shephard
Bryan Simcott
Robert Simpson
Caroline Sinclair
Kevin Skelhorn
Johnathan Smith
Matthew Spencer
Christopher Starr
Rhys Stewart
Richard Taylor
Linda Terrell
Paul Thomas
Jackie Thompson
Julian Thomson-Hill
Jan Thomson
Graham Thurley
Christopher Tranter
Ian Twyford
Richard Unwin
Nicola Vernon
Martin Wakefield
Janet Wakeling
Wayne Walker
Stephen Ward
Chris Watkins
Simon Wheatley
Alex Wilcock
Andrew Williams
John Williams
John Wilson
Alex Wilson-Fletcher
Dave Wood
Cary Woodward

Also Available from Hirst Books

'Self Portrait' and 'Naked'
by Anneke Wills

Best known for her iconic role as Polly in *Doctor Who*, **Anneke's extraordinary life, filled with tears, laughter and discovery, will leave you breathless.** In two extraordinary volumes, Anneke's autobiography is hilarious and heartbreaking in equal measure. A unique childhood, living and breathing swinging sixties London, a turbulent marriage to a leading actor, and life with the eccentrics, actors, film-makers, satirists and drunks who were changing the world, fill the first volume, 'Self Portrait'. In the second volume, Anneke leaves the limelight of television for rural family life, fully embracing the liberal zeitgeist of the seventies and travelling to India to become a disciple of the notorious spiritual teacher Bhagwan Shree Rajneesh. In the eighties, she lives among unique artists on a small Canadian Island, works as a designer and gardener in California, endures unbearable tragedy and two more unorthodox marriages. She returns to the folds of *Doctor Who* in the nineties, which leads to worldwide travels, emotional reunions and new adventures. To this day, Anneke's life continues to be unpredictable and bizarre. These books cover the whole of Anneke's life, laying bare the story of a true renaissance woman. You couldn't make it up.

'Shooty Dog Thing'
by Paul Castle and friends

Cool and accessible, Shooty Dog Thing is the fanzine that's inspiring a new wave of *Doctor Who* fandom. Forget the facts and figures, half-remembered anecdotes and continuity errors – Shooty Dog Thing will make you remember why you fell in love with *Doctor Who* in the first place. This is the best in contemporary fan writing; challenging established views, exploring the many worlds of *Doctor Who*, and finding reasons to love the show just that little bit more than the casual viewer. The best of the first 10 issues is compiled here for your enjoyment, along with some lovely, juicy new stuff. Love *Doctor Who*? You'll love this.

www.hirstbooks.com

Coming Soon from Hirst Books

Doctor Who: Time Regained
A Memoir in Four Episodes
by Matthew Waterhouse

Flight Risks
a contemporary thriller by Douglas Schofield

A Comedian's Tale
by Charlie Ross

Spies, Smuggler and Spook Trains
The Making of "Enid Blyton's The Famous Five" in the 1970s
by Gary Russell

Whether you Like It Or Not
A second volume of columns from Colin Baker

Pre-order these titles and as a thank you we'll list your name at the back, and you'll receive a signed, dedicated copy.

www.hirstbooks.com